ON THE DAY FORT SUMTER SURRENDERED TO Confederate authorities, General Braxton Bragg reacted to a newspaper report that might have revealed the position of gun emplacements by arresting the correspondent, a Southern loyalist. Thus the Confederate army's first detention of a citizen occurred before President Lincoln had even called out troops to suppress the rebellion. During the civil war that followed, not a day would pass when Confederate military prisons did not contain political prisoners.

Based on the discovery of records of over four thousand of these prisoners, Mark E. Neely Jr.'s book undermines the common understanding that Jefferson Davis and the Confederates were scrupulous in their respect for constitutional rights while Lincoln and the Unionists regularly violated the rights of dissenters. Neely reveals for the first time the extent of repression of Unionists and other civilians in the Confederacy and uncovers and marshals convincing evidence that Southerners were as ready as their Northern counterparts to give up civil liberties in response to the real or imagined threats of wartime.

From the onset of hostilities, the exploits of drunken recruits prompted communities from Selma to Lynchburg to beg the Richmond government to impose martial law. Southern citizens resigned themselves to a passport system for domestic travel similar to the system of passes imposed on enslaved and free blacks before the war. These restrictive measures made commerce difficult and constrained religious activity. As one Virginian complained, "This struggle was begun in defence of Constitutional Liberty which we could not get in the United States." The Davis administration countered that the passport system was essential to prevent desertion from

(continued on back flap)

SOUTHERN RIGHTS

A NATION DIVIDED
NEW STUDIES IN CIVIL WAR HISTORY

James I. Robertson, Editor

SOUTHERN RIGHTS

POLITICAL PRISONERS AND THE MYTH OF CONFEDERATE CONSTITUTIONALISM

MARK E. NEELY JR.

UNIVERSITY PRESS OF VIRGINIA

CHARLOTTESVILLE AND LONDON

The University Press of Virginia
© 1999 by the Rector and Visitors of the University of Virginia
All rights reserved
Printed in the United States of America

First published 1999

The paper used in this publication meets the minimum requirements of the American
National Standard for Information Sciences—Permanence of Paper for Printed Library
Materials, ANSI Z39.48-1984.

Library of Congress Cataloging-in-Publication Data

Neely, Mark E.
    Southern rights : political prisoners and the myth of Confederate
constitutionalism / Mark E. Neely, Jr.
        p. cm. — (A nation divided)
    Includes bibliographical references and index.
    ISBN 0-8139-1894-4 (cloth : alk. paper)
    1. Confederate States of America—Politics and government.
2. Political prisoners—Confederate States of America. 3. Civil
rights—Confederate States of America. 4. Constitutional law—
Confederate States of America. 5. Martial law—Confederate States
of America. I. Title. II. Series.
E487.N44 1999
973.7'72—DC21   99-25230
                                                                    CIP

CONTENTS

ACKNOWLEDGMENTS

I WAS ABLE TO WORK ON THIS BOOK with support from various institutions over the years. The Virginia Historical Society in Richmond got me started with a Mellon Research Fellowship. The Interlibrary Loan Department of Saint Louis University expedited loans of the microfilm edition of the Letters Received by the Confederate Secretary of War, sent from the University of Virginia and from the University of Southern Mississippi for three years. The Henry E. Huntington Library in San Marino, California, made me the R. Stanton Avery Fellow for a year.

Robert Bonner of Michigan State University read the whole manuscript and offered valuable criticism and advice. John David Smith of North Carolina State University read several chapters and also provided helpful commentary. The members of the Legal History Seminar at the Huntington Library read and criticized the chapter on the Confederate Bar. The critics for the University Press of Virginia, Richard F. Bensel of Cornell University and an anonymous reader, offered extremely valuable criticism from two quite different perspectives.

My colleague in the Civil War Era Center at Penn State, William Blair, gave me constructive criticism of the Jefferson Davis chapter. The funds attached to the McCabe-Greer Professorship at Penn State purchased for the library the crucial microfilm edition of the Letters Received by the Confederate Secretary of War, 1861–1865, published by the National Archives, and thus facilitated the final checking of the principal source for this book. Richard B. McCaslin of High Point University and Kenneth H. Williams of the *Papers of Jefferson Davis* project each furnished searching and deep commentaries on a paper based on this book presented at the annual meeting of the Southern Historical Association, 13 November 1998.

Sylvia Neely read, criticized, encouraged, and formatted.

I am grateful for all the help.

INTRODUCTION

AT THREE O'CLOCK IN THE AFTERNOON of the day Fort Sumter surrendered to Confederate authorities, General Braxton Bragg summoned a correspondent for the local newspaper named Lawrence H. Mathews to his headquarters in Pensacola, Florida. "By what authority," demanded General Bragg, "did you assert that the Confederate States were to raise Sand batteries on the island of Santa Rosa?" It was a common rumor, Mathews replied. Bragg maintained that an article Mathews had written gave the impression that the information came from the general himself. "You are a traitor, Sir," Bragg asserted.

At that accusation Mathews exploded with indignation, "General Bragg, whoever calls me *traitor,* speaks falsely of me. I would shed my last drop of blood for the South." "I place you under arrest, Sir," was the general's unfeeling response. And without giving Mathews a chance to go by his home for a change of clothes, Bragg expelled him from Pensacola. What was done with the reporter's motherless five-year-old son in the circumstances is not clear from the surviving record, but Mathews was soon writing from the Confederate capital of Montgomery, Alabama, where he was apparently under house arrest. Authorities sent him to the Exchange Hotel, and from there he asked the War Department what were the charges against him and who were his accusers. He expressed a desire to have a trial to clear his name.[1]

Thus the Confederate army's first arrest of a citizen occurred on 14 April 1861, even before President Abraham Lincoln called out troops to suppress the rebellion. There would never be a day during the Civil War when Confederate military prisons did not contain political prisoners. This book is a study of those prisoners and of the system that created them.

What made the book possible was the discovery of records of 4,108 civilian prisoners held by military authority in the Confederacy. There were many more political prisoners than these, but I was able to locate records by name for only 4,108 in some five years of searching. To find even those required considerable effort, as the logical sources of information—the records of southern military prisons captured by Union armies after the war and now housed in the National Archives—in fact contained only fragmentary lists. More complete records of the prisoners lay elsewhere, improbably filed and, as explained in chapter 5, not easily identified.

Knowledge of the existence of thousands of political prisoners now reverses our basic understanding of the Confederate cause. Instead of protecting the southern rights and liberty to which politicians had extravagantly pledged their society before the war, the Confederate government curtailed many civil liberties and imprisoned troublesome citizens. Moreover, many white Confederate citizens submitted docilely to being treated as only slaves could have been treated in the antebellum South. Some, here and there, protested the system, but it operated throughout the existence of the Confederacy.

Almost daily Confederate citizens faced the test of their willingness to sacrifice liberty. For example, if they had to travel any distance on trains or carried products to market, they were likely to have irritating encounters with military officials who asked them nosy questions about their identity and destination. Guards and inquisitors confronted citizens on every railroad and at many crossroads. Thus in March 1863 a Virginian named Eppes complained to the secretary of war that "there are guards between Franklin and the City of Petersburg, who have instructions to 'stop' and 'search' on the *public highway* all carts and wagons and if they have '*bacon*' they are ordered back to Franklin under guard." Eppes bitterly reminded the secretary of war that "this struggle was begun in defence of Constitutional Liberty which we could not get in the United States."[2]

Men like Eppes recalled the pledges of the antebellum past and protested the Confederate system, but protests were not numerous. Although a great number of citizens traveled, the domestic passport system in place in much of the Confederacy during the war required the issuance of a government document each time a citizen wished to travel. It affected all railroad travel for most of the war and imposed restrictions on other modes of travel in places far from the military front. The system caused delays and often subjected citizens to impertinent scrutiny, whatever their rank in society.

The passport system can best be characterized as a gradual adaptation to the needs of mobilization and internal security. Unlike the more famous controversial measures often dwelt upon by historians of the Confederacy, conscription, impressment, or the tax-in-kind, for example, the passport system originated in the War Department and not in the Confederate Congress, but it had extensive reach without being the law of the land. The passport system quietly but firmly ruled the lives of citizens who traveled, whether they came from Indian Territory in the West or Richmond in the East. Passports were necessary for travel in some places as early as the summer of 1861 and nearly everywhere by the summer of 1864.[3]

Those unsympathetic to the Jefferson Davis administration noticed the system right away and pointed out its resemblance to the antebellum system requiring passes for slaves and free African Americans.[4] In East Tennessee, for example, where martial law was declared in 1861, opposition leader William G. "Parson" Brownlow commented, "Every little upstart of an officer in command of a village or crossroads would proclaim *martial law,* and require all going beyond, or coming within, his lines to show a pass, like some negro slave."[5]

Foreign visitors to the Confederacy, even sympathetic ones like the British guardsman Lieutenant Colonel Arthur J. L. Fremantle, could not help noticing the domestic passport system. Traveling from Meridian, Mississippi, to Mobile, Alabama, late in May 1863, he found that "on the railroad every person's passport was rigidly examined." Fremantle moved on to Montgomery, Alabama, and there boarded a train for Chattanooga, Tennessee. "A sentry stands at the door of each railway car," he wrote in his diary, "who examines the papers of every passenger with great strictness, and even after that inspection the same ceremony is performed by an officer of the provost-marshal's department, who accompanies every train." Always eager to excuse any unattractive feature of life in the Confederacy, Fremantle added that the "officers and soldiers on this duty are very civil and courteous, and after getting over their astonishment at finding that I am a British officer, they do all they can to make me comfortable."[6]

Not everyone was as fortunate in encounters with Confederate inspectors on the trains. Senator James L. Orr of South Carolina watched a provost guard turn out of a railroad car two young women who were traveling with the senator at three o'clock in the morning.[7] Some members of Congress grumbled about the system for years. In 1863 Senator Williamson S. Oldham of Texas objected to the passport system, under which he, though a "free citizen, was not allowed to go from [Richmond] . . . to North Carolina without going to the Provost Marshal's office and getting a pass like a free negro." Senator John W. Lewis of Georgia also complained that it did "not seem . . . just or proper that I cannot be permitted to go from this city to my home without obtaining a pass like a negro." Lewis offered a vivid portrait of travel in the Confederacy: "When Congress shall adjourn I wish to go home, but before I can be permitted to do so I must get some one who can identify me to go along with me to the Provost Marshal's Office to enable me to get a pass. At the Provost's I shall be met at the door by a soldier with a bayonet. After getting the pass, I shall be again met at the cars by other armed men, and be obliged to obtain other passes and undergo other examinations."[8]

Senator Lewis said that he would also like to carry some seed wheat back with him, but, he continued, "I, a free citizen of this Confederacy, cannot and will not humiliate myself by submitting to go through the required forms and circumlocutions." Finally, Lewis explained to the Senate that he felt it his duty to call attention to these subjects "because the practices complained of are having the effect of alienating from the Government the affections of the people. They are beginning to doubt whether they are really gaining much by this revolution."[9] But Lewis did not speak for all the people by any means. Others, like the editors of the *Charleston Courier,* fearful of "strangers, who come to us or go from us," felt that the "Passport system, well enforced, may answer so far as our Rail Roads are concerned; but it may be questioned whether some additional and stringent regulations are not required in reference to other modes of leaving the city."[10]

Some Confederates desired more restrictions; others, less. Most said nothing on the subject. Some of the critics, moreover, could definitely be termed extremists and idiosyncratic personalities. Sharp-tongued and dyspeptic Henry Foote of Tennessee, for example, complaining about a bill to devise a State Department passport for members of Congress, said "he did not want to go to the Confederate Government for authority to walk around here, or travel about. He would feel like a free negro if he did."[11] And Vice President Alexander H. Stephens, a shrill critic of the president, later denounced "the whole system of passports and provost-marshals" as being "utterly wrong and without authority of law."[12]

It could be exasperating to ordinary citizens. Dr. R. D. Craighead, of Dalton, Georgia, for example, inquired in the autumn of 1862 "if it is in accordance with the Spirit of the Constitution of the Confederate Government, that [in] each Small Town on the line of our Rail Roads through Georgia that Martial Law, be proclaimed by deputy Provo-Martials and So rigidly executed the Citizens or Soldiers must be under painful necesity every five or ten miles to have passes granted either to go to the Cars or from them."[13]

The passport system interfered with religion, business, journalism, and government itself. It could keep dying Catholics from receiving last rites and government assessors from appraising property for vital taxation. Thus O. H. Sears, a Catholic priest in Lynchburg, Virginia, wrote the secretary of war late in 1864, asking for "a general pass." The necessity of obtaining a pass for each trip caused him great "trouble and annoyance" and, he pointed out, "will sometimes prevent the sick and dying from . . . the rites of religion, a matter of great importance to us Catholics." Sears then received a sixty-day pass.[14] The head of the Southern Express Company in Richmond, a vital message and package service, complained in June 1862 that "our Messengers are being taken up in the street every day & put in the Guard House on account of military duty." He had obtained exemptions for all his employees, but they apparently did not suffice, and, he warned, "It will be impossible to conduct our business as it should be done haveing this annoyance every day."[15] As for the press, L. G. Reid complained to Secretary of War Leroy Pope Walker as early as July 1861 that passports restricting newspaper correspondents' travel muzzled the press.[16] A member of the House of Representatives informed the secretary of war that two government commissioners who were supposed to assess the value of products in the countryside each needed a general pass. "They are now subjected to some annoyance in traveling in discharge of their duties," he explained. The passes were given.[17]

The libertarian protests against the passport system made by such members of Congress as Lewis and Oldham were the stock-in-trade of southern politicians. Their lament was formulaic: a domestic passport system was suited to African Americans but not to free white Southerners. These protests thus fit a historically familiar scheme. The odious system exposed white Southerners to the erosion of liberty certain to remind them of the perils of slavery. In southern society before the war, slaves and free African Americans needed passes to travel, and free white people did not.

Of all people in the United States, antebellum white Southerners had once been the loudest in their protestations that they would not abide restriction, but the Davis administration was not about to abandon the passport system, despite occasional protests from politicians. In truth, the pressure on the administration to reform the system was never very great. The House of Representatives got around to inquiring about the irritating passports only in January 1864, after almost two and one-half years of operation.

Answering Congress's inquiry, J. B. Jones, the famous Richmond diarist and War Department clerk, testified that "the origin of the passport office consisted merely in a verbal order from the first secretary of war, and subsequently, I . . . was requested to take charge of the office . . . in August, 1861." Jones held the post until martial law was declared in Richmond in 1862, when he continued to operate under the orders of General John H. Winder. No one could explain how the system had spread to other cities, though it seemed likely that it was often an outgrowth of local and temporary impositions of martial law (such as the ones Brownlow protested in East Tennessee). The significant point, as Jones noted in his diary before the investigation, was that "There was no law for it."[18]

According to Jones, no one could leave Richmond by rail or any other conveyance without a pass, and he oversaw the issuance of 1,350 passes a day. His office stayed open long hours, sometimes until after one in the morning, but even so some latecomers were disappointed. Often the crowds and consequent delays were so great that people waiting in line missed their trains. The government provided separate offices to issue passports for men and women, but despite all their attempts to satisfy the public, the system remained, by the admission of the Richmond provost marshal, "obnoxious." It "trenches odiously upon personal liberty," Major Elias Griswold added; it was "attended with vexatious delays, and sometimes with questionings and interviews, wounding to the self-respect of worthy and good citizens."[19]

Even so, the domestic passport system remained a Confederate institution, for it had long since been tied to the prevention of desertion from the army. As Major Griswold put it, "Only a few days in this office will convince any one that without passports, deserters from our armies would increase to such an extent as to be truly disastrous. Nothing could prevent the soldier, who desired to do so, from putting on citizens' dress and returning to his home or going where he chose. Now a passport must be obtained, every person whose age subjects him to military service must give an account of himself [and] must produce his discharge or evidence of substitution &c." Jones pointed out proudly, "Cases are daily occurring where deserters and persons with fraudulent papers are . . . arrested."

In the end, Congress let the system survive—for ordinary people—and created by law a special pass for members of Congress, so that they could travel with one readily identifiable document. The system otherwise outlived congressional investigation, as it did all criticism. In retrospect, the criticism seems desultory and tepid. Justifying the system as a measure for preventing desertion surely did not meet the objections of women travelers, for example. In the last analysis, the government never needed the authority of law nor a systematic explanation for the southern public. Most Confederate citizens resigned themselves to getting passports if they had to travel. Freedom to travel—something that before the war had set white Southerners apart from black Southerners—was surrendered with little protest for the sake of the war effort.[20]

The passport system was a minor irritant in a society locked in deadly combat for national existence, and the remainder of this book focuses on much greater infringements of civil liberties, namely, the arrest and imprisonment of more than 4,100 citizens by Confederate military authorities. But a description of the passport system begins our construction of an accurate image of daily life in the Confederate state and gives us a feel for the atmosphere of the South at war. There were guards in many places and military posts throughout the South—"too much of brass button and bayonet rule in the country," as one disenchanted North Carolina congressman expressed it. By and large, though, most Confederate citizens reconciled themselves to the restrictions on freedom typical of modern wars. Their experience mirrored that of the northern society with which they were at war.[21]

PART ONE

LIBERTY AND ORDER

HISTORIANS OF THE CONFEDERACY today are divided into what might be called the "moderns" and the "populists." Neither school of interpretation is centrally concerned with constitutional issues, and therein lies an important tale. It is not that the historians consider constitutional issues unimportant to Confederate history but rather that the historians believe that the constitutional issues are settled. Most interpretations assume that restrictions of constitutional liberty went decidedly against the grain of the white people of the South. Despite their other disagreements, on that point the historians have reached a tacit consensus.

The leaders of the "modern" school, historians Frank E. Vandiver and Emory M. Thomas, emphasize, as Vandiver once put it, "the techniques of administration and business management [Jefferson] Davis adopted during the war, the experiment he conducted in rudimentary economic planning, in social control, in national mobilization." These "all represented fundamental changes in the South—changes which wrenched it rudely into modern times."[1]

Vandiver's student Emory Thomas, instead of invoking "modernization" or "institutionalizing," hit upon "revolutionary" as the concept to describe a similar phenomenon. He pictured a Confederate "revolution" somewhat out of control of its instigators and propelling dramatic changes in the South: "The Confederate government, albeit unwittingly, transformed the South from a state rights confederation into a centralized, national state. In so doing the government, or more usually Jefferson Davis as leader and symbol of the civilian Confederacy, incurred the displeasure of those who felt the government had gone too far, and of those who thought it had not gone far enough. Within the limits of its ability the Davis administration dragged Southerners kicking and screaming into the nineteenth century."[2] The "modern" point of view has become a standard feature of biographies of Jefferson Davis. Biographer William C. Davis, for example, said:

> More than anyone else, Jefferson Davis built the system and organization that kept . . . armies in the field another four years. Cajoling the governors, dominating Congress, having the courage to call for and enforce conscription, taxation, and the impressment of agricultural produce did not make him popular, but it kept the legions manned, armed, fed, and moving. Moreover it was Davis who, more than anyone else, accounted for what little sense of Con-

federate nationalism grew in the South. It came at the price of some of his cherished states' rights beliefs, and cost him the goodwill of men like Stephens, Brown, Toombs, Vance, and more.[3]

Despite the invocation of such concepts as "system," "organization," and "control," with their connotations of increased national government power, the "moderns" never quite made up their minds on the question of liberty. Vandiver, for example, said in 1964 that "Irritation with State-righters helped [Davis] . . . condone a political police force charged with arresting sedition. This doubtless was a mistake, for it contributed to the image of a dictatorship which his political enemies repeated gleefully across the country."[4] But only four years later Vandiver seemed less sure and made a more restrained statement: "although he boasted of thriving civil rights in the Confederacy—in contrast to the Union— and kept his hand carefully off the public press, Davis took an active part in social change." "Social change" seems milder than "social control," and Vandiver by no means said that Davis's boast on "thriving civil liberties" was empty.[5]

Emory Thomas seemed uncertain, too. In 1971 Thomas cited "the operation of martial law in Richmond" as "a clear case study of how far the Confederacy was willing to depart from state rights individualism." He vividly described the controls imposed on the Confederate capital by General John H. Winder and concluded that "apparently most Richmond Confederates accepted arbitrary rule with . . . docility."[6] When he returned to the subject in 1979, however, Thomas termed Winder's actions "perhaps atypical" and said nothing of the willingness of the citizens to go along with the authoritarian regime in Richmond. Instead of docile acceptance of government restriction, Thomas spoke of "the Old South's fundamental attachment to individualism and its jealous regard for civil liberties."[7]

The most thoroughgoing of the "moderns" is political scientist Richard Bensel, who carried the argument to the point of saying that "the all encompassing economic and social controls of the Confederacy were in fact so extensive that they call into question standard interpretations of southern opposition to the expansion of federal power in both the antebellum and post-Reconstruction periods." That statement probed the assumptions of southern historiography boldly, yet Bensel remained substantially captive to the myth of Confederate constitutional conservatism in regard to civil liberties. Discussing the suspension of the writ of habeas corpus, he asserted that "even when granted this power, Davis never used suspension as sweepingly or with as much overt political purpose" as Lincoln did. Bensel concluded that "the Confederate experience with suspension of the writ and martial law was considerably less statist than the administrative structure and implementation in the North" and asserted that "most arrests under martial law were probably related to the sale of liquor by civilians to enlisted men, usually in camps."[8]

The "populists" challenge the "modern" preoccupation with the organizational innovations of the Confederate elite—"economic planning," "social control," and "national mobilization"—and accuse them of failing to take into consideration the ordinary citizens who were controlled, mobilized, and fit "kicking" and "screaming" into others' "plans." The "populists" focus instead on the suffering and sacrifice of the common people and what, in certain areas, seemed to approach class warfare between planters and yeomen or Confederate authorities and poor whites. Their gaze fixes on economic questions, and the nature of constitutional liberty is seldom a concern with them.

The "populist" depiction of class warfare tends to come in social histories, which are necessarily limited by methodology to small geographical areas of the Confederacy, typically a county or group of counties.[9] But the most important formulation of the "populist" critique of the Davis administration appeared in Paul Escott's *After Secession: Jefferson Davis and the Failure of Confederate Nationalism* (1978). Escott criticized Davis for failing to develop an ideology adaptable to programs that might meet the economic needs of the common people. After Gettysburg and Vicksburg, Escott concluded, "Confederate ideology . . . practically ceased to exist as an ideology. No organized body of doctrine, principles, and goals remained, only the prod of fear."[10]

As a planter himself and a longtime representative of the planter class, Jefferson Davis had nothing to offer the common people in their distress. "Ideology meant less . . . to the common people of the Confederacy. Their prime need was immediate economic assistance, and they did not hesitate to seek or accept it whenever it was offered."[11] In the end, Escott pronounced an avowedly "harsh" judgment on Davis for proving "insensitive to the problems of ordinary southerners, who suffered greatly from inflation, shortages, speculation, and impressment." Critical though he was, Escott nevertheless still gave Davis higher marks on constitutional issues: "At no time did he totally abandon his claim to be a defender of states' rights and individual liberties, and indeed in these areas his record was much better than that of his northern counterpart."[12]

Thus the current great debate on the nature of Confederate society is only peripherally concerned with constitutional questions. Because their central focus falls elsewhere, both "moderns" and "populists" tend to accept without question the view that the people of the Confederacy were not about to tolerate circumscription of civil liberty. To this day the subject of civil liberties in the Confederacy rests substantially where Jefferson Davis put it in his memoirs written in retirement—a matter of sharp contrast to the practice of the Lincoln administration.

The traditional view of civil liberties in the Confederacy remains dangerously untested by documentary research. Focusing on the history of legislation and public executive pronouncements on the writ of habeas corpus, the only well-known part of the story, renders a misleading picture. The Confederate

Congress authorized suspension of the writ of habeas corpus for only about one-third of the war's duration, and President Davis actually suspended the writ of habeas corpus or imposed martial law over only a fraction of the territory within those seventeen months. Statutes limited suspension to the period from 27 February 1862 to 13 February 1863, and from 15 February 1864 to 31 July 1864.[13] By contrast, President Lincoln without congressional authorization suspended the writ of habeas corpus in some places within two weeks of the fall of Fort Sumter, and in certain cases it was suspended throughout the North for twice as long as the Confederacy allowed suspension. The bare public outlines of policy history thus suggest sharp contrast between North and South in constitutional history.

But public policy and administrative practice diverged sharply in the Confederacy, and liberty was more severely restricted for longer periods and over larger areas than mere legislative history suggests. All the chapters that follow help prove this point. The two chapters immediately following examine the subject of civil liberty in relation to modernization, as the current historiographical debates dictate. Chapter 1 deals with civil liberty in an area of the Confederacy as underdeveloped in comparison with the rest of the South as the Confederacy itself was in comparison with the North. Chapter 2 deals with attempts to control alcohol, as such attempts are often taken to be a sign of modernization. In the case of the Confederacy, it appears that modernization went hand in hand with proscription of civil liberty.

I

THE ROGUE TYRANT AND THE PREMODERN STATE

A "REMOTE DOMAIN"—SO ARKANSAS APPEARS to modern historians of the Confederacy. Yet its history in the rebellion presented in microcosm the general problems of the Confederacy, and the attempts of General Thomas C. Hindman to cope with these problems severely challenged civil liberties in the state.[1] For a time Arkansas was the fiefdom of this rogue military tyrant, a remarkable politician turned general, with a gift for stirring phrases.

In an amazing seventy-day period while he was commander of the Trans-Mississippi Department, General Hindman mobilized this prostrate state and created a minor economic miracle. Without hope of aid from the East, Arkansas, under Hindman, scorched its cotton crop and began establishing essential war industries. In the course of modernizing the state for war, General Hindman sacrificed individual liberties that had once been the obsession of "southern rights" politicians like himself and created the first great controversy over habeas corpus in the Confederacy.

Hindman probably could not have turned in his brief bravura performance had Arkansas not been remote from Richmond. However, to marginalize his activities as "fanaticism" ignores the uncanny qualities of the episode, not the least of which was its encapsulation of the problems of Confederate nationhood. Moreover, Hindman, unlike Jefferson Davis, was able to articulate his program in one of the most forceful documents from all of Confederate history. It has previously been difficult to take seriously Hindman's report on Arkansas as a manifesto of Confederate policy because of its forthright authoritarianism. But under differing assumptions derived from new knowledge of the existence of thousands of political prisoners in the Confederacy, it is time to reconsider Hindman and his eloquent manifesto.[2]

Hindman attempted to accomplish for the one-crop primitive agricultural economy of Arkansas, one of the least advanced Confederate states, what Jefferson Davis attempted to accomplish for the Confederacy as a whole—the strenuous manpower and economic mobilization in the face of an enemy superior in population and war resources—and all without practical hope of immediate outside intervention. Ironically, Davis would remove Hindman for doing in the West substantially what Davis himself soon recognized must be done in this region a year later—and for doing what Davis eventually attempted to do for the whole Confederacy.

Arkansas had a total population below 450,000, and three-fourths of the state had average land values below those in notoriously impoverished East Tennessee. In 1860 the state contained only sixty-six miles of railroad track and was dependent on river navigation for trade and commerce. It ranked below only Florida among the Confederate states in the value of its manufactured products.[3] Yet the state was growing, and the economy could be said to be booming.[4] Cotton was king. Like the Confederacy itself when compared to the North, Arkansas was a land of one-crop staple agriculture, otherwise underpopulated and backward in terms of transportation and manufacturing development.

Arkansas under Hindman went to extremes that the Confederacy as a whole never matched. As Union general John M. Schofield observed about a month after Hindman left the department, "Desperate measures are the only ones left to the rebels west of the Mississippi."[5] Hindman proved willing to attempt desperate measures in underdeveloped Arkansas before the Confederate cause as a whole was desperate. But unlike Jefferson Davis, General Hindman was not a democratically elected official. From the start, he operated blatantly without authority of law. When Hindman provoked civil libertarian opposition from an articulate but eccentric politician, Albert Pike, much as Davis did with Georgia's Joseph E. Brown and Alexander H. Stephens, he could not prevail. Davis would survive the opposition of Brown and Stephens while president—and in reputation afterward. Hindman was relieved of overall command and all but disappeared from history.

Because of a poor transportation and communications network, made worse in the western theater by early Union penetration and occupation, the possibilities of rogue military commanders who ignored or trampled civil liberties in remote regions was greater in the Confederacy than in the North. The Trans-Mississippi West was already considerably isolated before the fall of Vicksburg. Following the maps in Richard McMurry's *Two Great Rebel Armies,* we can see that dispatches from Richmond, if they traveled the most direct rail route, came down the Shenandoah Valley and the mountains of eastern Tennessee to Chattanooga, then looped a little south through Decatur, Alabama, and Corinth, Mississippi, to Memphis. There was no direct rail route from Memphis to the state capital in Little Rock.[6] After Corinth and Memphis fell early in June 1862, the upper west of the Confederate States grew still more isolated. A letter Hindman sent to the War Department on 9 June 1862 reached its destination on the 27th. The general in charge of the Trans-Mississippi Department was on his own. In some ways that suited Thomas C. Hindman. He was never one for keeping his superiors posted with reports. He sent none to Richmond on his operations in Arkansas until almost a year after Theophilus Holmes succeeded him in overall command there.

The document he finally sent to the War Department on 19 June 1863 was a minor masterpiece that should be reprinted in any compilation of important Confederate documents. Hindman wrote it in Richmond, using the official records in the adjutant general's office. He apologized for its length, some 9,900 words, but he need not have: the document is a model of organization, energetic prose, and clarity.

Hindman began the report by re-creating for his readers an image of the plight of Arkansas upon his arrival in Little Rock on 30 May 1862. The Confederate troops, defeated at Pea Ridge, had withdrawn and were then transferred to concentrate forces east of the Mississippi. The commander in Indian Territory, Albert Pike, had drawn back to the Red River. "Thus Missouri was left hopeless of early succor, Arkansas without a soldier, and the Indian country undefended except by its own inhabitants." The Federal forces under General Samuel R. Curtis advanced to within thirty-five miles of Little Rock.

Hindman drew a vivid portrait of a prostrate state:

A Federal force of 5,000 strong was organized at Fort Scott, under the name of the Indian Expedition, and with the avowed intention to invade the Indian country and wrest it from our control. Hostile Indians began collecting on the border and Federal emissaries were busy among the Cherokees and Creeks inciting disaffection. Detachments of Federal cavalry penetrated at will into various parts of the upper half of Arkansas, plundering and burning houses, stealing horses and slaves, destroying farming utensils, murdering loyal men or carrying them into captivity, forcing the oath of allegiance on the timid, and disseminating disloyal sentiments among the ignorant. A regiment of Federal Arkansians was organized at Batesville, another commenced in Northwestern Arkansas, and the work of recruiting for the Federal service went on prosperously. Tory bands were organized or in process of organization in many counties, not only in the upper but in the lower half of the State likewise, and depredations and outrages upon loyal citizens were of constant occurrence. Straggling soldiers belonging to distant commands traversed the country, armed and lawless, robbing the people of their property under pretense of impressing it for the Confederate service. The Governor and other executive officers fled from the capital, taking the archives of State with them. The courts were suspended and civil magistrates almost universally ceased to exercise their functions. Confederate money was openly refused or so depreciated as to be nearly worthless. This, with the short crop of the preceding year and the failure on all the uplands of the one then growing, gave rise to the cruelest extortion in the necessaries of life and menaced the poor with actual starvation. These evils were aggravated by an address of the Governor, issued shortly before his flight, deprecating the withdrawal of troops and threatening secession from the Confederacy.[7]

Hindman needed to act "with promptness," but he did not have a single soldier nor authorization to raise an army, "the instructions of General [P. G. T.]
Beauregard limiting me to the enforcement of the conscript act, which prohibited new regiments."[8]

When Hindman crossed the Mississippi to assume command of the department, he effectively crossed the Rubicon:

> To wait until the necessary authority could be applied for and received from
> Richmond, even if the Government should not deem itself precluded by the
> conscript act from granting such authority, would be nothing else than the sur-
> render to the enemy of the country from which the troops must be obtained.
> I therefore resolved to accept the responsibility, which the situation imposed,
> of raising and organizing a force without authority of law, and that I would do
> all acts necessary to make that determination effective. In coming to this con-
> clusion I considered that the main object of all law is the public safety, and that
> the evident necessity of departing from the letter of the law in order to accom-
> plish its object would more than justify me in the eyes of my superiors and
> of intelligent patriots everywhere.[9]

Willing from the start to work "without authority of law," General Hindman
began to raise an illegal army, "laying off the state into convenient districts,"
appointing a commander in each, and "authorizing him to purchase or impress
arms, ammunition, and the necessary supplies."[10]

Hindman adopted measures for manufacturing the sinews of war:

> salt, leather, shoes, wagons, harness, gun-carriages, and caissons, powder, shot
> and shell, and accouterments, all of which were soon produced in consider-
> able quantities. Preparations were made for mining and smelting iron, with
> the view to cast field and heavy artillery, and molds, furnaces, and lathes were
> constructed for this purpose. Machinery was made for manufacturing per-
> cussion caps and small-arms, and both were turned out in small quantity, but
> of excellent quality. Lead mines were opened and worked, a chemical labora-
> tory was established and successfully operated in aid of the Ordnance Depart-
> ment, and in the manufacture of calomel, castor oil, spirits of niter, the various
> tinctures of iron, and other valuable medicines. Most of these works were
> located at and near Arkadelphia, on the Ouachita River, 75 miles south from
> Little Rock. The tools, machinery, and material were gathered piecemeal or
> else made by hand labor. Nothing of this sort had been before attempted on
> Government account in Arkansas to my knowledge, except the manufacture
> of small-arms, the machinery for which was taken away by General [Earl] Van
> Dorn [when he departed the state with Confederate troops], and there was
> neither capital nor sufficient enterprise among the citizens to engage in such

undertakings. Considering the isolation of my district and the virtual impossibility of supplying it from east of the Mississippi, my purpose was to make it completely self-sustaining. With a reasonable amount of money I should have accomplished this design if left to my discretion in its execution. The natural resources of that country are truly wonderful in their abundance and variety. Energy and a liberal foresight might develop them to an immensely valuable extent.[11]

The report also makes clear that General Hindman was ruthless. He authorized guerrillas to operate in Missouri, including the notorious William Quantrill. He also decided to destroy all the cotton in Arkansas and northern Louisiana to "keep it out of the enemy's reach." A recent act of Congress authorized this, and Hindman's superior, General Beauregard, had already blazed the trail in the West with orders to burn cotton within reach of the Mississippi River, a program willingly carried out by Hindman on his way to Arkansas.[12] Hindman had definite ideas about how the destruction should take place:

To defer taking it into possession until the enemy should get in the immediate vicinity and then rely upon the owners to destroy it would be puerile. Wherever that had been tried the enemy got at least five bales out of every ten. Whether this resulted from the fears or the cupidity of the owners was immaterial. I determined to dispose of the matter differently and effectually. An order was issued seizing all the cotton which I regarded as in danger, and directing receipts given for it by agents appointed for the purpose. The same order directed that all cotton adjacent to the enemy's lines should be burned immediately; that the remainder should be removed 20 miles from any navigable stream and burned upon the approach of an enemy; but that out of all, as far as practicable, 10 pounds should be issued as a gratuity to each member of every family for domestic manufactures. The distribution in 10-pound parcels was as certain a mode of keeping the cotton out of the enemy's hands as to destroy it, while in fact it extorted from misfortune a great public benefit.[13]

Thus considerations of general public welfare also entered his military plan. It was efficient to bring about the end, Hindman argued, and it offered relief to "the wives and children of soldiers, and other necessitous persons" who obtained thereby "the material for clothing themselves and their relations in the army." He furthered that development by aiding "persons skilled in the manufacture of cotton and wool cards, spinning-wheels and looms, and caused wool to be brought from Texas and exchanged at cost and carriage for army supplies." He helped develop "home industry and production never before equaled . . . which was an essential element of my success in the creation and maintenance of an army."[14]

Desertion presented a serious problem for Hindman, as it would later for the Confederacy as a whole. The scarcity of supplies for the troops in the field and their families at home, the consequent dismounting of cavalry regiments to save corn, and irregularities in pay caused many men to depart. Because the new Arkansas regiments had been organized without authority of law, Hindman at first "shrank from inflicting the death penalty," but that seemed only to encourage desertion. Eventually convinced of an organized conspiracy to desert in numbers, Hindman convened a military commission of three officers to try deserters. Twelve men were executed, including one civilian for enticing desertion. "These summary measures had the intended effect," the general reported later.[15]

Finally, Hindman declared martial law over the whole state on 30 June 1862. Arkansas had experienced "a virtual abdication of the civil authorities," and "as the only man having the requisite force," he instituted "a government *ad interim*." He appointed a provost marshal in each county and put independent companies of nonconscriptable men under their command. The result, Hindman maintained, was gratifying:

> Martial law and the regulations enforcing it put an end to the anarchy by which the loyal population had been so long afflicted. They exorcised the devil of extortion that was torturing soldiers into desertion by starving their wives and children; they restored the credit of Confederate currency and saved the army from starvation; they broke up trading with the enemy and destroyed or removed out of his reach thousands of bales of cotton that selfish and venal planters were ready to sell for Federal gold; they insured the exclusion of spies, the arrest of traitors, stragglers, and deserters, and the enforcement of the conscription. Occasional acts of injustice may have been committed, but in the main the greatest good of the greatest number of loyal citizens was promoted. That was certainly the result, because these citizens themselves, as members of the independent companies, carried martial law into effect in their respective localities. Many arrests were made; but, though the order proclaiming martial law plainly invited the civil authorities to reassert their jurisdiction, I never heard that the writ of *habeas corpus* was even spoken of, except in the case of a negro man who had attempted the rape of a white woman whose relations were in the army. The writ was not sued out and the negro was hanged, as he deserved to be.[16]

Hindman said resistance to martial law came only from "tories, speculators, extortioners, and deserters and a few of the smaller politicians, who mistook the clamors of these malcontents for the voice of the people." All "good citizens" wanted martial law, including the two leading secessionist newspapers in the state.[17]

Hindman never had a doubt about his right to declare martial law.[18] "Precedents had been set by commanding generals in every part of the Confederacy," he noted. Martial law was in effect in Little Rock, under a Beauregard order, when Hindman arrived on the scene. Generals Earl Van Dorn and Sterling Price had declared it at Van Buren and Fort Smith. General Paul O. Hebert had declared it in Texas. General Braxton Bragg had declared it in Kentucky, and Hindman himself had declared it at Murfreesboro on his retreat from Kentucky before being called to Arkansas. "But," Hindman concluded in characteristically strident style, "if there had been no precedent at all I should nevertheless have taken the responsibility, risking myself upon the justice of my country and the rectitude of my motives."[19]

I have allowed General Hindman to speak largely for himself to this point. His statement makes clear how bold were the measures for which he was willing to take full responsibility. It should make clear as well the considerable ability shown in the composition of the document. This was no ordinary man. The words leap from the pages of the *Official Records* and sound less like a routine report on military operations than the economic manifesto of a nation-building visionary.

Of course, historians cannot take Hindman entirely at his word. He was a politician and a lawyer—and by the time he wrote his report, a general scorned. He could craft a self-serving case in broadly plausible and politically appealing terms. Hindman may have been either a fanatic or an unprincipled despot or both, but he put together in his report a careful list of precedents for imposing martial law. Checking his accuracy for the most part bears him out. Braxton Bragg had declared martial law over Memphis on 5 March 1862, and Albert Sidney Johnston had proclaimed it in Jackson and Grenada, Mississippi, on 30 March 1862.[20] On the Confederate retreat from Kentucky in the winter, Hindman declared martial law on 17 February 1862 in Murfreesboro.[21]

However, Hindman ignored one obvious precedent—from Arkansas itself: a declaration of martial law by Colonel Solon Borland in late November 1861. Borland's order, intended to alleviate Arkansas's severe economic disorder, declared it illegal to export or to monopolize certain commodities. He vowed to arrest violators and seize the commodities involved. The governor of the state protested and tried to annul the order himself; he wrote the War Department, and they revoked it.[22] General Hindman knew better than to cite as precedent an order for martial law overturned by the War Department; since his retirement from command in Arkansas he had evidently found time to put on his lawyer's hat and scour the record for those precedents that had not been overturned.

This rogue military commander was an energetic, explosive, unpredictable, and abrasive Democratic politician. Thomas C. Hindman was born in Tennessee in 1828, the son of a Whig merchant and Indian trader. The family moved to Mississippi, and Thomas went north to preparatory school. He became active in the

Sons of Temperance in Mississippi, and he practiced law. Though his background seemed to dictate Whiggery, Hindman entered politics as a Democrat opposed to the Compromise of 1850. He moved to Arkansas in 1854 and dived into its brawling political scene right away. Fighting with Bowie knives, signing on for a Cuba filibuster, and embracing extremist political positions all marked the five-foot-tall Hindman as a fire-eater. He advocated reopening the African slave trade and expelling free blacks from Arkansas.[23]

Hindman served a term in the Mississippi legislature and was twice elected to Congress from his Helena, Arkansas, district. He was an active secessionist. He had military experience as well, having served in a Mississippi regiment in the Mexican War, and after Arkansas seceded he became colonel of the Second Arkansas Infantry. In less than a year he made major general.[24]

Typical of his bombastic style was his proclamation of 4 December 1862 to the Confederate soldiers before the Battle of Prairie Grove, Arkansas: "Remember," he told them, "that the enemy you engage has no feeling of mercy or kindness toward you. His ranks are made up of Pin Indians, free negroes, Southern tories, Kansas jayhawkers, and hired Dutch cut-throats." Then he reminded his men of the homes, women, children, neighbors, and graves of kindred threatened by the invasion of these "bloody ruffians."[25]

Hindman was an extremist. From Corinth, for example, on 3 May 1862 General Beauregard ordered the Confederate quartermaster in Arkansas, W. Warren Johnson, to "Burn all the cotton within probable reach of enemy—You are vested with ample authority to destroy cotton." From Helena, Arkansas, the next day came an order from Hindman spelling out what to do:

> [You] will proceed immediately up Arkansas river as far as practicable, destroying all cotton on that stream[,] its tributaries or the country beyond which he can reach, without respect to persons or places. He [Johnson] will appoint such agents as he may deem necessary, with powers equal to his own. And he or they will summon such assistance of citizens as may be required to effect the purpose, arresting as Traitors to the Confederacy all persons resisting the execution of this order. . . . Receipts will be given.

Authority to burn cotton was surely not the same as authority to arrest as "traitors" those who resisted the burning. The Confederate Constitution defined treason as the U.S. Constitution did, and Hindman's use of the term could hardly be taken seriously. He added not only extremist exaggeration but also a certain populist edge to his order: Johnson was to be no respecter of persons among the cotton planters along the river.

More extreme yet was Hindman's order of 13 May 1862, a printed order presumably circulated in Arkansas:

All Cotton in Arkansas is considered in danger within the meaning of the act of Congress.

General Beauregard therefore directs that every bale of Cotton in the State be burned at once.

. . . The immediate, total destruction of the Cotton will be the best preventive of invasion, under present circumstances.

Beauregard had not ordered the destruction of every bale in Arkansas, at least not in so many words, but Hindman's mind—and his language—naturally worked toward extremes. In June Hindman ordered Johnson to "collect the remainder of the cotton in the District, not otherwise directed to be disposed of, at points in Arkansas and Louisiana no nearer than twenty miles of any navigable stream, distribute to necessitous persons enough for clothing for their families and contract for manufacturing the balance into army clothing, tent-cloth, etc. You will leave every planter enough for clothing for his family, but no more." Again, Hindman supplied an edge of class consciousness to his order, using the confiscation of cotton as a southern Robin Hood might to take from the planters to help the southern poor whites and the ragged privates in the ranks. In the end, 102,870 ¾ bales were destroyed in eleven Arkansas counties, along with 59,200 pounds of seed cotton in Arkansas County. The cotton destroyed was equal to about 28 percent of total cotton production in the state in 1860.[26] "Many planters complained," Hindman said in his report.[27]

Neither Hindman's predecessor nor his successor in Arkansas could get along without martial law.[28] The governor of Arkansas and other authorities there reported to the War Department in Richmond that some 266 civilian prisoners had been taken up in the winter of 1861–62 on vague charges of disloyalty and treason—long before Hindman came back to the state.[29] Some Little Rock civil leaders urged General John S. Roane, who, like Hindman, was also a successful Arkansas politician before the war, to declare martial law around the city in the spring of 1862. Roane, only recently appointed, asked Beauregard to clarify the extent of his authority, and Beauregard replied that Roane could declare martial law. He did so on 17 May 1862. Roane used his authority to prohibit the sale of liquor and to seize distilleries. He instituted a passport system and prohibited price gouging and hoarding of food. Hindman's successor, General Theophilus Holmes, wrote President Jefferson Davis a letter shortly after his arrival in Arkansas, justifying Hindman's controversial course of action while in command and seeking essentially to continue the policies.[30]

Drastic though the measures eventually became under Hindman, he followed the precedents of predecessors in meeting Arkansas's dire problems.[31] Furthermore, he put martial law in place gradually.[32] Hindman seemed sincere in his belief in the necessity of martial law, and he was consistent in urging its impo-

sition even when it brought him unpopularity with the people and with his superiors in Richmond. After his defeat at the Battle of Prairie Grove in December
1862, Hindman submitted the customary military report but added to it an
unusual reflection on what was needed to win the war:

> the last suggestion I have to make will be . . . decidedly unpopular. It will be
> odious in the eyes of speculators, extortioners, refusers of Confederate money,
> evaders of conscription, deserters, harborers of deserters, spies, marauders,
> federalists, and that less respectable class who regard these others as the peo-
> ple, and pander to them for their votes. The obnoxious suggestion is, a vigor-
> ous and determined system of martial law, covering all classes of evil-doers
> mentioned above, and compelling them, by stern and swift punishment, either
> to leave the Confederacy or to bear their due part of the burdens of the war.
> Without martial law, loyal citizens and the fighting soldiers of the country,
> their wives and children are literally the prey of the basest of the population.
> The civil laws, State organizations, rights on paper, and penalties on statute-
> books, are inert and powerless to help them.

Emerging from his rationalizations for martial law was a hazy version of a
warrior critique of bourgeois society and a radical nationalistic vision. Materi-
alism headed the list of enemies ("speculators, extortioners"), and Confederate
money was vindicated for the sake of national honor, not for any material lure.
If parliamentary democracy was not denounced, there were definite reservations
expressed about the political system: politicians "pandered" not to the real "people" but to speculators and shirkers.[33]

Hindman's successor, General Theophilus Holmes, a North Carolinian and a
man of very different temperament, was ordered to take command on 30 July
1862, and essentially he continued many of Hindman's policies. For example,
Holmes seized the salt works in Arkansas and Indian Territory on 1 October
1862.[34] It is not clear exactly what orders reached the generals in the hinterland,
but on 3 August President Davis had sent via the governor of Mississippi this dispatch to be given to Holmes on his way to Arkansas: "It has been reported to me
that the military authorities in the department to which you have been assigned
have usurped powers and displayed needless rigor by declaring martial law, by
forcing persons into service not subject to enrollment, by needlessly impressing private property, establishing arbitrary prices for commodities, and enforcing the discipline of a camp upon towns remote from the enemy and not
occupied by troops. You will endeavor to correct these abuses as rapidly as is consistent with the defense of the country."[35] By November, even the somewhat
obtuse Holmes seemed to understand that there was discontent with martial law.

Hindman's excesses provoked the publication of the only Confederate States equivalent of the great pamphlet wars of the North waged over the suspension of the writ of habeas corpus by the Lincoln administration. Albert Pike, the poet-lawyer, author of the most widely known words to "Dixie," mystic Freemason, self-styled friend to the Indian tribes, and commander of the Indian Department adjacent to Arkansas, managed to publish five separate titles dealing with the controversy over martial law in Arkansas.

It is difficult to tell whether paper and ink shortages rather than lack of keen interest dictated the scarcity of pamphlet literature on questions of civil liberty in the Confederacy. But the fact is that they were scarce. The standard bibliography of Confederate imprints does not even have an index heading for habeas corpus. The identifiable pamphlets on military arrests of civilians, the suspension of the writ of habeas corpus, and martial law, excluding Pike's output, number about a dozen for the whole Confederacy during the entire war. By contrast, northern pamphlets published on the habeas corpus question in Philadelphia alone exceeded by a considerable margin the number printed in the whole Confederacy. Civil liberty was certainly discussed in anti-Davis newspapers from time to time, but the intensity of the discussion often fell short of the systematic and steady drumbeat of opposition produced by the Democratic newspapers of the North. In fact, if history judged by the amount of literature of protest against government restrictions produced by the two societies during the war, then the obvious conclusion would be that the North was obsessive about liberty and fearful of falling into slavery and the South was less excitable on the question.[36]

Albert Pike's infatuation with opposition to martial law grew apace until it reached grand ideological proportions as well as a tidy bundle of pamphlets. The first production was an ill-fated *Letter to the Chief Magistrate of the Confederacy, Calling His Attention to the Enclosed Orders of Major General Hindman*, a circular dated 2 July 1862 and sent to Jefferson Davis, who rebuked Pike, as a general, for addressing the president directly through a printed circular.[37] *Albert Pike's Letter Addressed to Major Gen. Holmes*, published 30 December 1862, appeared in three editions, including one printed on wallpaper. In 1863 allies in Richmond printed Pike's *Charges and Specifications Preferred August 23, 1862, by Brigadier General Albert Pike, against Major Gen. Thos. C. Hindman*. Pike's *Address to the Senators and Representatives of the State of Arkansas in the Congress of the Confederate States* came to the public on 20 March 1863. On 20 April 1863 the indefatigable pamphleteer arranged to publish in Richmond his *Second Letter to Lieut.-General Theophilus Holmes*. This curious lot constitutes the principal pamphlet literature produced in the Confederacy on martial law and the writ of habeas corpus.[38]

It is possible to sum up the issues by focusing on Pike's *Address* to the Arkansas legislators, published in 1863. There Pike charged that General Hindman had committed the following offenses: (1) declared martial law without rightful authority; (2) appointed provost marshals throughout the state who placed "an arbitrary tariff of prices" on certain goods; (3) forced merchants to keep stores open "during certain fixed hours," to sell their goods at the fixed prices, and "to receive in payment Confederate paper at par"; (4) authorized provost marshals to establish punishments for offenses against these orders; (5) "declared Confederate money to be of equal value with any other, and required all persons . . . to receive it at par in payment of old debts as well as new," and had arrested at least one man, "an aged citizen of Little Rock," for disobeying the order; (6) "declared all cotton in the District, except in the Choctaw country, seized for the use of the Confederate States; appointed persons . . . to distribute large quantities to the necessitous persons of the community; authorizing them to call all persons to their assistance, and making it *treason* to refuse to give such aid, or for the owner of any cotton to conceal it"; (7) ordered the arrest of "all suspected persons and strangers" to be held until they could establish their loyalty; (8) unlawfully appointed officers in the army; (9) "caused several persons, citizens of Arkansas, to be put to death, without any legal trial by any competent tribunal known to the laws, for assumed offences against the military law"; and (10) "allowed his Provost Marshal General to try, condemn and execute, by hanging, a slave, for an alleged offence against the criminal laws of . . . Arkansas."[39]

Hindman had established a "reign of terror," said Pike. Hindman's military commission, consisting of officers whom he appointed without Confederate authority—one of whom may not have been twenty-one years old—sentenced nine men to be shot for desertion, treason, and disloyalty, with "Hindman himself witnessing the execution." Hindman also ordered "Brigadier General Roane to hold a military commission for the trial of offenders at the Pine Bluffs, in Arkansas; *and to preserve no records.*" Pike asked, "*Have the records of the proceedings of any trials by military commissions ordered by General Hindman, wherein men have been sentenced to die, ever been received in the War Department? Ask the question, and insist upon an answer, Senators and Representatives of Arkansas; for with and without trial, as many, it is said, as thirty, forty, or perhaps fifty, of your constituents have been put to death.*" Pike said that military commissions were unknown to law and that trials by them were illegal.[40]

Pike's address also reiterated the charges he had leveled against Hindman's successor, General Holmes, in November: that he had not rescinded martial law, as instructed, and that he had interfered with supplies bound for Indian Territory. He concluded with the ultimate Confederate insult, the unfavorable comparison with the record of civil liberties in the North: "The subservient Congress of the United States has lately passed an act to indemnify Abraham Lincoln and his minions from the illegal exercise of the same powers of despotism that have been exercised by Thomas C. Hindman in our State of Arkansas, and to authorize him for the future to exercise those powers, not quite so tyrannically as they have been exercised by the individual who was for some months the lord of Arkansas. . . . A more galling and degrading tyranny than that of Abraham Lincoln has been enthroned and reigned for months in Arkansas."[41]

The contents of these pamphlets and circulars must be measured against their origins. A careful look at the chronology of the conflict between Pike and Hindman suggests that Pike seized upon civil liberties issues to reach out for support in his already inexorable dispute with Hindman. The problem at first was jurisdictional rather than ideological and may ultimately have had to do with power and not with principle.

Indeed, one of the first complaints to Richmond about Hindman arose from another jurisdictional conflict, this one over recruiting districts. A conscript officer in Louisiana who found Hindman's subordinates seeking conscripts in his district sent the secretary of war copies of what he regarded as illegal orders from Hindman on 17 July 1862. The orders forbade substitutes in the army, called for the designation of officers for regiments Hindman had no right to appoint, and arrogated to the general and other local commanders powers that were probably congressional in nature. They also demanded the acceptance of Confederate currency in transactions and regulated prices for commodities. The orders called for the arrest of anyone refusing to sell or holding out for a higher price to be "sent to these headquarters, to be dealt with as such inhuman and disloyal conduct may deserve."[42]

Likewise, the root of the Pike-Hindeman conflict lay not in libertarian ideology but in confusion of Confederate jurisdiction. It also lay in Pike's egotism and in Hindman's inveterate power grabbing. As General Pike himself put it on 31 July 1862, "The beginning of mischief was the creation of the Trans-Mississippi District embracing the Indian Territory, and the assigning to the command of that district of Maj. Gen. Earl Van Dorn."[43] Pike's original understanding had been that he would administer the Indian Department independently, reporting directly to Richmond. When it became a part of the Trans-Mississippi Department, that was no longer possible.

Hindman arrived in Little Rock from Kentucky on 30 May. The full declaration of martial law was one month away. On 31 May Hindman ordered Pike to send part of his forces to protect Arkansas. Pike received the orders at 5:30 p.m. on 8 June and wasted no time drafting a reply running to well over three thousand words. The order, Pike responded, "destroyed" all his plans, paralyzed his efforts, and completed "the ruin of this command" (Pike had already been quarreling with Hindman's predecessors).[44] The real issue was the independence and control of the Department of Indian Territory, which Pike identified with strongly, lamenting particularly the departure of the artillery he had built up through great personal exertion and machination. By curious coincidence, he did mention in passing, while describing to Hindman his achievements in Indian Territory, "I have not even found it necessary to proclaim martial law, except in the immediate vicinity of the camps."[45]

The earliest of Pike's complaints against martial law came in a letter to Secretary of War George W. Randolph, sent on 30 June 1862. Referring to the limits of martial law in Hindman's initial order of 17 June 1862, which imposed martial law on Van Buren and Fort Smith, Pike declared that he would not allow martial law to be enforced in the Indian Country. It was not needed. Moreover, Hindman's subordinates should not impress supplies in the Indian Country, or Pike would order their arrest.[46]

At this point, General Pike protested martial law only as something not needed in his own jurisdiction. By 20 July, when the stakes had grown higher, the denunciations of martial law had grown louder and more systematic. He told the secretary of war then that he had submitted his resignation, "and also there is no power on earth short of actual force that could take me within the sphere of his martial law and the jurisdiction of his cloud of provost-marshals, and no power whatever that could compel me to aid in enforcing that martial law while I regard it as a simple usurpation and the substitution of a despotism in place of a constitutional government."[47]

By 6 July 1862, six days after General Hindman declared martial law over the entire state of Arkansas, the War Department ordered General Holmes to assume command of the Trans-Mississippi Department and to repair to Little Rock without delay, but the conflict over martial law continued.[48] The political questions churned up by Pike and Hindman simmered the whole time Hindman remained in Arkansas as a subordinate of Holmes. Congress asked the secretary of war for information on Hindman's actions, and on 5 September 1862, Secretary of War Randolph replied that Holmes had been sent to inquire and rescind martial law if the allegations of illegal actions were true. Randolph also stated evasively that Hindman had not been made commanding general of the Trans-Mississippi Department by the War Department. That was technically true because of Beauregard's confusion over the extent of his authority. The department's pusillanimous dodge of responsibility infuriated Hindman.[49]

The president began to feel the political pressure, too, and on 11 October Randolph, on Davis's instructions, told Holmes that

> reports have reached him [Davis] from reliable sources of the continued enforcement of martial law in Arkansas and of arrests of persons and seizures of property by officers of the army and provost-marshals. He is confident that it is only necessary to call your attention to this state of things to insure the adoption of prompt measures for the prevention and punishment of infrac-

tions of law. I am aware of the difficulty of restraining subordinate officers from exceeding their authority, and that with every effort on your part cases must still occur which afford well-grounded cause of complaint.[50]

On 13 November 1862, a general order issued from Little Rock stated: "The Legislature of Arkansas being in session, it is no longer necessary for the military authority to take action in any matter having regard only to the well-being of the people."[51] In all these documents evasive and euphemistic language reigned. No one stated clearly and forthrightly—in so many words—that martial law must be rescinded and not declared again.

By autumn, the president and the War Department had curtailed Hindman's power and denounced his methods. Outgoing Secretary of War Randolph disavowed any War Department role in Hindman's appointment to command in Arkansas. Randolph's successor in the department, James A. Seddon, regarded the general the same way. In March 1863 he told General Kirby Smith that Hindman was "admitted to have shown energy and ability" but "rendered himself, by alleged acts of violence and tyranny, perfectly odious."[52]

Arkansas's six-man congressional delegation agreed with the governor that martial law should be rescinded entirely or restricted to special cases and places and so informed the president late in January 1863.[53] When Davis seemed to ignore their warnings, all the representatives complained that Arkansans had been "outraged already by Gen Hindman with the silent acquiescence of the administration," and they protested "against the declaration of martial [law] in that state while Gen Hindman is there, and if he is to execute the law, under any & all circumstances!" The surprising outcome of this complaint is discussed in chapter 9, but for Albert Pike the ideological drama was not over yet.[54]

Pike's resignation had not been accepted, and he remained at his post in Indian Territory. His distaste for martial law grew, and he was now prepared to lecture the War Department on the subject at length. He did so by enclosing for the secretary's edification an answer he crafted on 26 October 1862 to a question raised by an agent of the Seminole Indians, who had asked him about the possible appointment of provost marshals in Indian Territory. Pike said he would not appoint them, and the reasons he gave ran to roughly two thousand words of political philosophy, accusing Van Dorn, Bragg, and Hindman of Caesarism and insisting that there was "no such thing as martial law in the sense in which it is popularly used."[55] Pike was clearly aiming beyond the Seminoles' agent at a broader audience.

By the fall of 1862, Pike had found powerful intellectual allies in his attack on martial law, including the vice president of the Confederate States of America, Alexander H. Stephens, who, Pike pointed out to the Indian agent, "has lately pronounced as his opinion that even Congress cannot declare martial law, which in its proper sense is nothing but an abrogation of all laws."[56] Pike had seen Stephens's denunciation of the prohibition on liquor selling in Atlanta by the local provost marshal (discussed in chapter 2) and recognized useful doctrine.

Pike likely also recognized doctrine coming from friendly and safe political forces, for Pike, like Alexander Stephens, had been a Whig before the Civil War. He had helped found the Whig party in Arkansas, in fact, and later became a Know-Nothing when he came into conflict with Hindman for the first time. Civil libertarian philosophy in the Confederacy was not old Whig philosophy, but it was often voiced by old Whigs. Politicians of Whig background in the North—like Abraham Lincoln—had little trouble reconciling their old beliefs with the suspension of habeas corpus and the imposition of martial law, but in the Confederacy, where mostly former Democrats rather than former Whigs now ran the country, opposition to martial law and the suspension of the writ of habeas corpus came often from former Whigs. In other words, the pattern tended to be the opposite in the South because the opposite faction was in power. Pike latched onto such opposition doctrine because of his jurisdictional grievance against former Democrat Jefferson Davis and especially former Democrat Thomas Hindman. Had he been left alone to fulfill his imagined destiny as protector of the Indians, Pike might very well have remained forever silent on civil liberties no matter what course Hindman took in Arkansas.

It is possible to write about the conflict between Pike and the Confederate generals in Arkansas without mentioning martial law, and one of Pike's modern biographers has done so, emphasizing not only the ego conflicts over power but also the legitimate and sizable disagreements over Indian policy and administration. Even the balanced David Y. Thomas in *Arkansas in War and Reconstruction, 1861–1874* discussed Hindman's fall without mentioning issues of civil liberties between Pike and Hindman, quoting Pike's denunciation of the general's despotism over a hundred pages later in a sort of coda on political issues. Conversely, it is possible to write about the conflict focusing almost exclusively on the principles involved in the argument over martial law, as more recent historians of Confederate Arkansas tend to do, for Hindman in his practical way and Pike in his windbag way had made the case for and against rather fully and well. Neither approach seems quite accurate if embraced exclusively. Both ambition and ideology as well as practical wisdom on both sides played their roles in the dispute.[57]

Hindman's ruthless methods resembled Pike's acid and uncompromising depiction of them. Hindman misrepresented what he was up to. In his self-vindicating report of 1863, Hindman had laid ground for depicting Pike as inconsistent on the question of martial law, saying that Pike by his own admission had declared martial law in some parts of Indian Territory. Pike's letter of 8 June 1862, which turned up in War Department files only later, not in time to influence the dispute between the two generals, actually had the opposite import from what Hindman maintained. What Pike had written was "I have not even found it necessary to proclaim martial law, except in the immediate vicinity of the camps."[58] Some confusion arose from the terms: properly, Pike should have said he imposed "military" law over the camps—a power universally acknowledged as embodied in the Articles of War passed by Congress and legitimate for men enlisted in the armed forces.

Pike attributed Hindman's actions ultimately to political ambition. "The difference," he told President Davis on 31 July 1862, "between General Hindman's views and mine is a radical one. He is an Arkansas politician, looking for future civil honors as a reward of a successful defense of his State, and his sole object is to effect her deliverance and safety. The Indian country to him is nothing, except so far as it affects the safety of Arkansas." Pike was hardly exempt from political ambition himself, however, and what better way could he find to establish credentials for the judiciary than to produce a string of pamphlets arguing constitutional issues? Whatever his aim—the purity of the Indian Department or the Arkansas bench—Arkansas governor Harris Flanagin appointed Pike associate justice of the state supreme court in June 1864.[59]

In February 1863, Hindman, bridling in subordination to "granny" Holmes and attempting to return to command under Braxton Bragg in Tennessee, had frankly admitted that the bold measures he took to arm the state, imposed without waiting for word from Richmond, had "greatly embittered the disaffected population against me." Now, he told General Bragg, he wanted out of "this grave of ambition, energy, and system."[60]

Both sides in this dispute agreed on one thing: civil liberties in Confederate Arkansas were sharply curtailed.[61] Pike complained about it, and Hindman proudly took responsibility for draconian measures as matters of military and civil necessity. At this point, President Jefferson Davis and Vice President Alexander H. Stephens both professed disapproval. When Hindman's successor, Theophilus Holmes, suggested the reinstitution of martial law, Davis told him, "Many complaints were made against the attempt to subject the people of Arkansas to a military police. The effort was certainly unwise, and no doubt much of your embarrassment has resulted from the necessity of restoring things to their normal condition. A people called upon to sacrifice everything in resistance to usurpation and oppression should always have before them unmistakable evidence of a strict regard for their rights on the part of those who invoke their assistance."[62]

Hindman proved to be both modernizer and populist, demonstrating perhaps that the two need not always be contrasted. But there were victims. The actual toll in political prisoners in Arkansas will not likely ever be known. There is no list by name of the 266 prisoners inquired about at the War Department in the winter of 1861–62 before Hindman's appointment, and these Arkansas prisoners—but a fragment of the whole number—form no part of the 4,108 prisoners providing the basis of this book. Arkansas's political prisoners were not transported to Virginia and North Carolina military prisons, the institutions from which almost all War Department records of political prisoners survive. Historians today know only what Jefferson Davis knew in the winter of 1862–63 at his post far from remote Arkansas, that there were many complaints from Arkansas politicians about civil liberties in the state in 1863.

Such information was at first enough for Davis, but he would change his mind. Thomas C. Hindman would not be alone in straying from the path of southern rights. He blazed the trail for Confederate policy.

2

ALCOHOL AND MARTIAL LAW
THE PROBLEM OF ORDER IN THE CONFEDERACY

A WHISKEY BARREL FIGURES AS THE main character in Phoebe Yates Pember's memoir of life as a nurse in Richmond's Chimborazo Hospital during the Civil War. Around that barrel's coveted contents swirls a tragicomedy of intrigue in the sprawling Confederate military hospital. An English "lady" working as a nurse turns out to be a comically staggering sot, and the precious barrel is the objective of various ingenious campaigns plotted by hospital personnel. At one dramatic point a drunken doctor kills a patient by amputating the wrong leg. Pember's whiskey barrel was a stroke of genius, for it mirrored the importance of alcohol in the society at war, a factor otherwise neglected in the literature on the South's experiment in nationalism—and one curiously important to the problem of civil liberty in the Confederacy.[1]

Early scholarship on alcohol in the Confederacy—now substantially forgotten—emphasized the progress of prohibition. William M. Robinson Jr.'s article "Prohibition in the Confederacy," published in 1931, argued that the Civil War brought prohibition briefly to the South. He noted that all but two Confederate states outlawed liquor distilling at one time or another during the war. The naval blockade made importation from abroad more difficult, and after February 1864, when the Confederate government regulated the amount of nongovernment cargo on blockade runners, importation became virtually impossible.[2]

But the image of a hard-drinking plantation regime and corn-liquor subsistence farmers in a backward economy—like Thomas Sutpen and Wash Jones drinking together in William Faulkner's *Absalom, Absalom!*—lived on. More recent work tends to ignore the moves toward prohibition in the Confederacy. "Not until the South began to industrialize and urbanize *after* the Civil War," says historian Ian Tyrrell, "did the region generate a powerful temperance movement."[3] Folk habits aside, many Southerners also sniffed abolition on the garments of temperance reformers and wanted nothing to do with modern reform movements.[4] If it had any effect, historians now say, the war may well have accelerated the trend away from temperance. In *Liquor and Anti-liquor in Virginia*, C. C. Pearson and J. Edwin Hendricks see the Civil War as wiping out whatever modest gains the temperance movement had thus far made in the South: it "played havoc with temperance and temperance work. Despite the examples of Lee, Jackson, and Stuart [none of whom was a drinker], drinking and drunkenness became the subject of serious discussion in the daily press."[5]

If the Confederacy moved away from temperance reform, then, in the opinion of most, it moved just that far away from modernization. Temperance to modern social science appears to have been a reform meant to bring habits of a precapitalist workforce into line with the discipline of the bourgeoisie.

But if the statute books can be believed, the Confederacy did witness a temporary triumph of prohibition, remarkable in the annals of nineteenth-century reform in the South. Prohibition is relevant here because it served to hasten the advent of martial law in the Confederacy. The neglect and misinterpretation of this development, which may at first seem far afield from the traditional problem of civil liberty in the Confederacy, have distorted our understanding of the powers exercised by the government and the nature of southern society that sustained it.

By the time of the Civil War the South shared with the North, if not the same impulse toward temperance reform, at least the same general attitude of the mid-nineteenth century toward alcohol: it was more a luxury than, as the previous century had regarded it, a necessity.[6] A stubborn exception to this attitude lay in the military and naval subcultures—especially in the realm of military medicine—where strong drink was still considered a necessity. The Confederate War Department consistently sought to guarantee a supply of alcohol in the face of hostile state laws and public opinion. Thus the Confederate government played a role as "modernizer" in hastening prohibition of distillation, often with the encouragement of local community leaders and the press, but the retrograde military demand for alcohol caused the government to leave many loopholes for distillation. The record of the Confederacy in the end was mixed—which helps to explain the varying interpretations, for there is evidence for both sides in the debate.

The drama of the whiskey barrel in the Confederacy began with mobilization.[7] The important underlying social circumstance was the generally rural and sparse settlement pattern of the South. When mobilization concentrated tens of thousands of young men in camps of instruction, they were for the first time in many cases out of sight of parents, wives, and preachers. Many seized the opportunity for drinking sprees. Southern communities near Confederate camps reeled in shock from the tipsily liberated behavior of the young rural roughnecks on their own. The problem was exaggerated by provinciality bred of scattered settlement: for some citizens *their* local young men had departed and *strange* and wild young men from other places now camped nearby and caused social disorder, especially when drunk.

The problem may have appeared greatest in Richmond. A South Carolinian there in February 1862 commented on the scene for his hometown newspaper:

The evils of intemperance among the soldiers, particularly among those from the country, are doubtless apparent in Charleston. But even with your experiences you can hardly imagine the scene presented in Richmond daily. The city is crowded with re-enlisted soldiers on furlough. A hundred whiskey shops are in operation on Main-street and the side alleys. Drunken men reel in and reel out, tumble into the gutters, sprawl over the sidewalks, brandish knives and pistols, and oftentimes indulge in those deadly conflicts which fill our prisons with candidates for the gallows. Something should be done to stop this all over the Confederacy. Not only should the distilleries be abolished, but every drop of whiskey, except such as is needed for the hospitals, should be poured upon the earth.[8]

"I have been a great deal on the rail road," wrote another Charlestonian a week later about conditions in his own state, "and during the last three months in particular have witnessed more drunkenness than I have ever seen altogether before, and most of it has been among our young and ardent volunteers."[9]

The most infamous single incident involved the arrival of city boys in a Tennessee village. After their organization as the First Regiment of the Polish Brigade (later the Fourteenth Louisiana), some 850 men from the Pelican State headed for the front in Virginia, stopping en route at Grand Junction, Tennessee, in August 1861 to cook dinner. Their commanding officer, Colonel Valery Sulakowski, took the precaution of requesting that all persons who sold intoxicating liquor "close their shops during the few hours the regiment would there encamp to cook rations." Nevertheless, some members of one company, the Franko Guards, became intoxicated and started quarreling with companies of sober men. A few of the Franko group also started a riot at a hotel. When the colonel rushed there, all order broke down, the men threatened to set the hotel on fire, and Sulakowski wound up shooting two of the men with his revolver. Altogether four men were killed and seven wounded in the incident. The Franko company was disbanded afterward. Colonel Sulakowski blamed "the cupidity of one or two *shop keepers* in the village, who forfeited their promises" not to sell liquor to the soldiers.[10]

Naturally officers often desired to issue orders prohibiting the sale of alcohol to their men. They could easily do so in camp, but their jurisdiction did not extend outside camp, and soldiers took leaves in neighboring towns. Proclaiming martial law would allow prohibition beyond the camp's boundaries as well. This idea occurred to Confederate authorities in Richmond, as we can see in the earliest declarations of martial law, almost all of which contained prohibitions against distilling or selling alcohol. The existing literature on civil liberties in the

Confederacy does not prepare us for this or for the surprising fact that southern citizens sometimes requested the imposition of martial law on their own communities so that they could deal, not with the approach of the enemy, but with the Confederacy's own drunken soldiery.

After President Jefferson Davis gained authorization from the Congress to suspend the writ of habeas corpus and impose martial law in February 1862, the initiative passed to the hinterland. The president waited to see what requests came in. He received several, and some had to do with alcohol.

From Lynchburg, Virginia, for example, came a petition with more than sixty citizens' signatures requesting martial law for the town and the area five miles around it. The petitioners, led by Merchants Bank of Virginia president Samuel McCorkle, explained that many citizens were away in the army but that there were large numbers of soldiers now on the local scene, whom the citizens could not restrain from disorder and acts of violence. The petitioners requested a declaration of martial law *"chiefly,* and *especially,* from the difficulty of suppressing the sale of spiritous liquors, whose intemperate use by soldiers and others"* lay at the heart of their problems.[11] Davis did not respond.

A committee of safety consisting of the mayor and commissioners and eighteen other prominent citizens sought the imposition of martial law in Wilmington, North Carolina, to prepare for attack, to counter disloyal persons, and to suppress the sale of alcoholic beverages. The committee cited the following as the dangers that threatened the town's safety: communication with the enemy in nearby New Bern and in ships off shore by disloyal persons and the "use of spirituous liquors . . . demoralizing alike to the soldiers and citizens in this town and its vicinity." Wilmington's civic leaders thought it "indispensable that during the existing exigency the civil power should to the necessary extent be subordinated to the military." Davis chose not to order martial law in this case but promised he would "upon further application."[12]

Despite the military subculture's endorsement of spirits, many in the military services saw alcohol as a serious threat to the efficiency of the war effort. Captain John Taylor, commanding the post at Charlottesville, Virginia, in the spring of 1862 urged the closing of liquor shops to keep alcohol from the Confederate soldiers recuperating at the area's military hospital. He followed with a more insistent letter on "the importance of declaring military law here, that the numerous Liquor shops may be closed—the importance of such a step forces itself upon me more & more every day, & nine tenths of the population concur in the importance of stringent laws to keep the soldiers here from that worst of all poisons to a soldier *Whiskey."*

Taylor had other concerns, among them draft dodgers and persons using treasonable language, but he never let up his drumfire on alcohol: "We have very nearly 800 patients here now," he wrote, "& the grog shops are at every corner.

I have been using the Jail as a Guard House. Those I have been obliged to confine, have been so destructive of the furniture in the Jail, & the windows, that the jailer this morning has refused to take any more." Apparently, the captain organized the Confederate surgeons at the hospital and other prominent locals, like John B. Minor, Basil L. Gildersleeve, and T. J. Wertenbaker, professors at the university, to sign a petition requesting the imposition of martial law to the extent of granting the commanding officer of the post the power to close liquor shops. Taylor's successor proved of like mind. Captain William B. Mallory also asked the War Department for authority to confiscate liquor stocked by unlicensed sellers. The problem, as usual, was not the enemy but the Confederates themselves: "since the Maryland line went into encampment about a mile from town," Mallory complained, "it is hard for me to keep order with the small guard at my disposal." The War Department instructed Captain Mallory to apply to the local county court to revoke the licenses of liquor sellers.[13]

A major center of trouble was Atlanta, Georgia, a small town made large by the war. Its residents were unaccustomed to the heavy railroad traffic of mobilization through this crossroads, and citizens grew uneasy with the transient population of soldiers. The most active pursuit of martial law and order came, not from Atlanta's citizens, but from the local military establishment. The colonel commanding the post was G. W. Lee, who told the secretary of war in October 1862, "The City of Atlanta . . . is a . . . point secondary in importance to that of Richmond. It is the great Center thoroughfare—and radiating point [for] . . . the Cotton States." However, this central position and role made the city, in Lee's view, "ever since the commencement of the revolution—a point of rendezvous of traitors—swindlers—extortioners—and counterfeiters. The population as a predominant element is a mixture of Jews, New England Yankees, and refugees shirking military duties. Besides it is the great 'Gate Way' for the passage of soldiers to Virginia the West and to the seaboard departments."[14]

Foreshadowing the sensational temperance tactics of the future, Lee seized liquor barrels, broke them open, and poured their contents in the streets.[15] He confiscated liquor from wagons coming into the city and apparently made numerous arrests—he collared a man named Harford seven times. Harford eventually employed a lawyer, who commented "that between Capt. Lee and the tyrant [Benjamin F.] Butler there is only this difference that Butler persecutes his enemies while Capt Lee persecutes his friends."[16]

Provincialism added to the early hostility to alcohol. The mayor of Selma, Alabama, explained that in his small town the young men were away, but three gunboats were being built by "strangers gathered from every quarter[.] Many of them are bad men as any. They violate our laws continually. . . . They crowd the drinking establishments night & day and it is dangerous to pass them." The Confederate provost marshal in Selma closed the bars for a time, and "during that time they were closed the city was quiet enough," the mayor reported. However, the secretary of war informed the provost marshal of the limits of his powers, the order was rescinded, and the mayor had a problem of order once again. "One of these Retailers does us, more harm than fifty open enemies. And if the Military authorities cannot suppress this evil it is a sad reflection," he complained. He went on to make this threat: "The Charter of the City authorizes me as Mayor to arrest & send out of the city all suspicious persons and if these hands which have been sent here to do government work are not controlled by the Government I will be compelled to call out & arm the citizens [to] arrest them [and] send them out of the city. I would regret this but cannot help it." Secretary of War George W. Randolph informed President Davis there was nothing he could do without martial law in the city except have the army used as a "civil posse," and so he telegraphed Governor John Gill Shorter authorizing him to call on the Confederate general for assistance if requested. Davis approved.[17]

Even some of those who did not believe in martial law admired the results it got in curtailing the sale of alcohol. The mayor of Atlanta, James M. Calhoun, writing to the secretary of war to defend the controversial actions of Provost Marshal Lee, said that he "never believed our government admited of" martial law. "Still," he added, "I hope & believe there is some legal way in which the retail of spirits can be prohibited at such a time, in such a place, as this."[18]

A close examination of the press in Richmond reveals a steady drumbeat of complaints about the drunk and disorderly state of the persons in the streets immediately preceding the imposition of martial law.[19] The Confederate Congress that authorized Davis to issue martial law declarations, of course, resided in the city and must have been influenced by the evidence of public opinion so pressed on their attention—as Davis and the War Department must have been as well. In at least one instance, the order imposing martial law appears to have been prompted directly by a request from a community. On 4 March 1862 a public meeting in Petersburg adopted a resolution asking for the imposition of martial law on their community and the surrounding ten-mile area, as in the Richmond proclamation. The Petersburg resolution was offered by the Reverend Dr. Theodorick Pryor of the Second Presbyterian Church.[20] Davis's proclamation imposing martial law on Petersburg followed promptly on 8 March.[21] Most often, the Confederate government did not respond to such requests with an order for martial law, but sometimes local authorities could act on their own. The attitude toward authority revealed in the requests for martial law is important. It shows a longing for order in the South, released by independence from the North and quite at odds with the region's fabled desire for liberty or "southern rights."

Motives among those who desired martial law were mixed, but religion sometimes abetted the pleas to rid the countryside of alcohol. R. B. Lawrence of

Milton, North Carolina, invoked religious language of national covenant in seeking a halt to the sale of liquor and to stop smuggling: "I . . . think that marshal law in Every town and vilage in the Confederacy would be greatly to our interest as a nation. I believe the good Lord will Bless us and deliver us out of all our troubles and difficulties If we Could get Clear of those Shilocks and whiskey men." When Eli Phlegan and other men from Christiansburg, Virginia, urged the War Department to take steps to halt distillation of grain, they were joined by the pastor of the Methodist Church and a man who worked as minister for two Presbyterian congregations.[22]

A typical mixture of motives, with an invocation of religious language, came in the South Carolinian's observations on Richmond quoted in part earlier in this chapter: "The family of the absent soldier . . . cannot compete with the liquor maker, and is reduced to the point of starvation while, on the other hand, the poor soldier is encouraged to destroy himself with the vilest stuff that ever ran down mortal throat. . . . This is the poison manufactured by man's cupidity out of the most essential gift of a bounteous Providence."[23]

Sin and waste of grain both figured in the complaints of Thomas E. King, a wounded captain of the Seventh Georgia Infantry convalescing in Roswell, Georgia. "With others," he told Jefferson Davis in February 1862, "I deplore the damning vice of drunkenness so prevalent in our army. . . . We have in two neighboring counties near 100 distillerys all under full blast. . . . They destroy thousands of bushels of corn weekly, which is causing a material advance and scarcity in this abundant section. . . . Corn which would only command 50 to 60¢ is now sold reluctantly at $100 per Bu. and unless a stop is put to this criminal waste of the 'staff of life' it will soon be out of the power of the families of our volunteers to get any and there will be suffering." King added, "It makes me tremble when I think of the evils intemperance is bringing on us through our army. I think most of our disasters can be traced to that cause." The president did not yet have an answer for the problem. "What is the remedy?" Davis asked the secretary of war.[24]

In the same month Rufus W. Folger, of Spartansburg, South Carolina, said that distilleries were "raising the price of bread beyond the reach of the poor Families of thousands of our Brave soldiers now upon the Battle Field Fighting in the noblest cause men ever fought for." Folger also referred to the national covenant, noting recent reverses after God's having blessed the nation for twelve months. Alcohol could hold back the realization of the Confederate mission of nationhood. A North Carolinian invoked the idea of the national covenant, complaining of drunken officers "making beasts of themselves," setting a bad example for the common soldiers, and thus inviting the disfavor of the "God of Battles."[25]

The greatest concentration of protest came in the early months of 1862, but as late as June 1864 Joseph Taylor, of southwestern Georgia, complained about the continued distillation of corn into whiskey:

> No country, particular our infant friendless Republic can prosper until Such a curse as the distilling of corn into Liquor be in toto prohibited. We can hear crys for bread daily younder on an other Street[.] we can see Some one lying beastly drunk off of this miserable Stuff. Even our Soldiers when they come make beasts of themselves, distroy their own families and insult them at home. The Great God the Ruler of the Universe will never bless a people like us until this great evil is entirely abolished. We may have our national "Fast" days, assemble to pray for the success of the Confederate cause. Suppose our independence to day was achieved and our Soldiers returned home[—]do you doubt that three fourths of them would be drunk and continue So as long as the poison could be had. . . . As a People making pretensions of Christianity, I can say and feel it that the Nation is not prepared for *Peace*. Everything tending to corrupt and interrupt the morals of the Land ought to be prohibited.[26]

Albert G. Graham, of Jonesboro, Tennessee, suggested to Jefferson Davis that the copper from whiskey stills could be seized by the government to make the barrels of cannon. "Why should churches give up their bells?" he asked. "Why should planters? why should the women give up their copper kettles?" Graham added, "Temperance men say that half a million drunkards die annually. . . . If [the stills] . . . are now taken, & their brass and copper turned to war purposes, it will mark an era in temperance which will be spoken of in history." A railroad official, concerned about drunkenness on the trains, wrote Secretary of War Randolph, "For the safe transportation of Govt. Troops & stores over this Road It is necessary that a guard of Confederate Soldiers say 12 or 15 should be placed at different stations on one line of Road to prevent the Sale of Liquor to troops."[27]

Religious temperance advocates apparently had no problem with the accomplishment of their goals by military means. Thus W. H. Christian, speaking "as a representative of a Division of the Sons of Temperance," wrote to the president requesting the continuation of martial law in Richmond. Organized religion was also in evidence at a meeting in Botetourt County, Virginia, urging War Department control of alcohol production. A mass meeting on 10 February 1862 appealed to the Confederacy's material interests, arguing that "*grain* is more necessary than money for the sustenance of our troops." The meeting began, however, with an "address by the Rev. William McGuire, explaining the object of the meeting."[28] B. M. Ednery, of Polk County, North Carolina, urged the secretary of war not to give permits to distillers, who were "stilling up all the corn from the Soldiers Wives" and would "ruin & starve our poor people." There was no explicit religious language in this formulation, but Ednery did say that the "whole moral community" had implored him to address the secretary.[29]

In the end, the argument that most often prevailed was secular and nationalistic, and the people did not go unheard. As soon as Congress allowed the president to suspend the writ of habeas corpus, prohibition of liquor became an
objective of martial law. On the day he signed the bill authorizing him to suspend the writ of habeas corpus, President Davis hastily sent a telegram placing
Norfolk and Portsmouth, Virginia, under martial law. Within days the administration had settled on wording for such proclamations, declaring martial law in
Richmond on 1 March 1862 in this language: "I, Jefferson Davis, President of the
Confederate States of America, do proclaim that martial law is hereby extended
over the city of Richmond and the adjoining and surrounding country to the distance of ten miles; and I do proclaim the suspension of all civil jurisdiction (with
the exception of that of the mayor of the city) and the suspension of the privilege of the writ of habeas corpus within the said city and surrounding country
to the distance aforesaid."[30] The adjutant general, Samuel Cooper, then added
the following orders:

> All distillation of spirituous liquors is positively prohibited, and the distiller-
> ies will forthwith be closed. The sale of spirituous liquors of any kind is also
> prohibited, and establishments for the sale thereof will be closed.
>   . . . All persons infringing the above prohibition will suffer such punish-
> ment as shall be ordered by the sentence of a court-martial, provided that no
> sentence to hard labor for more than one month shall be inflicted by the sen-
> tence of a regimental court-martial, as directed by the Sixty-seventh Article
> of War.[31]

The order for Petersburg, following the same format, came a week later.

Other methods were explored as well for curtailing alcohol production. For
example, a reporter noted in February 1862, at the height of popular enthusiasm
for action on alcohol, that "From every part of Virginia petitions are pouring into
the General Assembly, praying for the prohibition of the further distillation of
grain into whisky."[32] The state legislature in Virginia would respond within
weeks, and other states would move, too, but the quickest results came from the
imposition of martial law. Commenting on the results in the behavior of soldiers
on furlough in Richmond, a Charleston reporter noted the contrast "with the
drunken revelry and abandoned licentiousness of the soldiery which crowded
this place in autumn last" and no longer "despair[ed] of the Republic." "Through
absolute fear, or disgust of them, respectable travel had almost ceased. . . . Rev-
elling and brawling, revolvers and bowie knives, bleared eyes, dishevelled hair,
muddy boots, dirty clothes, sick stomachs, aching hearts and dethroned reasoning faculties were *then* the order of the day. *Now*—glory be to Martial Law!—
things are changed. . . . It is seldom . . . that you meet with a drunken or
refractory soldier."[33]

Influential Richmond newspapers waxed enthusiastic. The *Dispatch* concluded on 12 March 1862 that the result of the imposition of martial law "makes us almost wish that cities were always governed by martial law. The rascals, rowdies, and rioters have all disappeared. . . . the dram shops have come to an untimely end."[34] The *Enquirer* also applauded the results in limiting the effects of whiskey on Confederate soldiers and lamented the passing of the president's authority to declare martial law a year later, saying, "So tender and jealous was our last Congress of vesting in the President a power to proclaim martial law that the evil is beyond his reach. No power can now be brought to bear on this nuisance."[35] The enthusiasm sweeping the Confederacy for curtailing alcohol production reached even the most improbable people. Governor Joseph E. Brown, of Georgia, who would take a different view later, in May 1862 consented to a plan to impose martial law on Savannah if the president endorsed the local military commander's plan.[36]

Problems arose almost immediately, however. A lawyer and member of the Virginia Assembly named Robert Collier got the War Department to end courts-martial for violation of the anti-liquor ordinances under martial law. Collier's protests, published in newspapers and as pamphlets, were among the earliest systematic defenses of civil liberties in the Confederacy and offered vivid proof that alongside the yearning for order there still existed among many Southerners sharp anxieties about liberty.[39] Complaints from other lawyers caused the government to alter the language of the proclamations so that most ordinary work of civil courts—probate of wills, administration of estates of deceased persons, qualification of guardians, property sales, orders concerning roads and bridges and county levies, and payment of county dues would not be suspended.

The War Department duly amended the proclamations, but the later orders—for various counties in Virginia, for part of South Carolina, and for East Tennessee—all retained prohibition of alcohol. State legislatures began passing prohibition laws, too. All along, various authorities banned liquor sales and production from place to place—occasionally the head surgeon of a military hospital, altering the pattern of military medicine's insistence on the availability of alcohol, would oblige the local residents and suppress liquor sales.[38]

Other allies of the prohibition movement among the military were General John C. Pemberton, General Lucius B. Northrup, and General Elias Griswold. Pemberton brought about a strict prohibition in Charleston, South Carolina, for a time.[39] Northrup, as the commissary general, naturally felt the scarcity of food supplies and wanted the South's grain in its natural condition.[40] Griswold, as Richmond's provost marshal, witnessed the welter of tippling and related crime in the Confederacy's greatest boomtown.[41] As a Richmond resident, even President Jefferson Davis had to agree sometimes, though after the war he would become an anti-prohibitionist: "It is necessary that the introduction & sale of liquor in this City be prevented," he said on 15 October 1862, "the peace of the city, the welfare of the army, the care of the sick, and the safety of the place demand it. Call upon the city authorities to withhold licenses if that be done the military & civil police may through the courts maintain order, if it be declined orders will be given to meet the necessity."[42]

Ultimately the military establishment, especially the doctors, kept distilling alive in the Confederacy. In Virginia, for example, the manufacture of whiskey after 12 March 1862 was illegal, unless it was made on contract with the Confederate government.[43] As at Mrs. Pember's Chimborazo Hospital, Confederate medical doctors retained the whiskey barrel and deemed brandy, sherry, whiskey, and other alcoholic beverages medical necessities. When they grew scarce, a doctor might report, as one did in 1865, that "the men in the Hospitals were dying for the want of stimulants."[44] Alcohol regularly appeared on lists of supplies needed for the medical department.[45]

Though we may see it differently today, tradition was on the army's side. No less venerable an American soldier and Virginian than George Washington had recommended alcohol's military virtues. In a letter to the Continental Congress during the Revolution, Washington wrote, "I would beg leave to suggest the propriety of erecting public distilleries in different states. The benefits arising from the moderate use of strong liquor have been experienced in all armies and are not to be disputed."[46]

George Washington's attitude was echoed by the comments of James Lyons, a member of the Confederate Congress from Virginia, who called the secretary of war's "attention to the suffering of our troops for the want of a little whiskey—Every day and night almost when it rains the poor fellows come into me for it, complaining often that after 24 hours of picket duty they are still without a mouthful to drink, and with great pleasure I feed them, dry them and reanimate them with a drink, but the latter cannot hold out much longer unless the strange phenomenon of Martial Law, which, in the very teeth of an act of Congress, forbids a private citizen to purchase spirit for private use is corrected—While the deprivation was confined to the well it might be borne but . . . even the sick suffer from it."[47] Even the enthusiastically pro-martial law *Richmond Dispatch* recommended a spirit ration for the army, as a small quantity of whiskey twice a day was essential for the health of men undergoing exposure.[48]

Some members of the worldly Confederate elite, always excluding Lee, Jackson, and Stuart, of course, tended to have a mellow outlook on the subject. Secretary of War Randolph, for example, talked as a man does who has tasted and appreciated the product of the distiller's art. When a proposal from a firm to make whiskey for the government came to the War Department, Randolph endorsed it this way: "This is a long established concern famous for its good whiskey."[49] As late as 31 January 1865, Mrs. Chesnut attended a ladies' luncheon at the Confederate White House, where the president's wife served claret soup and champagne. Mrs. Davis apparently had a famed recipe for apple toddy as well.[50]

Moreover, the distilling industry was an interest, a sector of the southern economy, and there were men interested in profiting from it and promoting it. There were also farmers with corn and orchardists with fruit for brandy who were used to disposing of their perishable crops in the production of alcohol. Among the interested great men was Alexander Hugh Holmes Stuart, the former Whig leader, who vigorously pressed on the War Department the interest of his brother, a distiller named G. B. Stuart. After explaining the favorable terms his brother could offer the government, Alexander Stuart added, "Whiskey is now regarded as essential to the health of the army." The network of southern hospitality among the elite proved useful, for Stuart noted that "Mr. Randolph may have seen some of the whiskey of G. B. Stuart & Co at the home of his brother T. J. Randolph."[51]

To be sure, some could rise above narrow self-interest on the issue. Lewis G. Harvie, for example, who was president of the Richmond and Danville Rail Road, told the secretary of war, "Of course it is the interest of the R Road to transport what is offered, but that interest I did not & do not regard if it conflicts with the policy of the Government in time of War." He ordered that no liquor be carried on his trains to Coalfield, a gathering point for smuggling into Richmond.[52]

The struggle over alcohol in Atlanta had important consequences because the Confederate vice president, Alexander H. Stephens, wrote one of the milestone documents on civil liberty in the Confederacy when he was asked for his opinion on prohibition there. The "civil governor" of Atlanta, appointed by General Braxton Bragg, wrote Stephens to ascertain the extent of his authority. The official was not able to find any printed guidelines for his office, and he was faced with conflict over the control of alcohol in the city. Stephens replied from Richmond on 8 September 1862 in the blistering prose that increasingly marked his style. "The truth is," Stephens wrote, "your office is unknown to the law." "General Bragg," he asserted, "had no more authority for appointing you Civil Governor of Atlanta than I had; and I had, or have, no more authority than any street-walker in your city." Pointing out that the Confederate Constitution "was made for War as well as Peace," Stephens asserted that "in this country there is no such thing as Martial Law." The so-called civil governor had "no jurisdiction" in cases of selling liquor to soldiers. As for a practical solution to the problem of drunkenness in the Confederacy, Stephens offered only this advice: "If the proper discipline and good order of the army require that the sale of liquor to a soldier by a person not connected with the army should be prohibited, (which I do not mean to question in the slightest degree,) let the prohibition be declared by law, passed by Congress, with pains and penalties for a violation of it, with the mode and manner of trying the offence plainly set forth."[53]

The questions of law were complicated. General Simon Bolivar Buckner's attempt to ban liquor in Knoxville met the opposition of local interests who gained the ear of their congressman, N. G. Swan. On behalf of a number of bar-keepers in his district, Swan asked for clarification of the extent of General Buckner's powers to close barrooms in Knoxville. Swan acknowledged the general's authority to ban liquor in a garrison, but the camps were a mile or two outside of Knoxville, and Swan could not see why a general "may . . . not likewise declare any other town or locality where no troops are encamped a 'garrison' and place it under military law."[54] Yet for many southern citizens, being located near a camp brought frightful horrors from Confederate troops. The board of trustees of the town of Manchester, Virginia, for example, in the spring of 1863 asked for protection, not from the enemy, but from General John Bell Hood's command. Though stationed three or four miles outside town, the "unrestrained" soldiers committed murder, beat old and unoffending men, and brought "unprovoked drunken broils" when they came to town.[55]

In the end, most of the doubts were dispelled by state legislation. In the state-houses the argument that prevailed was the one of scarcity of grains. Only laws against distilling and not against sale or consumption were passed, and the pre-ambles to prohibition laws generally stated relief from rising grain prices as the purpose of the legislation. Temperance thus marched across the South in the guise of patriotism with the most effective strides it had ever made or would make until near the end of the century: Virginia, 12 March 1862; Georgia, 22 November 1862; Alabama, 8 December 1862; Florida, 15 December 1862; North Carolina, 17 December 1862; Mississippi, 3 January 1863; Louisiana, 20 June 1863; and Texas, a county option law on 16 December 1863.[56]

The actual effect of these measures is difficult to assess. S. S. Barber of Hunts-ville, North Carolina, for example, complained that despite state law, the state authorities were ineffectual in controlling distilleries, that a hundred or more continued to operate in North Carolina, and that, "as the necessities of the army are so urgent, . . . the military authorities ought to take the matter in hand." He reminded the secretary of war that old General Andrew Jackson, when he imposed martial law on New Orleans in the War of 1812, "sent a military force who seized the still caps & put them under guard."[57]

In his pioneering article on the subject, historian William M. Robinson argued on the basis of the state laws of 1862 and the well-known regulations of block-ade-running that prohibition was "the enforced product of war conservation. It was never a high moral issue." Likewise, May Spencer Ringold in her 1966 book on state legislatures in the Confederacy concluded that "few of the general laws relative to the production of whiskey passed by Southern legislatures were inspired by concern for morals or law and order; rather, the object seems to have been conservation of foodstuff for soldiers and for home consumption."[58] Such conclusions rely too completely on the preambles to the state laws for evidence of motivation. There is other evidence available now—revealing the early and sharp reactions to the tipsy violence of the Confederate soldiers in camps of instruction in the first winter of the war. Some of these invoked the national covenant in pleas for prohibition.

Most significantly, Robinson and Ringold overlooked the origins of prohibition in martial law. Indeed, some Confederate citizens asked for martial law in order to regulate alcohol. The legislation was only the later phase of a movement begun for the sake of law and order and with high hopes of maintaining the national covenant. That alcohol should be the subject of specific and special regulation in almost all of the early martial law orders speaks volumes about southern society. The willingness to embrace such means in a people allegedly wed to constitutional form is surely a sign of a deep longing for order—not a social force emphasized in much recent literature on the antebellum South.[59]

The prohibition provisions in the orders likewise disprove the customary assertion that Jefferson Davis used the power to suspend the writ of habeas corpus and impose martial law sparingly even after the legislature granted him authority. In fact, Davis employed the power for social ends beyond the constitutionally described ends of repelling invasion and providing for public safety. Ironies abound in this. None of President Abraham Lincoln's proclamations suspending the writ of habeas corpus and imposing martial law included the prohibition of alcohol (and Lincoln, unlike Davis, was a teetotaler). There were some protests against the restrictions imposed by the Confederate government, but most came from people with a direct pecuniary interest in alcohol production, from their lawyers, and from the farseeing but dyspeptic Alexander H. Stephens. His role in articulating dissent in this matter was somewhat analogous to Albert Pike's in the case of Arkansas. These men were, at this time at least, eccentric Confederates.

Faced with a problem of order early in their nation's brief history, the Confederates asked for and received the requisite government force to achieve it—sometimes in impositions of martial law and in most places by state legislation. Though largely overlooked by historians, the relationship between alcohol and martial law nevertheless is deeply revealing of the yearning for order in the Confederate States of America.

PART TWO

THE CONFEDERATE BENCH AND BAR

THERE IS NO "ADEQUATE HISTORY of the southern legal system in relation to the national," according to the modern student of slavery, Eugene Genovese.[1] This leaves a major gap in southern social history, for as historian Vernon Burton comments, "Although most professional opportunities were in short supply in the agrarian South, attorneys abounded."[2]

The need for basic study of the southern bar seems acute for the period of the Civil War. The existing literature offers no distinct image of the Confederate bar, and the lingering myth of the "Southern lawyer-statesman" who was supposed to be "a far cry from the dusty rider of the plains," that circuit-riding attorney of the West, does not really aid our understanding.[3] Southern lawyers came in all types, including circuit riders, because of the crazy quilt of social conditions in the states that formed the Confederacy. As historian Charles S. Sydnor observed of the South, "Some parts of it had been settled less than a generation when the Civil War began, while older settlements in pine barrens and mountain coves were in a sense retarded frontiers, relatively out of reach of sheriff and court."[4] Men practicing in the two- hundred-year-old courts of Virginia, practitioners of law according to the Napoleonic code in Louisiana, and quick-study frontier circuit riders contributed to the mix of the Confederate bar.[5]

Modern scholarship on the bar is only emerging.[6] The bench now is better served, perhaps, but in general law in the South is a subject too much neglected given the common assumptions that the region was obsessed with constitutionalism, that the southern people were especially legal minded, and that the South had lawyers in excess of their society's simple agrarian needs.

Naturally, the bench and bar had much to do with civil liberties in the Confederacy. Works of Confederate history offer two different images of the lawyer's role. In one, lawyers appear as nettlesome troublemakers who aided treason without committing it themselves. In the other, they appear as self-sacrificing patriots who adapted the American legal system to the peculiar need of the Confederate States of America despite the strains of war.

The hostile image came from the Richmond journalist Edward A. Pollard, who combined hatred of Jefferson Davis with a lofty contempt for the masses of Confederate citizens. The people lacked "patriotic devotion to the South," he complained. "Only the utmost rigor of conscription," he argued, "forced a majority of its troops in the field; . . . half of these were disposed to desert on the first opportunities; and . . . the demands for military service were cheated in a way and to an extent unexampled in the case of any brave and honorable nation engaged in a war for its own existence." "We have," Pollard pointed out as proof, "the remarkable fact that in one year the Confederate States Attorney in Richmond tried *eighteen hundred* cases in that city on writs of habeas corpus for relief from conscription!" Pollard expressed rare contempt for the writ of habeas corpus: "This honored writ . . . became the vilest instrument of the most undeserving men; and there is attached to it a record of shame for the South that we would willingly spare. Mr. Humphrey Marshall, a member of the Confederate Congress . . . , added to his pay as a legislator the fees of an attorney to get men out of the army; he became the famous advocate in Richmond in cases of habeas corpus; and he is reported to have boasted that this practice yielded him an average of two thousand dollars a day!"[7]

The work of twentieth-century scholars has rehabilitated the images of the Confederate lawyer and judge. They seem now almost models of moderation and believers in the rule of law. Legal historian Maxwell Bloomfield, for example, describes Texas attorney William Pitt Ballinger as a reluctant secessionist who nevertheless loyally supported the Confederacy. With few clients during the war, he made ends meet only by combining his private fortune with income from a government job sequestering the property of enemy aliens.[8]

Descriptions of the Confederate judiciary verge on the unctuous. The landmark work on the subject, William M. Robinson Jr.'s *Justice in Grey: A History of the Judicial System of the Confederate States,* concluded that the "course of justice was preserved in practice as well as in constitutional and statutory contemplation."[9] Kermit Hall remained in the Robinson tradition in his able study of the work of Confederate circuit judge West H. Humphreys. The "commitment to the rule of law and to fairness, bred by judicial and legal experience," Hall wrote, "kept him from judicial excess. . . . his conception of the Confederate nation included a place for the operation of justice."[10]

Writing at the same time Hall did, legal historian B. Patricia Dyson commended the written opinions of the Confederate attorneys general, saying that they

> all fall in the . . . pattern of following orderly precedent. While it would have been possible for the Confederate attorneys general to establish the office as a one-man supreme court or a legal dictatorship, none of the office holders did. The temptation to look at the difficulty of war rather than legal precedents must have been strong. . . . This reluctance to seize legal power and the unwavering adherence to precedent says something not only about the Confederate legal system, but about the strength of the American legal heritage itself. The Confederate attorneys general made no new contribution to American

legal theory, thought, or precedent, but their refusal to depart from the principles of the system when they were no longer charged with following it, stands as a commendation to its force and vigor.[11]

Even the troublesome North Carolina Supreme Court, whose chief justice, Richmond M. Pearson, sharply challenged Confederate authority, has recently received similar commendation. "The court and its members," wrote Jennifer Van Zant, "diligently relied on precedent and their principles in construing the statutes of the Confederate Congress. While the war raged around them, the justices refused to compromise personal liberties and judicial review for necessity."[12]

There is much truth in these rather sanguine modern views. No one has discovered another example of irresponsible opportunism as Pollard did in Humphrey Marshall.[13] The judges of the states by and large upheld Confederate authority while quietly dispensing justice as usual on the American model.

Yet the history of the Confederate bench and bar remains largely undeveloped.[14] It is difficult to reconcile the strident libertarian rhetoric of southern rights and constitutionalism, the stock-in-trade of southern lawyer-politicians, with the thoroughness of Confederate mobilization. Chapter 3 investigates the institutional setting of law practice in the Confederacy. Then chapter 4 provides a description of the institutional setting of judicial power in the Confederacy. Within that context, the work of the most famed and important justice voicing libertarian dissent, North Carolina Chief Justice Richmond M. Pearson, is analyzed.

Chapter 5, the final chapter in this section, skirts the attorney general's office and seeks evidence of "innovation" in Confederate justice elsewhere—in the War Department. Any historian studying a nation as consumed by war as the Confederacy was ignores the War Department only at great peril to the truth. There, in fact, government lawyers, one of them a former United States Supreme Court Justice, overcame southern reluctance to seize legal power.

LIBERTY AND THE BAR OF THE CONFEDERACY

AMERICAN LAWYERS PLAYED a leading role in the practical definition of civil liberty in wartime. When General Andrew Jackson for the first time in American history imposed martial law in New Orleans at the time of the great battle there in 1815, an event well known to many Southerners and often recalled during the Civil War, an anonymous lawyer took an important part. He represented a Louisiana legislator and journalist arrested on Jackson's order. They sought a writ of habeas corpus from a federal judge. When the judge issued the writ, Jackson defied it and arrested the judge, too. Later, after the judge's release, he fined the general $1,000 for contempt of court.[1]

Forty-six years later the arrest of Marylander John Merryman led to Roger B. Taney's famous 1861 decision, *Ex parte Merryman,* denouncing President Abraham Lincoln's suspension of the writ of habeas corpus. Taney was given the opportunity because a clever lawyer bypassed the Baltimore jurisdiction and went directly to the chief justice of the United States Supreme Court, who had original jurisdiction in habeas corpus cases of federal prisoners.[2]

The availability, skill, and political willingness of lawyers to make issues of civil liberties matter. To understand civil liberties in the Confederacy we must therefore take a look at the institutional setting of law practice in the Confederacy. This chapter is based mainly on the War Department records, where lawyers make appearances fairly often and in a variety of roles. The Confederate bar might look different in the light of other sources, but War Department records suffice at least for an introduction to this neglected subject.

This chapter seeks to provide a sober look at the Confederate bar—not the withering cynicism of Edward Pollard but something perhaps more critical than the emerging modern interpretation stressing uninterrupted justice and moderation following "American" precedents. Experiences varied widely, but without a supreme court to focus attention on "landmark" decisions and without political parties to create dramatic "martyrs" like Clement Vallandigham in the North, historians must probe the local corners of the Confederacy to find the varieties of legal experience.

Courtrooms and Clients

Modern emphasis on the continuity of Confederate practices with American legal traditions underestimates the extent of disruption of legal institutions in the Confederacy. Whatever the internalized values of the lawyers and judges, they could do nothing if the courts were not open. In many places, no legal work got done. The historian of Nicholas County, Virginia—on the frontier between Union-controlled West Virginia and Confederate-controlled western Virginia—noted: "From the 9th day of September 1861, when Judge Evermont Ward signed the last court order under . . . Virginia until October 16, 1865 when Judge Robert Irwin signed the first court order under . . . West Virginia, Nicholas County was in a condition of anarchy—During this time there were no public officials to control crime, enforce legal rights, or keep records. For this *interregnum* Nicholas County still has no land book records or reports on vital statistics."[3]

Unfortunately, historians do not know how many counties shared the plight of Nicholas County. Nor do we know, therefore, how many lawyers suffered the plight of David A. Barnes, an attorney from Jackson, North Carolina, who wrote William A. Graham, an influential Tar Heel legislator, on 26 August 1862 "upon a subject entirely personal. The suspension of the courts has left me without active employment," he explained. His health would not permit him to endure the hardships of a military campaign, and he sought aid in gaining "some place" in the governor's administration.[4]

The historian William M. Robinson Jr., on the other hand, argued that anarchy did not reign in as many places as one might think, and that some courts were held at least some of the time even in East Tennessee.[5] Only systematic work, state capital by state capital and county seat by county seat, month by month, will ultimately settle the question, but that task lies well beyond the scope of this book. Thus far the nondisruption view seems more persuasive. The amount of legal stasis caused by Union occupation may not have been great until near the end of the war.[6]

Confederate mobilization also took a heavy toll of clients, resulting in reduced land and business activity where courts remained in session, as legal historian Maxwell Bloomfield has pointed out. William Webb, a lawyer in La Grange, Texas, which was untouched by invasion, wrote in January 1864, "I regularly attended Columbus Court before the war, but since that time I have not been there once. The attys & parties of all the cases civil & criminal I have there are nearly all in the army and the cases by common consent are to lie over till the war ends: hence I should have no other business to call me to Court."[7] Lawyers who maintained a practice during the war were naturally grateful for work generated by the war. The patriotic William Pitt Ballinger, an apologist for the government's suspension of the writ of habeas corpus, apparently accepted clients seeking writs of habeas corpus to release them from the army.[8]

Taken all in all, the legal institutions of the Confederacy were at least adequate to protect civil liberties in wartime. Though fewer courts were in session, the apparent effect was to create a surplus of lawyers rather than a shortage of courts—especially in so far as civil liberties were concerned. For those purposes, as President Jefferson Davis ruefully pointed out, there were courts aplenty: "Every judge has the power to issue the writ of *habeas corpus,* and if one manifests more facility in discharging petitioners than his associates the application is made to him however remote he may be." Even Richmond's lowly municipal hustings court was hearing habeas corpus cases.[9]

Some Lawyers at Work in the Confederacy

Some southern lawyers thought themselves specially charged to protect civil liberty. An obvious example was Robert R. Collier, the Petersburg lawyer and member of the Virginia Senate who set out to correct abuses under the early martial law orders. Collier, though vigorously patriotic and hopeful of the establishment of a southern nation, proved to be a stickler for individual rights. When civilians in his area were tried by courts-martial for selling liquor to soldiers, he showed the government the error of its ways. "Unemployed as counsel by anyone," Collier on 27 October 1862 wrote the secretary of war simply as "a warm admirer and determined advocate of civil liberty."

The Petersburg lawyer thought there could be no such thing as martial law under the Confederate Constitution—Congress provided only the Articles of War, and these governed only members of the armed forces. Therefore, he argued, even with the writ of habeas corpus suspended, a civilian could be put in prison but not tried by court-martial.[10] Secretary of War George W. Randolph did not reply immediately, and on 3 November Collier followed up with another letter.[11]

Collier also wrote Jefferson Davis to protest the conviction of William H. Moore by court-martial for retailing liquor without a license. Moore, he explained, had already been discharged from the army when the alleged offense was committed and could not, as a civilian, be tried by court-martial. Davis asked Adjutant General Samuel Cooper to investigate, and Cooper agreed with Collier that the military could not try Moore. On the eleventh he so informed President Davis, who ordered that "the error be corrected. The writ of Habeas corpus is a remedy which will bring discredit on the military authority and should be avoided by doing justice voluntarily. The Provost Marshall cannot institute a court to try a citizen for offences against the statutes of the state."[12]

It appears that Cooper and Davis learned their lessons from the case, but the president had not said that the provost marshal could not try citizens for offenses defined under martial law or by Confederate statute. He had given up as little ground as possible, even while volunteering justice. By 24 November Collier was writing again to protest the court-martial of a Richmond civilian named Handly, arrested for selling liquor in camp. He enclosed a clipping from the *Petersburg*

Express, an article he had written on the subject. Using Bouvier's *Law Dictionary,* Blackstone's *Commentaries,* and Greenleaf on evidence, Collier argued that whatever might be the case in countries less free than the Confederacy, under this government citizens could not be brought before courts-martial. "We already live under the shadow of a gigantic despotism," Collier now concluded.[13]

The attention the lawyer's protests gained brought him clients with grievances against the army, and he protested the suspension of habeas corpus and the imposition of martial law. He still identified with the Confederate cause, however, and congratulated Davis on the recent victory at Fredericksburg.[14]

Near Christmas 1862 Collier wrote a long letter of protest to the president. "The people," the Petersburg lawyer explained, "or rather a small portion, at the time, . . . not understanding Martial law, applied months ago, and you acceded to their solicitation, to declare martial law." Courts-martial of civilians ensued, with Collier representing some of the defendants, and finally he received Adjutant General Samuel Cooper's 22 November order "to the effect that civilians are not lawfully triable by Courts-martial." Cooper had nevertheless interpreted the law narrowly, and since by chance the letter was acted on in October while Congress was renewing the authority to suspend the writ of habeas corpus, Cooper gave expiration of the law as the grounds for ending military trials of civilians. To Collier's dismay, Cooper's order went on to say that "In the mean time although the power to *arrest* offenders continues in the Provost Marshal till the order '(General orders Number 11)' is revoked, action under the 4th paragraph requiring them to be punished by sentence of a court Martial, would be suspended." "Now, Sir," Collier complained, "who knows what is the condition we are left in. . . . We trust you will cause us to be relieved of the perplexities of a quasi condition of 'Martial law.'" He warned Davis that the Confederacy was "tending too much to resemble Lincolndom."

Davis referred the letter to the War Department, which prepared a reply on 30 December stating that "the Department has appointed an additional person to examine the prisons with instructions to discharge all those who are illegally" held. Far from satisfying Collier, that answer only caused him to demand to know by what authority of law the additional person was appointed and whether he was civilian or military. To Collier's way of thinking, such a person was unnecessary while the writ of habeas corpus was not suspended because illegally detained prisoners would then have access to a judge through the writ. Even while the writ was suspended, only Congress could create such an office. Collier claimed to have halted the practice of allowing civilians to be court-martialed. Moreover, he had now become one of the earliest critics of the origin and authority of the shadowy figures appointed by the Davis administration to examine political prisoners, the habeas corpus commissioners (who are discussed in chapter 5).

To give Collier his due, it made more sense to think of securing the future of civil liberty in the Confederacy in the victorious winter of 1862–63 than it would later. But to some lawyers, sticking up for civil liberty knew no limits of time, place, or circumstance. There were, in other words, troublemakers among the lawyers of the Confederacy, as Edward Pollard knew. Desperation for clients might drive them to cause trouble, greed might, and the adversarial ethic of American law certainly did nothing to discourage such behavior. Finally, the extreme client loyalty of nineteenth-century law likewise removed barriers to the employment of all means to gain freedom for clients.[15]

An example of a troublemaker was David Chalmers Glenn, of Enterprise, Mississippi, who was twice the state's attorney general and by the time of the war was retired from public life to private practice on the coast of Mississippi. Glenn, who had connections with both Henry S. Foote and Jefferson Davis, prominent Mississippians in the Confederacy but arch enemies, felt confident in writing to Richmond officials to offer advice or to seek appointive office.[16] Davis repeatedly gave him glowing endorsements. Nevertheless, receiving no appointment at first and with "poverty staring" him "in the face," Glenn was still practicing law when Ulysses S. Grant invaded Mississippi on his fateful Vicksburg campaign.[17]

The western Confederacy suffered a minor misfortune in that this decisive campaign of the war coincided with a congressional election year. A majority of the politicians in Richmond apparently felt that they dare not limit civil liberty formally and then face their constituents.[18] Besides, the war was still going well for the Confederates in the East; they were at high tide there, and the legislators, resident in Richmond, tended to be influenced by the Richmond mood.

The Confederacy was reaching a low ebb in the West, however. General Joseph E. Johnston, charged with recruiting an army to raise the Yankee siege of Vicksburg, felt the perennial Confederate desperation for manpower keenly in the late spring and early summer of 1862.[19] One potential recruit in Enterprise, Mississippi, a man named Louis Frenkel, claimed exemption from conscription by virtue of having furnished a substitute. Conscript officers arrested him, declaring his exemption papers faulty. Frenkel hired Glenn as his lawyer, and Glenn sued out a writ of habeas corpus for his client before a state circuit judge. The judge found Frenkel illegally detained and ordered his discharge. Immediately thereafter the commander of the conscript district, Major M. R. Clark, had Frenkel rearrested and declared that he would not obey an order of a state judge interfering with his command. Major Clark, it must be admitted, more than once took a broad view of his powers to identify legal conscripts. When, in another controversy, British authorities complained that he enrolled aliens, Clark replied, "I consider that persons who come here for the purpose of making money and remain here for several years, without returning to their homes of nativity, are domiciled"—and subject to conscription. It never seemed to occur to him that such might be matters of law or diplomacy rather than individual moral judgment.[20]

Glenn told Secretary of War James A. Seddon, "This at once leads to a direct and dangerous conflict between the Civil and military Authorities." Both sides showed determination, and he said it might well come to "an issue of force & arms in our midst while our common foe is encompassing us about on all sides." Glenn would delay further action until he heard from the War Department, but if Richmond upheld Major Clark, Glenn warned, "I shall regret the issue, which is thus forced but duty to my client will compel [me] to exhaust every remedy known to the laws of Miss to obtain the liberation of my client & for the consequences which may thus ensue I will not be responsible." In this extreme instance of loyalty to client, the lawyer from all appearances sought legal relief even at the risk of internal civil war![21]

Glenn also asked the attorney general of the Confederacy, Thomas Hill Watts, how he might rule on the case, vehemently arguing the constitutional aspects of the Frenkel dispute:

Even in the old Government the jurisdiction of state Judges in writs of personal liberty was rarely questioned. In one or two cases U.S. Judges have leaned that way & Kent once, alone of a Court so ruled while his Commentaries & the great body of the State decisions are clearly otherwise. In the present Government, we claim above all things to have established forever the sovereignty of each of the States. And yet it is claimed that the personal liberty of the Citizen is taken from without the protection of the judiciary of the States and handed over to officers owing their existence to the very Government which may be seeking to oppress them.[22]

Watts refused to reveal to the Mississippi lawyer his own views on the matter but quickly wrote Seddon, offering him no very specific legal advice but warning vaguely against conflict between civil and military authority in Mississippi.[23]

General Grant was about two weeks away from claiming Vicksburg and control of the great river. Hindsight alone does not suggest the peril: people on the ground at the time knew the situation was desperate. Enterprise was a long way from Grant, being located directly south of Meridian, about 140 miles due east of Vicksburg and almost on the Alabama line. The Union armies, which had laid waste to Jackson, roughly midway between Vicksburg and Enterprise, stood between the little eastern Mississippi town and the famous river fortress in the West. Presumably the citizens of Enterprise could go to the state capital only under special restriction (which might well have hindered Glenn's recourse to the ultimate legal remedy in the state) because General Johnston was attempting to gather his army there. Enterprise itself was barely rescued by Confederate soldiers from a contingent of Union cavalrymen seeking the town's surrender in late April, part of Benjamin Grierson's famous raid conducted in eastern Mississippi to distract attention from Grant's movements on the other side of the state.[24]

Enterprise citizens had other good reasons to feel the urgency of the military situation. With the advent of the Union forces that would burn the capital on 14 May, the governor fled Jackson and set up office temporarily in Enterprise.[25] While the governor was there, President Davis was calling desperately for Mississippi to provide "large accessions to . . . Joseph E. Johnston's army, when advancing to attack, by the junction of militia and less organized bodies of citizens."[26] The president telegraphed the governor twice at Enterprise, on 20 and 21 May, about arms and ammunition being made available to Johnston for reinforcements.[27] The terror of the citizens of Jackson encountered by Johnston's staff, who happened to arrive on the night the governor evacuated the capital, was palpable, and surely some of this was communicated to citizens of Enterprise when the state government contingent arrived there.[28]

But for some lawyers and judges, life in Mississippi's Eighth Circuit Court went on as before. The judge in the Frenkel case, William M. Hancock, wrote to Mississippi representative Ethelbert Barksdale apprising him of the dangerous legal situation in Enterprise. "You are aware," he told the congressman, "that there has been for some time and is now a great deal of soreness & irritation existing in the public mind in this region in connection with the writ of Habeas Corpus & the assumption of military authorities over the liberty of the citizen." The judge said matter-of-factly that he concluded that Frenkel was held illegally and ordered his release. He pointed out that "No appeal or writ of Error was prayed for, or sued out to the High Court, which is the only tribunal vested with the power to reverse the judgment of the circuit court." Hancock warned, "When this matter is once publicly known it will create intense excitement."[29]

Representative Barksdale, who cooperated with the Davis administration in efforts to suspend the writ of habeas corpus, cautioned the president that the case was "one of serious moment, involving important principles and questions of high political expediency and consequences." He assured Davis that Judge Hancock was thoroughly loyal to the southern cause and expressed his own opinion: "The privilege of the writ of Habeas Corpus not having been authorized to be suspended in any case whatever, I can scarcely think that the course of the commandant of the camp of Instruction is warranted by orders of the War Department." Davis endorsed the note: "Secty of War for prompt attention"— a routine notation for the president.[30]

Not one of the documents of the Frenkel case surviving in the War Department records describes or analyzes the facts of the case or the merits of Frenkel's cause. The whole dispute, once it reached Richmond, was conducted at the abstract level of power and liberty, of jurisdiction and constitution. The alleged fault of the substitution documents remains to this day a mystery.

What the record shows is that David Chalmers Glenn willingly put loyalty to his client above justice or the survival of the infant republic. Louis Frenkel wished to escape military service by paying someone else to serve for him, but Glenn did his part in elevating the cause to one of civil-military relations, and he did so without explaining the merits of Frenkel's case. His warning of possible civil-military conflict appears to have served his client's cause by attempting to frighten officials with the social consequences of retaining their prisoner. It was not necessarily based on impartial observation or sincere conviction: it sufficed for this Mississippi lawyer if the gambit were necessary to free his client. If the fear of civil-military conflict expressed by Glenn was sincere and not a legal tactic, then he could be accused of putting loyalty to his client above loyalty to the republic. Barksdale, who was definitely sympathetic to Confederate mobilization, shared the alarmist view, it must be said.

Glenn's actions did not hurt his cause with the administration, filled as it was with lawyers inured to the adversarial absolutes of the American legal system. After the fall of Vicksburg brought disaster to Confederate Mississippi, Glenn grew distressed over "the present critical state of affairs in Mississippi" and sought to counteract treason and disaffection in the state politically. In the midst of this campaign to save the state for the Confederacy, he wrote Jefferson Davis pleading for an exemption from conscription, to which he became liable under the most recent law. He claimed physical disability, admitting however that he could not obtain a surgeon's certificate to prove it. He also pointed out the domestic difficulties of his two daughters. President Davis was sympathetic, but Secretary of War Seddon proved reluctant to grant Glenn a favor without a surgeon's certificate. The administration found him a job as judge of a military court with the Army of Northern Virginia, and Glenn somewhat reluctantly abandoned his speaking campaign to save Mississippi from traitors. He thus avoided conscription by becoming a colonel and judge.[31]

Some lawyers in Mississippi held rigidly libertarian opinions on civil rights uncomplicated by client loyalty. Judge William Lewis Sharkey, for example, blamed the plight of the Confederacy on Jefferson Davis's inability to hold New Orleans and Vicksburg, but he was alarmed by proposals to allow the president to suspend the writ of habeas corpus. Sharkey drafted an opinion that such legislation was unconstitutional on the ground that suspension of the writ was a legislative power and could not be delegated to the executive. In the course of the discussion he expressed shock that martial law had been declared within a ten-mile radius of Vicksburg before its fall.[32]

Other lawyers saw themselves as essentially peacemakers.[33] An example was Benjamin Gardner of Troy, Alabama. Late in 1863 he warned Governor John Gill Shorter of the increasing tendency of the conscript bureau to ignore the freedom of citizens and the judges of the state courts. The local conscription officer, a Colonel Morehead, had arrested a man named John D. Rhodes, who claimed exemption as a Confederate States tax collector. Judge Fitzpatrick issued a writ of habeas corpus, but military authorities ignored it, and soldiers eventually drew their guns when a sheriff came to enforce the court order. The sheriff arrested Morehead, and the next morning Colonel Morehead arrested Judge Fitzpatrick. The colonel cooled off temporarily, released the judge, and then threatened to arrest him again.

At that point, Benjamin Gardner, whom the colonel hired to defend him, advised him "not to do so—told him he had no right to arrest him [Rhodes]—that he was not answerable to the military authorities, nor was any other noncombatant citizen." Gardner felt the weight of Confederate power and authority keenly, saying, "The community is greatly disturbed—they feel that their rights and liberties are in danger, and no man feels safe from arrest. An armed guard patrols our square every moment, and the citizens feel that they are under military surveillance." Gardner did not threaten confrontation but rather counseled peace—against the inclinations of his client, Colonel Morehead.[34]

Robert M. Barton, a lawyer from Russellville in East Tennessee's Grainger County, also took responsibility for the consequences of his advocacy in seeking justice for his clients. On 4 May 1863 he informed the secretary of war about a long-simmering dispute between judicial and military authorities in his troubled part of the country. When Colonel E. D. Blake had called up conscripts for examination for service the previous January, the examining physician had exempted three men on grounds of physical disability, but in March these men were ordered by a physician to report to the camp of instruction in Knoxville. They obtained writs of habeas corpus from G. W. Gorlay, judge of Tennessee's Second Circuit. At a hearing on 2 April 1863 the judge ordered the men discharged from military custody. On 17 April Colonel Blake had the men arrested, and the judge had Blake brought in for contempt of court.[35] By 4 May Blake had called up all men with disability exemptions for reexamination, listing by name those discharged on habeas corpus and threatening to treat them as deserters if they failed to appear. So the case stood when Barton wrote to the War Department.

Could citizens be reexamined after discharge, the lawyer wondered, or was a certificate of discharge from a surgeon final for three years or the duration of the war? Was it useful only for the time being? Could the War Department recognize discharges on habeas corpus when there were calls for reexamination?

Barton, though he represented the three men, did make the sort of assurances that Glenn never made. He told the secretary of war that his clients were loyal and desired "only . . . to be fairly heard, learn their duty and obey." He would not vouch for the loyalty of the others on Colonel Blake's reexamination list.[36]

A Defenseless Government and Lawsuits as Political Sabotage

Lawyers sometimes appeared ready to take cases that involved veiled political opposition to the government in Richmond. In North Carolina, especially, where political opposition to Jefferson Davis's administration seemed as near to being organized as in any other Confederate state, there was a bevy of former anti-secessionist lawyers available to take cases against the government.

Among these was former Unionist John A. Gilmer of Greensboro. He served in 1864 as counsel, for example, for John J. Welch, B. Y. Clarke, and M. M. Kester, exempted blacksmiths who were conscripted and quickly sent from the Raleigh camp to Virginia before writs of habeas corpus could be served.[37] Gilmer appeared for the plaintiff in 1863 in the case of another blacksmith claiming exemption from conscription, called *In the matter of Solomon N. Guyer.*[38] In addition, he was counsel for the plaintiff in the important case *In the matter of Nicholson,* also involving an exempt worker, a miller.[39] William A. Graham, a former Whig and antisecessionist, appeared as counsel in the case called *In the matter of Curtis,* which concerned Samuel Curtis, who was exempted as a primitive Baptist minister and then served as a substitute. A conscription officer arrested him as a conscript because he had given up the trade that exempted him. Graham appeared for Curtis, who lost his appeal.[40]

Graham also played a substantial role in the celebrated case of R. J. Graves, a naive clergyman who was arrested after going north for his health, answering questions asked by northern military officials on his return through the lines, and writing an article for a Richmond newspaper describing the North's determination to fight a long war. Graves was arrested in Orange County, North Carolina, and removed from the state by Confederate military authorities, an action that Carolinians protested vigorously as a violation of states' rights. Graham led the protest, introducing a resolution in the state legislature demanding Graves's return. Graham had taken a $25 fee from members of Graves's congregation to serve as part of his legal defense; the defense was well coordinated, and Graves's lawyers in Richmond included the former secretary of war, George W. Randolph.[41]

The legal deck was stacked against the army and in favor of the civilian shirkers. With less business than usual in the courts, lawyers, even pro-Confederate ones, were surely eager to pick up business in suing out habeas corpus writs for clients attempting to avoid military service. Moreover, representing such clients provided an outlet for political opposition in lieu of formally organized party activity. Those clients who had paid for substitutes, moreover, tended to be well-off financially and, at least from the standpoint of the army, offered lucrative fees to the lawyers. The anti-Semitic clerk John B. Jones noted on 20 December 1863: "There was much consternation among the Jews and other speculators here, who have put in substitutes and made money. They fear that their substitutes will be made liable by legislative action, and then the principals will be called for. Some have contributed money to prevent the passage of such a law, and others have spent money to get permission to leave the country. Messrs. Gilmer and Myers, lawyers, have their hands full."[42] On the other hand, the War Department did not have a judge advocate's department and did not have on staff a battery of lawyers to represent the government in suits.[43]

The commissary department, for example, despite numerous conflicts over the value of property impressed for government use, had no lawyer. When a case pressed by sugar wholesalers appeared before the Georgia Supreme Court in 1863, the commissary major who was sued by the companies hired his own counsel. The War Department thought the case so poorly managed that the government stood a chance of losing in this "deliberate effort to break down the impressment law" without the vital issues even being raised. Despite the major's receiving what the department regarded as poor legal advice, several law firms filed bills in the department for $1,000 each. The clerk who received them regarded them as "enormous." The Confederacy eventually won the case, but the legal disarray was symptomatic.[44]

After more than a year's experience with conscription and some nine months' experience while the writ of habeas corpus was not suspended anywhere, the War Department had discovered that conscription was so unpopular that the government needed lawyers to fend off the suits of those who wished to escape the Confederate ranks. On 19 November 1863 the secretary of war directed that "standing counsel" be employed in those areas of each congressional district lacking a Confederate district attorney to represent the Bureau of Conscription "in cases of habeas corpus sued out for discharge of persons from military service." The department suggested a fee of twenty dollars a case where the lawyer had to make an appearance in court plus a ten dollar per diem and travel expenses of ten cents per mile.[45] Inflation and the heavy demand for lawyers to save citizens from military service, as we shall see, quickly drove up the standard fee and made the guideline unrealistic. Lawyers worked in the War Department, of course, but they served as administrators mostly and seldom argued cases in court or offered legal advice to officers. Occasionally the department hired counsel in important cases, but before the law of 19 November 1863 there does not seem to have been a clear procedure in instances where officers were hauled into court. Defense of the government's interests in all areas was the responsibility of the Confederate States district attorneys, and they sometimes filled the void by hiring local counsel to help in habeas corpus cases.[46] For their parts, the military officers likely to be sued had no idea whether they were allowed to employ counsel to defend themselves and were not likely to do so. Thus the civilian could contract legal representation to sue officers who were not systematically defended by attorneys.

Lack of counsel for the government in important cases may have damaged the Confederate cause. In the case called *In the matter of Austin,* decided by Richmond M. Pearson of the North Carolina Supreme Court, the justice commented that he heard arguments only from lawyers for the plaintiff. Richard M. Austin, a North Carolina Home Guard member, was challenging the authority of the governor to require him to arrest deserters from the Confederate army. Pearson felt "not really apprised of the ground on which the Governor rests his claim of authority."[47] In the case called *In the Matter of Cain,* another Pearson decision, the plaintiff sought a writ of habeas corpus to escape conscription on the grounds that he had paid for a substitute. The privilege of the writ of habeas corpus was at the time suspended by the president in cases involving conscription, but Pearson ruled that the writ must issue because the form of writ suspended applied only to persons committed for a crime, not to persons illegally held to military service—a highly technical and somewhat abstruse ruling. "There was no argument on the side of the enrolling officer," Pearson commented.[48]

Some conscription officers took the initiative to seek counsel to protect themselves and the government. In Aberdeen, Mississippi, after the passage of the troublesome law making liable to conscription persons who had previously contracted for substitutes, E. W. Upshaw, commander of the conscript district of northern Mississippi, arrested one E. G. Shannon. Shannon, who had a substitute in the army, sought to avoid service by getting a writ of habeas corpus; along with others in a similar situation in the area, he employed able counsel. Upshaw, seeing that the cases would establish a precedent in northern Mississippi, "thought it prudent to procure" the services of lawyer Joel M. Acker. Upshaw promised that the government would pay "a reasonable compensation for his professional services in the case." Acker won after three days' argument in court.[49]

Months later, Acker wrote the head of Confederate conscription seeking payment for his work in Aberdeen. He had worked for four conscription officers, including Major Upshaw. The writs sued out against the Confederate officers came before the suspension of the writ of habeas corpus, he pointed out, thus emphasizing the difficulty of the government's position. He also noted that the "gentlemen" who could hire substitutes "were generally wealthy & gave large fees to their counsel." Acker maintained that he refused their offer of large fees because he "preferred to serve the government for less money, in defending a law which [he] . . . regarded as constitutional." The lawyer now asked for $3,000. He had not "applied for the money before" because he had "not needed it," but he needed it now.[50]

Though the outcome of Acker's application for his fee is not known, such initiatives on the part of nervous Confederate conscription officers sometimes embarrassed the government. Acker appears to have charged about $300 a case, and that rather than $20 may have been the going rate for such work in the late Confederacy—at least in so far as the attorneys saw it. But Assistant Secretary of War John A. Campbell saw it a little differently and sought an economical solution to the problem. A lawyer named Neeson had been employed over three months in twenty cases involving writs of habeas corpus sued out against Confederate officials. His bill came to $6,000, that is, $300 for each of the cases. Campbell replaced Neeson with B. R. Wellford Jr., a War Department lawyer salaried in Richmond. Campbell said Wellford's time was not all taken up with department office work and he was able enough to handle such cases.[51]

Conscription lay at the bottom of the great volume of cases, not espionage, sabotage, fifth-column activity, or states of siege. Since most cases dealt with conscripts or soldiers who thought themselves wrongfully held in military service, the detaining authorities were not usually law enforcement officers familiar with the justice system in their daily duties but officers of the army who might never have been inside a jail or a court of law in their lives.

The Legal Tender Cases

To emphasize continuity in legal and constitutional matters, as recent work on the legal and constitutional history of the Confederacy does, ignores a few significant sectional differences in laws and institutions. One of the most important differences, neglected by historians, came in money matters: the Confederacy never passed a legal tender act, as the North did. Therefore, the paper money with which the Richmond government funded the war in large part was not required by law to be taken in payment for debts. As previously discussed, in Arkansas, for example, generals were tempted to equate refusal to take Confederate money with deliberately debasing the country's currency and with treason. Serious problems could arise when a lawyer ran afoul of such military attitudes.[52]

The most important case occurred in Mississippi in midsummer 1862, following the declaration of martial law by flamboyant General Earl Van Dorn. His orders, published on 4 July 1862, included a stipulation that the "credit of the Government must be sustained" and that "any person who shall refuse to receive Confederate money . . . shall be subject to fine and imprisonment."[53]

Apparently because of the order, a lawyer named Samuel M. Hawkins was arraigned before the provost marshal of Grenada, Mississippi, in the north central part of the state, for refusing to take payment in Confederate money on two promissory notes. Hawkins was administrator for the estate in which the notes were held, and he did not feel that he could responsibly oversee the estate by accepting in payment depreciated Confederate paper. Provost Marshal R. H. Forrester told his superior, Brigadier General John Bordenave Villepigue, that Hawkins was an old man "of wealth and influence."[54]

Villepigue, placed in command in Grenada in June, was supposed to remove the supplies from this important military depot and transport them further south. Grenada was a railroad crossroads under threat of Federal attack (the campaign would come in the autumn). Evacuating supplies gave "the impression . . . that the upper portion of the State was to be entirely abandoned to the enemy," and such fears naturally caused a flight from Confederate currency, which would be worthless in trade with Yankees. In one case, Villepigue merely threatened a reluctant patriot who did not want to take Confederate money, and it worked. In another case—"that of a Jew," Villepigue noted—"a small fine made him desist." The lawyer Hawkins, however, was persistent, and General Villepigue authorized Forrester to deal with him severely.[55]

Arrested and fined $50 for refusing Confederate money, the irate Hawkins complained to the War Department in Richmond. Hawkins wanted to deposit notes in trust pending the decision of the secretary of war on the powers of the provost marshal. Military officers responded only with threats of incarceration in the guard house and cautioned him to have no communication with anyone. Forrester fined him another $100 and threatened to send him to prison in Tuscaloosa. Given another day's respite, Hawkins returned to be fined another $50 and threatened with trial on a "charge of high treason and rebellion." "Is there no check on him?" Hawkins asked about Forrester to Secretary of War Randolph on 15 July. "He claims that he is under no check of Constitution or law?"[56]

Hawkins solicited an opinion on the case from E. S. Fisher, formerly a judge on Mississippi's supreme court, the High Court of Errors and Appeals. Judge Fisher said that those who defended Forrester "are in so many words proclaiming the fact that he is a Tyrant—relying upon bayonets to uphold him." He reminded the secretary of his "*oath* requiring the Executive '*To preserve protect and defend the constitution.*'" "The constitution," Fisher lamented, "has not yet been in force five months and what is it to day but a snare, if this outragious proceeding can be sustained."[57]

War Department clerk Robert Garlick Hill Kean captured the mixture of the mean and the grand in this case: "Intrinsically the case is petty—as well in amount as in [the] spirit which appears to influence Hawkins. Its importance grows out of the *questions* he raises."[58] Hawkins had in fact raised this petty argument to the highest levels of political consideration of liberty and power—in what might be thought of as classic southern style. "When," he wrote, "the President announced, that under all the pressure of our revolutionary struggle the Constitutional rights of the Citizens had been faithfully observed, the sentiment swelled all hearts with pride throughout the Confederacy. What a contrast we presented to the Lincoln government, in which the Constitution became worse than a dead letter."[59] "I love my country," Hawkins protested, "and cherish as the best inheritance of my children, the rights which we have received from our British ancestry and our Revolutionary Sires; for many years I have made our political institutions my study—a labor of love; and I would ask what guarantee have the citizens of their rights, . . . if Marshal Law, as Gen. Van Dorn has defined it, 'The will of the military Commander' . . . [is] to be carried into effect in Mississippi by a man imported—a stranger—from Tennessee[?]"[60]

Kean's advice to his superiors in the War Department was to return to the status quo ante—refund the lawyer's fines and return the money paid by the debtor. Secretary of War Randolph sympathized with General Villepigue. Hawkins seemed "a litigious evil disposed person and possibly disloyal." The old lawyer, complained Provost Marshal Forrester, "insists that while the soldier who is exposing his life in the service of his country, must receive the notes of the Confederacy for his pay, he, the representative of some heir, some favored child of fortune, has the right to refuse to receive it . . . and shylock-like to demand the gold or silver. . . . His example if successful will be calculated to destroy the currency of Confederate notes in this country, which is very materially supported by the Knowledge . . . that the military authorities will not permit speculators to depreciate it."[61] But Randolph knew that the proceeding against Hawkins was "unauthorized by law" and essentially took Kean's advice to return to the situation before the dispute began.

The failure of the Confederate Congress to pass a legal tender act—perhaps a legacy of the hard-money Democratic party roots of many of its leaders— put a strain on the loyalty of the people. Responsible financial management would now be set athwart patriotism, and a wider rift was driven between suspicious military officers and civilians who often appeared to be speculators. Any lawyer who was a stickler was likely to cause problems over the issue of currency.[62] Sydney Baxter, who examined many cases for the War Department, could see the difficulties and preferred flexibility: "Congress has not made Confederate money a legal tender. To decline taking it is therefore in itself no offence against law. But as the support of this currency is necessary to sustain our cause the refusal to take Confederate money may be evidence of want of fidelity to our cause and its depreciation may be seditious. But whether in any particular case this be so must be judged by the circumstances."[63]

Conclusion

The behavior of the Confederacy's lawyers in dealing with war questions ran the gamut of possibilities. Many served in the armed services out of the same motives, patriotic or otherwise, that moved other classes and occupations. Of those who remained behind, some seized upon habeas corpus cases and defended their clients untroubled by patriotic conscience. Others tried to serve their clients and domestic peace at the same time. Still others seem to have taken such antigovernment cases only when their clients seemed loyal and had a reasonable case. Some preferred the government side in a case where constitutional ground seemed firm and where it helped the war effort. Some, more motivated by political feeling than legal consideration, used the law as a form of political criticism, another weapon in their partisan arsenal.

The legal landscape of the Confederacy might well have been a breeding ground of troublesome resistance to government authority. Enough courts were disrupted and so much normal business suspended that a surplus of lawyers was created. Yet courts remained open in the Confederacy where petitions for habeas corpus could be heard. The legal profession of the era imbued its practitioners with an ethic of adversary proceedings and of extreme client loyalty; it did not bother lawyers to be bothersome. That was their role, to some degree. Some, moreover, felt a special calling as guardians of individual liberty. If idleness, want of normal business, or libertarian principles did not drive lawyers to the defense of persons seeking protection of rights from the Confederate government, latent political disaffection with the secessionist government might offer special incentive for talented old Whig lawyers. Such seems to have been the case in fractious North Carolina, where the Confederacy witnessed the nearest thing, perhaps, to the resurrection of organized party opposition on a traditional American two-party model. The issues in court, conscription above all but also legal tender and others, were crucial to the war effort.[64] Because the government, especially the War Department, was poorly organized to respond to legal challenge, such cases might have become quite disruptive—of Confederate manpower and of Confederate finance.

But the lawyers did not cause Confederate defeat—far from it. Given the institutional biases toward freedom, it seems remarkable that there are no celebrated cases challenging the power of the Confederate government to interfere with the daily lives of its citizens. Confederate history does not have its equivalent of *Ex parte Merryman* or of General Andrew Jackson's fine for contempt. The failure to organize a Confederate supreme court was a major reason.

The extreme libertarian rhetoric of the antebellum period seems not to have had the effect one might expect among southern lawyer-statesmen, the very men who devised such rhetorical defenses of southern interests. In sum, given the political and institutional context, defenses of individual liberty seem none too numerous or prominent in Confederate history. The bar was largely complicit with Confederate government power.

In one state, North Carolina, decisions from its highest court on questions of civil liberty became a troublesome matter. Lawyers brought cases that found a sympathetic hearing from the chief justice. The next chapter explores the institutions and circumstances that conspired to make liberty a peculiarly important issue in that Confederate state.

4

"UNAFFECTED BY . . . THE CONDITION OF OUR COUNTRY"
THE PECULIAR JURISPRUDENCE OF RICHMOND M. PEARSON

WHEN A SOUTHERN LAWYER BECAME a judge, he left behind the client-advocate and adversarial culture of the bar—perhaps for the southern lawyer-statesman culture of myth. He certainly entered an arena important for the preservation of civil liberties. The justices of the North Carolina Supreme Court provide the most prominent example of judges attempting to protect liberties in the Confederacy. Because of his obdurate resistance to Confederate authority, in fact, the chief justice, Richmond M. Pearson, has become the single most important member of the bench in Confederate history.

Pearson and his court have been the subject of several specialized studies, and perhaps the best assessment of the court he led is that of Jennifer Van Zant.[1] Her interpretation is based on the ablest understanding of the issues involved in individual cases decided by the court. In the end she concluded that the "court and its members diligently relied on precedent and their principles in construing the statutes of the Confederate Congress. While the war raged around them, the justices refused to compromise personal liberties and judicial review for necessity. Although the members differed, they united to uphold the sovereignty of North Carolina when it was directly threatened."[2]

If Van Zant's is a fair assessment, then we have quite an anomaly on our hands, for the record of the North Carolina Supreme Court in the Civil War is unique. Its monument stands in the bound volumes of the state reports. The volume covering the period from June 1863 through December 1864 contains forty-six decisions dealing with the Confederate military and the writ of habeas corpus. Nothing in all of Civil War history, North or South, compares with that record of judicial engagement with war issues. Neighboring South Carolina, for example, reported only one decision dealing with a war issue (the exemption of a plantation overseer from conscription), and nothing else in their war-era reports touched on the war effort. Surely the other supreme courts were not ignoring precedent, compromising personal liberties and judicial review, and undermining the sovereignty of their states.

An account of civil liberties in the Confederacy must assess the extraordinary activity of Pearson's court. To do so requires proper understanding of its institutional setting.

The Power of the State Supreme Court

The chief justice shared the supreme court's powers with two associate justices, Matthias E. Manly and William H. Battle. Though wartime may seem an inhospitable setting for the least dangerous branch of government, in fact war greatly increased the concentration of power in the hands of any of these three men. Most important was a little-appreciated peculiarity of law that gave original jurisdiction to a justice in many cases in time of war. A justice of the supreme court could take original jurisdiction in applications for the writ of habeas corpus.[3] He did not have to wait passively for an appeal to reach him through lengthy court processes. In fact, this little-used power afforded United States Chief Justice Roger B. Taney his extraordinary forum in the early weeks of the war for challenging, as a supreme court justice in chambers, the power of President Lincoln in *Ex parte Merryman*. The power was of little significance in peacetime, as American judges in the nineteenth century rarely used the writ of habeas corpus.[4] But war, as the Constitution anticipated, brought a plethora of applicants for the writ.

Circumstance made Pearson and his colleagues even more powerful. The Confederacy itself enhanced their power, for it never organized a supreme court, and therefore the decisions of the state supreme courts were sovereign in many areas and could not be overridden. Moreover, cases involving conscription, which had been in place only since 16 April 1862, came to the courts in significant number beginning in 1863, and Congress happened to refuse to authorize the president to suspend the writ of habeas corpus in that year.

An important institutional augmentation of the power of an individual justice lay in the custom of sitting "in vacation." North Carolina was a poor state and, like other southern states, was little enamored of taxation.[5] The legislature limited the terms of the full court to three sessions, two of them in the state capital in Raleigh and one in Morganton, in the West. Stingy taxpayers got more for their money by having the three justices divide the state and serve alone most of the time, "in vacation," but each justice still had the power to speak with the authority of the whole court. Unless called together by a writ of certiorari, the court did not meet *en banc* except in term, and a single justice's decision could stand as the final interpretation of the law. As Chief Justice Pearson himself wrote in a decision challenging the authority of the governor, "I am aware of the responsibility under which I act. Jurisdiction is given to a single Judge in vacation—my decision fixes the law, until it is reversed by the Supreme Court, or amended by the Legislature, and I would not feel it to be my duty to stay the action of the Executive, except upon the clearest conviction."[6] The individual justice had the power to say what the law was at least until the whole court met for the next term. His decisions, though written alone, carried the weight and prestige of supreme court decisions and were printed in the state reports. They did more than dispose of an individual defendant's fate.

Still other circumstances increased the power of the individual justice. War reduced the number of times the court met in regular term. After 1861 the North Carolina Supreme Court ceased meeting its western term and had only June and December terms in Raleigh. Under such circumstances "in vacation" rulings had longer and broader sway. Moreover, for most of the June term of 1863, when many conscription cases were argued, Justice Manly was too ill to attend court. Sharing the bench with only one other justice in term, Pearson held half the supreme judicial power in the state for much of the period critical for conscription. The absent Manly also happened to be the justice most inclined to give the Confederate government leeway in exercising its powers over North Carolinians.

Any state supreme court justice in the Confederacy who had embraced the resonating rhetoric of liberty and southern rights in the political crises of the 1850s was well situated to protect liberty from the reach of the central government.[7] A lawyer with political roots in the opposition party of the secession era was in a good position as justice to put a stick in the spokes of the secessionist wheel. No other judge in the Confederacy so well demonstrated the power to obstruct the will of the administration as Richmond M. Pearson.[8]

Pearson was born in North Carolina in 1805. He graduated from the state university, entered the bar, and enjoyed four terms in the lower house of the legislature. In 1836 he was elected judge of the superior court and founded a law school, which, after 1848, was located in Richmond Hill in Surry County. In 1848 the legislature, despite its Democratic majority, elected Pearson, a Whig, justice of the supreme court. He became chief justice in 1858. With interruptions because of Reconstruction he managed to remain on the court most of the time until he died in 1878. Like many other former Whigs, Pearson opposed secession, but once war came, he never strayed into North Carolina's potent peace movements.[9]

Although the political climate of North Carolina was more unfavorable than most states to the Davis administration and must have created an atmosphere conducive to dissent, this alone did not determine the degree of judicial interference.[10] The extreme alienation of some of Georgia's political leaders from the Richmond government did not have a similar effect on the Georgia Supreme Court. As we have seen, the administration was pleasantly surprised by the Georgia court's ruling in the sugar impressment case in 1863. Apparently the individual proclivities of the justices go a long way toward accounting for the extraordinary record of the North Carolina Supreme Court on war issues.

Whatever the motivation, Pearson was willing to challenge the War Department. As soon as he gained a reputation for releasing conscripts, lawyers with clients in the clutches of the military naturally sought him out. Notoriety and his own willingness to seize these issues explain the disproportionately large number of such cases Pearson decided.[11] His actions, especially when contrasted with the records of other courts, amounted to massive judicial intervention in issues of mobilization. In some cases they were equivalent to judicial nullification of Confederate law.

The problem grew serious enough for Jefferson Davis to point it out to Congress in 1864:

> In some of the States civil process has been brought to bear with disastrous efficiency upon the Army. Every judge has the power to issue the writ of *habeas corpus,* and if one manifests more facility in discharging petitioners than his associates the application is made to him, however remote he may be. In one instance a general on the eve of an important movement, when every man was needed, was embarrassed by the command of a judge—more than two hundred miles distant—to bring . . . or send . . . before him, on *habeas corpus,* some deserters who had been arrested and returned to his command. In another, a commandant of a camp of conscripts, who had a conscript in camp, was commanded to bring him before a judge more than a hundred miles distant, although there was a judge competent to hear and determine the cause resident in the place where the writ was executed. He consulted eminent counsel, and was advised that, from the known opinions of the judge selected, the conscript would undoubtedly be released, and the officer was therefore advised to discharge him at once, and return the facts informally; that such a return was not technically sufficient, but would be accepted as accomplishing the purpose of the writ. He acted on the advice of his counsel, and was immediately summoned by the judge to show cause why he should not be attached for a contempt in making an insufficient return, and was compelled to leave his command at a time when his services were pressingly needed by the Government and travel over a hundred miles and a considerable distance away from any railroad, to purge himself of the technical contempt.[12]

When Pearson was "in vacation," he held court at Richmond Hill, which cannot be found on modern maps. It was located in Surry County, in the central northwestern part of the state, and the Western North Carolina Rail Road ran some forty miles south of the county. Richmond Hill was over a hundred miles from the seat of the supreme court in Raleigh, also the site of Camp Holmes, a conscript camp and camp of instruction for North Carolina troops.[13]

It is difficult to see Pearson's record with the North Carolina Supreme Court as the product of diligent reliance on precedent and principles in construing Confederate statutes, as Van Zant suggests. This seems obvious even before an examination of the content of his decisions, for the significant evidence is the sheer number of cases *and how he gained jurisdiction in them.* This was an unprecedented thrust of judicial power, and the problem that remains is to determine the purpose of the judicial intervention. Van Zant has made an excellent case that Pearson's court used judicial power for power itself (judicial review), personal liberties, and state sovereignty. What follows is an evaluation of the weight of Pearson's decisions in these three areas.

The Peculiar Jurisprudence of Richmond M. Pearson

Naturally Pearson did not himself see his work as enhancing the power of his own office, but he did see his client as "the law" and not the people. North Carolina's justices were chosen for good behavior by joint ballot of the legislature, not by the voters. The chief justice, in turn, was elected by the justices themselves.[14]

Pearson, who wrote most of North Carolina's decisions on conscription and habeas corpus, maintained steadfastly that he merely expounded the law, ignoring the beleaguered condition of the country and the likelihood he would be criticized for unpopular decisions. Pearson either saw himself or posed as an impartial interpreter of law constrained by his position to apply relentless logic, whatever emotion might otherwise dictate, and thus unswayed by other currents of political or social life. "The subject," Pearson wrote in the case called *In the matter of Austin,* "must be considered by a Judge 'as a dry question of law,' unaffected by collateral considerations growing out of the condition of our country, and for this reason," he said, his "conclusion may differ from that of those who are at liberty to look at it under the bias of feeling." In another decision in 1863 involving "a question . . . of great practical importance," Pearson explained that his "duty" was "simply to expound the law." In the decision reached in the case called *In the matter of Bryan,* he said that the court dealt with "a dry question of Constitutional Law, and its decision should not be influenced by collateral disturbing causes." He concluded that he had "no discretion and no right to be influenced by considerations growing out of the condition of our country, but must act with a single eye to the due administration of the law, according to the proper construction of the acts of Congress."[15]

To others, the distressed condition of the country seemed important. In the Bryan case, which determined whether a man who paid for a substitute was exempt from military service ever after, the government's lawyers argued:

> It cannot be supposed that Congress intended, without procuring thereby *the very slightest* advantage to the Government, to place it in the power of all men between the ages of 18 and 35 years, to put themselves beyond the reach of their country's call, *during the war;* at a time too, when the enemy were declar-

ing that our subjugation was a simple question of arithmetic, and depended upon the process of giving man for man, to death, or more if necessary, *till our last man was gone.* Such legislation would have been an act of madness unparalleled in the annals of time![16]

Pearson generally stopped short of the boldest judicial interventionism and activism. Most of his war decisions interpreted statutes and restrained national or executive authority under them. He declared an act of Congress unconstitutional only once. Though many Confederates expected it at any moment, and some historians have left that impression, Pearson did not rule conscription unconstitutional. He made rather a show of avoiding any ruling on it.[17] At Richmond Hill on 9 July 1863, for example, counsel for the plaintiff in the case entitled *In the matter of Irvin* asserted the unconstitutionality of conscription, but Pearson did not rise to the bait. His decision rested on customarily narrow reasoning instead.[18]

Chief Justice Pearson could maintain his pose of expositor of the law and appear to reason from precedent and principle in 1863 because it was easy for him to get his hands on the law, gaining jurisdiction in critical cases interpreting Confederate statutes. Since the Congress had chosen not to renew the president's authorization to suspend the writ of habeas corpus, Pearson could issue the writ, decide cases, and have his opinions printed later in the state supreme court reports. When the Confederate States district attorney in Raleigh hired General Braxton Bragg's brother Thomas in 1863 to help in habeas corpus cases before the supreme court, there were "some thirty" pending, and of those, apparently, twenty-seven had come to Pearson.[19]

Pearson's decisions, declaring that home guards could not be ordered to arrest Confederate deserters and upholding the exemptions of persons from conscription in complicated or questionable circumstances, brought him the hatred of North Carolina's conscription officers and Confederate generals (whose troops often eagerly interpreted Pearson's decisions to mean they could escape service if they could get back to their home states). The decisions caught the president's attention and vexed the secretary of war. They put loyal North Carolina politicians in a difficult position of upholding North Carolina sovereignty without impeding the nation's war effort. They caused other judges to caution Pearson and the War Department alike to avoid serious confrontation. All of this occurred in 1863, before Pearson began asserting fundamental principles more than merely expounding the law.[20]

In the cases he took on in 1863, Pearson could give the appearance of merely expounding the law because he was armed with original jurisdiction in habeas corpus cases. The Confederate Congress in 1863 chose not to authorize suspension of the writ of habeas corpus. In fact, Richmond Pearson's career on the bench suggests the utterly wrongheaded course of the Confederate Congress on the question. The legislators chose to authorize suspension early in 1862 before conscription and chose to end suspension early in 1863 just as conscription grew more and more vexatious. The Congress did not at first clearly realize that the need for suspension had less to do with sedition and states of siege than with the American hatred of the draft.

Like many thinking Confederates, Pearson realized that the new republic rested on different principles from the old, and these naturally entered his decisions from time to time. He enunciated them most clearly in 1864 in a case called *In the matter of Russell*. Daniel L. Russell Jr., an officer recently court-martialed and reduced to the ranks, was appointed county commissioner in Brunswick County while on furlough before transferring to another company. The appointment, which held the potential of exempting the incumbent from military service as an essential state worker, looked suspiciously like a ruse to escape service because Russell was under twenty-one years of age and probably could not legally claim the office. General W. H. C. Whiting refused to discharge Russell, who sued out a writ of habeas corpus and came before Pearson's bench in Richmond Hill on 25 July 1864. Brunswick County, presumably Russell's home and his residence on furlough, was located diagonally at the farthest remove from Richmond Hill, more than two hundred miles away, near Wilmington.

"The authority of the government to conscript," reasoned Pearson, "is derived from the power conferred on Congress to 'raise and support armies.' This power, from the very nature of things, is subject to the restriction that it shall not extend to the Governors, members of the Legislatures, Judges or other officers necessary for the proper administration of the State government; for as the Confederate government is a creature of the States, it is absurd to suppose, that the intention was to make a grant of power, which would enable the creature to destroy its creation, and cause the existence of the States to be dependent on the pleasure of Congress."

Pearson, as usual, did not search for precedents or survey commentaries on the constitution. The original law exempting North Carolina officials under the provisions of the Confederate Conscription Act was passed the year before and exempted only one county commissioner per county to distribute money and provisions to soldiers' families. The lucky Russell was Brunswick's choice for that position.[21] Pearson, reasoning mostly "from the very nature of things," ordered Russell discharged.[22] Pearson's fellow justice William Battle released a prisoner on habeas corpus citing the Russell decision as precedent later that summer.

To be sure, there was nothing remarkable in declaring states' rights doctrine as Confederate political or judicial philosophy. But in 1864 Pearson had to reach out even farther toward fundamental principles. He also had to assert his jurisdiction to decide war matters—which in a way had always been the secret of his jurisprudence. After 1863 Pearson's eagerness to intervene with writs of habeas corpus faced a more serious challenge than the opposition of exasperated conscription officers: the Congress finally suspended the writ of habeas corpus so that a military officer holding a conscript or deserter could reply to a writ that the person was held under the president's authority. Conscription grew more stringent, and Pearson was not about to miss the opportunity to insist that the judiciary and not the War Department interpret the laws. During 1864 he contrived a remarkable doctrine, unmatched by any other legal authority in the Union or the Confederacy, to get around the suspension.

Pearson began developing his argument in a case called *In re Roseman*. Pearson released a "conscript," accused by Colonel Mallett of "avoiding" service, on the grounds that a person "avoiding" service would escape to the woods; Pearson could not assume that seeking a law court was "avoidance." He distinguished between the criminal accusations protected by the writ of habeas corpus and civil accusations protected by other writs and pointed to the word *prisoner* in the statute authorizing suspension of the writ of habeas corpus.[23]

Later, the case called *In the matter of Cain* gave Pearson a chance to publish his novel argument. The suspension of the writ of habeas corpus by Congress, he argued, referred only to cases of petitioners held for criminal offenses. There were different kinds of writs of habeas corpus, and Congress referred only to the writ of habeas corpus *ad subjiciendum*. Others, like *de homine replegiando* or *de testificiandum*, initiated judicial inquiries into the restraint of persons not being held by criminal authorities for criminal acts—like children by improper guardians in custody disputes or conscripts in the army. These other writs had to do with "a civil remedy to assert a private right under a contract."

If no criminal act were specified in the return to the writ, a judicial inquiry could proceed even if the writ of habeas corpus were suspended. Pearson did not feel called upon in this remarkable decision (1) to specify by which of the other kinds of writs Cain was relieved; (2) to justify why, if such writs as *de homine replegiando* were, by his own admission, "ancient" and somehow "replaced" in modern times with the great writ of liberty, they were not also suspended; or (3) to explain why the framers of the U.S. Constitution, the framers of the Confederate Constitution, and the Congress of the Confederate States failed to discriminate among writs in the language of their documents if they intended to suspend only one kind. Even Pearson himself a year earlier had not seen any such distinction. In *Bryan* he had asserted that there were "several kinds of writs of habeas corpus," but he added that "the great Writ of Right, habeas corpus," could "bring any citizen alleged to be wrongfully imprisoned *or restrained of his liberty* before the Court, with the cause of his arrest and detention" (emphasis added).[24] More to the point, most people knew that these were precisely the sorts of problems the legislators thought they were solving by allowing the writ to be suspended. Pearson was seldom interested in the intentions of the legislators, who were more in touch with the condition of the country. Perhaps it is little wonder that after this decision the other justices on the court were emboldened to overrule Pearson.[25]

In *Cain,* Pearson overstepped his bounds. Afterward, his influence waned, though, as we have seen already, Justice Battle relied on Pearson's decision, made in vacation, to release a state official from conscription in a case Battle decided in vacation. Later Battle, joined with Manly during the full court session, changed his mind on this point. When these two justices agreed with Pearson in the later terms of the court in 1864, Battle wrote the majority decisions, with Pearson merely concurring, and they no longer hesitated to overrule Pearson. Thus Van Zant's interpretation lacks a proper periodization for the leadership of the court: Pearson's waned in 1864, and Battle and Manly took over.

The critical point came when Pearson at last attempted to overturn a Confederate statute. In *Ex parte Walton* Pearson ruled that the law empowering the Confederacy to conscript men who had previously provided substitutes was unconstitutional because it violated a contract. He had warned in *Austin* that he would resist such an action by the Confederate government. The original writ of habeas corpus in the Walton case had been issued on 27 January, but an agreement with Colonel Mallett delayed the hearing so that the Confederate colonel could obtain counsel for a full argument. Pearson's decision came on 19 February, but by agreement with Confederate authorities he bound Walton over to appear before the full supreme court in June 1864.

In a curious turn of legal events, two more Walton decisions followed. The first established the court's right to review a habeas corpus decision by a justice in vacation, and the second reversed Justice Pearson's ruling in the Walton habeas corpus case, on which he reached his decision while in vacation. Pearson sided with Battle in deciding that the court could review the decision made in vacation. In the second decision, Pearson was in dissent, as Battle and Manly upheld the constitutionality of the two acts of the Confederate Congress in language that matched their names in spirit. They were in line with judgments on the same question from the supreme courts of Virginia, Alabama, and Georgia. Battle reviewed the history of the U.S. Constitution and of Parliament, the models for the powers of the Confederate Congress, and pointed out that American governments were ones not of "limited" but "enumerated" powers. Enumerated powers were full and complete; the point of the Constitution was only that no others than those enumerated could be exercised by the central government. The power to raise armies was limited only by the stipulation that money could not be appropriated for the purpose for more than two-year terms. Battle spoke of the Confederacy's "unlimited war powers." Pearson merely reprinted his argument in *Ex parte Walton* and stated his protest "against the position, that the action of the Courts of other States can have any legitimate bearing on the action of this Government."[26]

Though influenced by Pearson's *Russell* decision later that summer, Battle wrote a majority opinion for the whole supreme court on a similar question in the October term and let it rest on less extreme ground than Pearson, whose concurring opinion went farther. In *William D. Johnson v Peter Mallett* the North Carolina Supreme Court upheld the states' rights doctrine popular with a wide range of politicians in the state, including Governor Zebulon B. Vance. The power to raise armies was limited in few ways, but an important one was that it could not be used to destroy the state governments. Johnson was a Raleigh policeman, albeit he mostly kept the city's water pumps in order. He could not be conscripted because the state legislature had specifically named Raleigh policemen as essential state workers in their act enumerating those who should be exempted according to the Confederate exemption law. Pearson's concurring opinion went a bit farther: "What officers are necessary and proper for the administration of the government, and laws of the State, is a matter confined to the wisdom of the Legislature. . . . Whenever the Legislature creates and fills an office, or authorizes a county or municipal corporation to do so, it is to be taken *conclusively*, as a 'principle of law,' that such office is necessary and proper." The state governor's certification of the office as necessary was an act of "supererogation": the Confederate government could not say that the governor's certification was necessary.[27]

But Pearson's authority was on the wane, and the condition of the country could hardly be ignored by the other justices. In the December 1864 term of the court, Justice Battle overturned Pearson in *Seth Bridgman v Peter Mallett*. There was a critical difference in the case of Mr. Bridgman, who had been elected a county register (an office exempted in the North Carolina act) while he was in service. This election would pull a man out of the army into state service rather than pulling a man out of state service to go into the army (as was the case with the policeman Johnson). Battle now sought the original intent of the Congress—anywhere he could find it, even in collateral legislation. He referred to the preamble of the 5 January 1864 act ending exemption to discover that the "country was then in very great need of soldiers." In this "life and death struggle for national existence" some persons were called to more than one duty. The problem, in other words, was that "the same persons are citizens of two separate and distinct sovereigns, to both of which they owe duty and allegiance."[28] "Although the war power of the Confederate government," Battle reasoned, "is . . . absolute and unlimited in terms, and the supremacy of that government over the States, in regard to that power, is thus clearly and distinctly asserted, it has been decided, and I think rightly decided, that the Confederate government cannot, in the exercise of the war power, destroy the States, by conscribing those officers who are necessary to the action of the State governments." He agreed fully that the "superstructure must fall away when its pillars are taken away or destroyed." But he finally came down on the other side:

> this case is reversed when the Confederate government has, in the exercise of its rightful supreme war power, conscribed into its service a man who is not an officer of the State, and the State is attempting to take him out of it, by electing him to office. The man, as a citizen, owed the duty to the general government, which it had called upon him to perform, just as much as he owed the duty to the State, to accept and discharge the duties, to which he was elected. Here are two obligations undoubtedly binding upon the man, but which being inconsistent, cannot both be performed at the same time. How can this conflict be settled, but by resorting to a principle of potent efficacy both in international and municipal law, that priority of possession gives priority of right?[29]

Battle now overturned *Russell* (and his own previous decision, which relied on *Russell*).

Battle shared Pearson's view of the Confederacy's first principles, more or less. He agreed that the states could not be destroyed in order to save the Confederacy. On the other hand, Battle reasoned, he was dealing with a dual sovereignty. It is not clear that Pearson ever recognized a dual sovereignty. He did not argue with Battle on this and preferred to heap contempt on arguments from necessity and national crisis.[30]

Once Battle discovered the governing principle, he applied it with great confidence. In *Matthew Johnson v Peter Mallett* he ruled that a man who applied for and was awarded a mail contract could not be removed from the army even though mail contractors were exempt from service. He was overruling another Pearson decision given in vacation.[31]

Battle's decisions lack the originality and penetration of Pearson's. The application of the priority rule in *Bridgman* seemed clumsy. On the other hand, he may have shown more statesmanship in reaching out to legislative preambles to remind North Carolinians of the condition of the country. A less aggressive use of habeas corpus might have solved the problem as well, but Pearson had already opened the door to its broad use in conscription cases—and the North Carolina statute imposing a fine for nonissuance may have been a factor. For all his originality and even brilliance, Pearson tended to hide behind his pose of logical expositor of the law. He may have operated from extreme states' rights principles, but he did not argue them in full against his colleagues.

Finally, Pearson's jurisprudence could not be characterized entirely accurately by his refusal "to compromise personal liberties."[32] During the Civil War, Richmond M. Pearson never protected anyone's speech or freedom to assemble. He never defended anyone's freedom of religion or right to print dissenting views in press or pamphlet. It would be at least as accurate to say of the court—especially of Pearson's decisions—that they served privilege rather than liberty.

The writ of habeas corpus, said historian Frank E. Vandiver, "was considered the surest protection of the common man," but there is a touch of the mythical in that statement, and there was nothing common about the men Pearson defended. The conscript officer quoted in chapter 3 was nearer the truth when he said that Southerners who could buy substitutes could afford able counsel. Daniel L. Russell Jr., the underage county commissioner attempting to escape service in the ranks after a court-martial robbed him of his officer's commission, was a future governor of the state. Some of those asserting Russell's rights against the Confederacy were only protecting him from loss of status. Governor Vance, for example, asserted Russell should be exempt, adding, "Should I be in error upon the law of the case, I must earnestly urge upon you not to wound the spirit of this gallant and promising young officer by sending him into the ranks."[33] Pearson aided the likes of Russell as well as exempt millwrights and mail route contract purchasers. He shielded overseers of Carolina's minority plantations while the state's vast majority of small farmers filled the ranks with an enthusiasm unsurpassed in any other state.[34] If Confederate conscription laws initially made the Civil War a rich man's war and a poor man's fight, Pearson's jurisprudence did nothing to right the balance. Its practical effect was to undermine congressional attempts to end the privileges of purchasing substitutes.[35]

In the end, no assessment summarizes with complete accuracy the work of the court or, more particularly, of Richmond M. Pearson. It is not possible to give an entirely satisfactory explanation of Pearson's jurisprudence, shaped as it was by several sources, including his position as leader of the court, his preference for analysis of logic and grammar to the exclusion of other legal or social principles, his extreme North Carolinian states' rights outlook, and probably other sources as well. But then, we do not need to. What is significant about Richmond M. Pearson's jurisprudence is that it was peculiar—very peculiar indeed.

In assessing his peculiarity, it is crucial not to envision him as a legalistic stickler oblivious to the political effect of his jurisprudence. The jurisprudence was informed by intensely held political views. Although Pearson never let his political disaffection from the Davis government take him down the path to peace movements, the politicization of his opinions has been overlooked by commentators. The strident language of the Walton cases was, after all, uttered in an election summer and departed from the rhetoric of "dry questions of law." He concluded that if the Confederate Congress could repudiate its own contracts under the war powers, it "may repudiate its bonds and notes now outstanding, a renovated currency being necessary to support the army, or it may conscript all *white women* between the ages of 16 and 60 to cook and bake for the soldiers, nurse at the hospitals, or serve in the ranks as soldiers, thus uprooting the foundations of society; or it may conscript the Governor, Judges, and Legislatures of the several States, put an end to 'State Rights,' and erect on the ruins a 'consolidated military despotism.'"[36] Dissenting later that summer when the Walton case was reviewed by the full court, Pearson despaired for law in the Confederacy, saying that the judges could put away their "books" and "indulge the hope that when peace again smiles on our country, law will resume its sway." Surely that was more the language of the hustings than of the supreme bench.[37]

Neither Pearson nor historians since his time realized quite how risky his judicial obstructionism was. War Department clerk Robert G. H. Kean was present on 26 February 1864 when Secretary of War Seddon and Assistant Secretary Campbell discussed a recent Pearson ruling: "The Assistant Secretary said, 'Suppose he decides that the act of Congress suspending the writ does not apply and continues to discharge them.' 'Then,' said the Secretary, 'I will not hesitate a moment to arrest him.' 'That is the point to which it is coming,'" said Judge Campbell.[38]

Seddon had written Governor Vance in March, saying that "Judge Pearson's decision . . . is, of course, until reversed, the law of the particular case, and will be respected as such. No effort will therefore be made to arrest or enroll the man temporarily discharged by him, and how then can any possible obligation be imposed on you to execute the judgment or protect that man?" But the suspension of the writ of habeas corpus was law, and any attempt to enforce a writ after an officer properly responded that the prisoner was held under presidential authority would bring a collision.[39] Jefferson Davis used equally ominous language two days later:

> The decision of Judge Pearson releasing the conscript in the case before him will of course be respected until the action of the appellate court, for the case was before him prior to the passage of the law suspending the writ of habeas corpus; and although I do not believe that his decision is right, the public interest will not suffer by awaiting the result of the appeal in the one case before him. But I understand that both the other judges of the supreme court of North Carolina have refused writs of habeas corpus since the passage of the law and since Pearson's decision, on the express ground that the act of Congress covers the case of the principals of substitutes, and thus we know that the appellate court will reverse the decision of Judge Pearson. The court of appeals of Virginia has just given an elaborate and unanimous opinion confirming the legislation of Congress as constitutional. In other States like decisions have been rendered, and if, under such circumstances, Judge Pearson should pursue the factious course you anticipate, and . . . put a Confederate officer in prison for contempt for making the exact return to a writ of habeas corpus which the law orders . . . I shall not shrink from the issue.[40]

Pearson's peculiar jurisprudence may have brought the Confederacy nearer to confrontation between the judiciary and the executive than the Pennsylvania Supreme Court's declaration that conscription was unconstitutional came to provoking armed conflict with the Lincoln administration.[41] Pearson was doing more than "diligently" relying "on precedent and . . . principles in construing statutes of the Confederate Congress."[42] Precedent had little to do with statements such as the one he made in the case called *In the matter of Irvin,* on 9 July 1863, months before Congress revoked substitution and made those who had hired substitutes liable to conscription: "Whether Congress has power to pass an act expressly making liable to conscription persons who have heretofore furnished substitutes and received an absolute discharge, is a question not now presented, and one which, I trust, public necessity never will cause to be presented, as it would violate natural justice and shock the moral sense."[43] "Natural justice" and "moral sense" were more the principles of the abolitionists than of the states' rights constitutionalists and were inimical to precedent. Pearson here threatened, warned, or challenged the Confederate government. More important, the repeated seizure of original jurisdiction was of necessity unprecedented because it was possible only in wartime's multiplication of habeas corpus petitions.

The Significance of Richmond M. Pearson for Interpreting the Confederate Bench

The question arises why states' rights principles or notions of individual rights like Pearson's did not more often put the Confederacy on the brink of conflict. Instead we find Judge Robert R. Heath of North Carolina's First Circuit Court writing Seddon on 2 March 1864 to plead for "a little patience" with Pearson. Heath was one of those who agreed with Pearson that the conscripting of men who had paid for substitutes violated a contract and was unconstitutional—that the substitution law was not merely an exemption from service like any other ordinary military regulation of the draft. But, he went on, "I am not prepared to go the length of holding, that the Law suspending the Habeas Corpus does not cover the case of those who put in substitutes: I had thought the act was passed *expressly* to effect that object, & many others." Heath warned the secretary of war that the re-arrest of particular individuals released on habeas corpus was "very dangerous" and threatened to pit Governor Vance and the state courts against Confederate authorities. A decision of the full supreme court on the habeas corpus would solve the problem and get Vance out of his adversarial relationship with Richmond on this case, and Vance was badly needed to defeat the movement for peace of William Woods Holden.[44]

Seeking the reason for Pearson's rarity misses the point. The point *is* his very rarity. Indeed, seeking an explanation might falsify, making what was abnormal seem explicable and even normal. It would be better simply to posit eccentricity and allow Pearson to join the other eccentric extremists of libertarian political thought in the Confederacy: Albert Pike, Henry Foote, and Alexander H. Stephens.

It is much more important to return to the institutional context of Confederate justice as a whole. The fate of liberty in the states' rights–oriented Confederacy lay in the hands of fewer than 37 lawyers. Nine of the states had supreme courts consisting of 3 men (27 justices altogether).[45] Two states, Louisiana and Virginia, had 5 men on their courts (adding 10 more justices).[46] Since the Confederacy never organized a supreme court, these 37 men reigned supreme in judging legislation affecting civil liberties in their states. At any moment the number was actually smaller. Virginia's western justice ceased sitting with the court after 1861, leaving only 4 justices there and 36 for the whole Confederacy. Justice Manly's illness in the summer of 1863 in North Carolina left 35 for a time. Other circumstances, including Federal occupation, reduced the number here and there.

All of the justices enjoyed roughly the same powerful position Pearson did.[47] Theirs was a small club. All of them basked in the prestige and enhancement of authority that accrued to them in a region saturated for a decade in noisy libertarianism, constitutionalism, and strict construction doctrines devised to combat the growing power of the northern nonslaveholding states. Pearson might have fit in with this group had they ever been brought together as a club. At first he was usually able to bring Battle and Manly along on his rulings. He earned the respect of his colleagues and had a sense of humor.

But there was only one Richmond M. Pearson, and he did not fit in. He was the only justice who came into dangerous conflict with the War Department and the president. Had there been another Richmond M. Pearson among the thirty-five Confederate lawyers robed with the awesome powers of the southern supreme judiciary in 1863, the Confederate war effort might have been seriously impeded, even blocked in some states, and the war actually lost because of internal opposition.

No such thing happened. In fact, the contrary situation prevailed. The Mississippi High Court of Errors and Appeals offers an interesting example. It decided only fifteen cases in 1861 and none in 1862. The court resumed meeting for its April term in 1863 but decided only two cases. It met for the October term in 1864 and decided two cases; it did not meet again until the war was over. Those courts that did meet took few war cases, and as Jefferson Davis exulted in his letter about Pearson, for the most part the courts upheld the essential war measures of the Congress and the administration when they did take them up.[48]

Thus the state judiciaries, by omission or commission, upheld order, as did most Confederate citizens except in certain regions of peculiar political geography. All the while the government in Richmond put in place a revolutionary economy sometimes described as state socialism, conscripted its young men, taxed, impressed supplies, and arbitrarily removed young women from trains in the middle of the night. All the while it imprisoned border state people hostile to the cause as well as reluctant conscripts, malcontents, and misfits.

"There was," said historian J. Mills Thornton III of antebellum southern politics, "always only one question which really mattered: how to maintain one's freedom." Theirs was a "society obsessed with the idea of slavery." Their inheritance from the American Revolution was a "fear of an imminent loss of freedom." In the South "this tradition was lent considerable urgency by a daily familiarity with black slavery, which served as a constant reminder of the terrible reality behind the politician's metaphor."[49]

That view confuses the rhetoric of the southern hustings with the realities of southern life. Antebellum politicians exaggerated sensitivity about southern rights as a means of combating northern power, but historians should not exaggerate as well. If such views were as prevalent and internalized as they are made out to be in recent literature, there would have been more than one Richmond M. Pearson produced by the southern political system to bedevil the Confederate authorities in Richmond from the secure power of the southern bench. The institutional power was there for all to seize, but only Pearson seized it.

The other thirty-six justices in the Confederate states shared to perhaps a surprising degree the views of their society at large. That society was not obsessive about liberty. That society was not paranoid with fears of slipping into the dread status of slavery. Southern society was, at bottom, American and much the same as northern society. It consisted of people who valued both liberty and order. They did not bridle more than normally at restrictive measures taken by the government to fight a war for national existence.

Southern society, or large portions of it, desired order. The politics of the 1850s stretched a thin veneer of libertarianism over these ordinary longings for order. The political ideas of the 1850s were artificial defenses from northern attacks and from expressions of disapproval from world opinion. When war came and tipped the political scales abruptly in the direction of order instead of liberty, many Confederate citizens were willing to go along, and their lawyers and judges usually went along with them.

5

GHOSTS OF THE DEAD HABEAS CORPUS
THE HABEAS CORPUS COMMISSIONERS

TRIALS BY MILITARY COMMISSION PROVED the downfall of the reputation of the Lincoln administration on civil liberties. In 1866 the United States Supreme Court, dominated by Lincoln appointees, condemned in *Ex parte Milligan* the common Civil War practice of trying civilians in military courts while civil courts were open. Such military commissions were common only in the North. Richmond authorities repudiated the scattered instances of the use of military commissions initiated by local commanders in 1861, 1862, and 1863 and backed away from their own imposition of courts-martial on liquor sellers and other persons detained under the initial martial law declarations. After that no more such trials occurred. In this respect the record of the Davis administration appears to have improved as the war went on.[1]

Yet the difference in practice from the North was not as sharp as it may seem. Not only did the Confederate War Department feel the need of military commissions, but in fact it quietly devised a little-known substitute for them. By the last year of the war, the War Department had improvised a shadow system of courts that played some of the roles of military commissions in the North. The Confederate Congress lethargically sanctioned them. Moreover, the War Department did not allow these useful institutions to lapse when the Congress refused to extend authority for the suspension of the writ of habeas corpus; the work of the War Department's shadow courts was never suspended, for there were *always* political prisoners in the Confederacy.

The Confederate counterpart of the military commission was the habeas corpus commissioner. The office had its origin long before the suspension of habeas corpus or presidential proclamations of martial law. General John H. Winder, keeper of the military prisons in Richmond and later provost marshal, suggested them to Secretary of War Leroy Pope Walker as early as 26 August 1861. Winder noted that many of those "arrested as suspicious persons and for other causes" could be released "if their cases were examined." He recommended "establishing a commission or . . . directing the C. S. commissioner to examine these cases and to prepare and digest them so that you can at once decide without the labor of wading through the investigations."[2] Secretary of War Walker wrote lawyers J. Randolph Tucker and James Lyons four days later, asking them "to pass upon the cases of persons who have been arrested under suspicion of disloyalty to the cause of the Confederate States." Lyons accepted the commission on 2 September 1861.[3] Walker's successor in the war office, Judah P. Benjamin, later persuaded Sydney S. Baxter to examine prisoners "in Richmond on charges of being spies, enemies, traitors, &c., with a view of discharging all such as ought not to be held in custody and bringing to trial and punishment such as seem guilty of the charges." Benjamin asked Baxter to make reports to him "as promptly as possible." Baxter would serve with no compensation.

The *statutory* creation of the office, which came well after the office in fact existed, is not easy to trace, but the Habeas Corpus Act of 13 October 1862 seems to be the first law to mention it. That act renewed the president's authority to suspend the writ of habeas corpus, which was expiring under the initial act of 27 February 1862. The second section of the October act stipulated that the "President shall cause proper officers to investigate the cases . . . in order that they may be discharged, if improperly detained."[4] In truth, legislative authority did not really matter, for War Department officials had already been interrogating political prisoners for a year and would keep on investigating them after this Habeas Corpus Act expired.

The evolution was analogous to the development of the domestic passport system. The initial lack of compensation to the commissioners permitted the department to avoid seeking funding from Congress—and thus having to explain to the legislators exactly what the department was doing to civilians. Such a strategy worked only up to the time when the number of civilians in military prisons grew too great to ask anyone to deal with them free of charge, and that time came soon. Lyons was already asking to be relieved of duty in December, as it took 80 percent of his time and left little for his private practice.[5] By 27 January 1862 Congress passed a gingerly worded resolution to establish amounts due Baxter and Lyons "for services rendered the Government in investigating charges against persons confined as prisoners in the city of Richmond."[6] Yet the initial habeas corpus legislation did not carry overt recognition of the office, nor did the commissioners receive their compensation. Baxter reluctantly appealed to Secretary of War George W. Randolph for compensation on 24 July 1862. "I really need money to support my wife and children," he explained and submitted a bill for $1,750, covering seven months' "services as commissioner to examine citizen prisoners" from 10 December 1861 to 10 July 1862 at $250 per month.[7]

Baxter's invoice went eventually to Secretary of War Randolph, who endorsed it vaguely: "The Secretary does not feel authorized to allow a rate of compensation equal to that of the Second Officers in the War Dept, for services which will probably be required while the war lasts and may to that extent be considered as a fixed salary. He is willing to allow $125.00 per month." The secretary of war knew that military arrests of civilians would continue as long as the war did.[8] In the end the commissioners were not left in quite as vague a condition as the passport system and were described as having the powers of district court judges in an act of 9 June 1864.

The institution was not at first called a court. It always functioned without juries, of course, and apparently without provision for counsel for the prisoners. In fact, there do not seem to have been any formal rules at all—no requirement for recording testimony, for example—and not many rules developed as practice went along. Commissioners were ordered to report their findings to the secretary of war, but no specific deadline was set, no uniform categories of information about the prisoners were required, and no standardized forms were ever developed, printed, or issued for the reports. The digests of cases constituted no more than notes jotted down from conversations with prisoners (and occasionally witnesses). They were not necessarily written in complete sentences. There was no requirement that every prisoner be reported on. The commissioners had no clerks and could not easily make copies of their reports. If an inquiry came after a report was sent to the secretary of war, the commissioner had to rely on unaided recollection. There were no penalties for failing to report, for inaccurate reports, or for lost or misfiled reports. The commissioner could recommend a prisoner be freed or turned over to civil authorities for trial, but no other powers were known or advertised. As a matter of fact, the commissioner had a very great power frequently exercised: he could simply *not* recommend their freedom and in effect sentence them to long confinement in military prison.

Casual reporting had terrible consequences for some prisoners, of course, but it had an unintended benefit to Confederate reputation after the war. The commissioners' digests of cases were filed alphabetically under each commissioner's name, as though they were ordinary letters written to the secretary of war. They were not treated as prison records or court records. There, under names unfamiliar to even diligent historians of the Confederacy—such as Baxter, Saffold, Hennen, Leovy, and Carrington—the records lay, in plain sight for any manuscript researcher, yet in a way invisible. The reports lay in the War Department files for more than a century, amidst the letters from would-be organizers of military companies, applicants for exemptions from military service, crackpot inventors, religious fanatics, and would-be travelers requesting passes. The prisoners' names were not listed on separate sheets for alphabetizing and easy reference. The reports were not made public; they were for the use of the secretary of war. The commissioners eventually had the authority and power of district courts but never the public accountability of courts of law.

The habeas corpus commissioners always saw themselves as judges and, to some degree, protectors of the people's rights. Their longings for the justifications of a legally established system of justice are everywhere apparent in form, if not in substance. Baxter thought of himself as examining men sent in from the front.

He did not much like the idea of martial law in the interior of the country.[9] Commissioner Isaac H. Carrington often headed his reports "Confederate States vs" followed by the name of the prisoner. In one instance among the hundreds, he noted carefully of the prisoner that "He was told that any statement he might make would be entirely voluntary, & that he might make the statement, or not, at his discretion." However, this prisoner, Daniel F. Dulaney, had been appointed an aide to loyalist Virginia governor Francis Pierpont, and Carrington was evidently taking special care that the record in this case of a politically well connected prisoner look scrupulously correct.[10] In fact, the detainees enjoyed none of the safeguards of defendants in courts of law.

Despite flourishes of legalistic style in the reports, the clerical practices typical of the century before typewriters invited injustice by clerical error. Samuel Simmers, for example, from Rockingham County, Virginia, was arrested in Harrisonburg on 18 August 1862. He entered the Eastern District Military Prison in Richmond on 7 September and died eleven days later in the prison hospital. His congressman, John B. Baldwin, inquired about Simmers, but at first he could elicit no information from the War Department. Baldwin described Simmers as an ignorant, simple, and harmless man with a wife and children, and was distressed to learn that the War Department had let him die without adequate record of his case. An investigation by Sydney Baxter exonerated the captain of the prison, who at the time was Henry Wirz. Baxter reported on 5 January 1863 that Wirz was "a faithful honest and efficient man—but the clerical mistake in transcribing the name has prevented the prompt account of the prisoner." With five thousand prisoners of war in the prison at the time, Wirz could hardly be censured for losing track of this one citizen. Baxter did recommend that in the future the names of citizen prisoners be kept in registers separate from those for POWs and promptly reported to the secretary of war or the person appointed to examine them.[11]

Other congressmen besides Baldwin grew curious about the work of the commissioners once they got wind of their existence. As early as September 1862, the House of Representatives passed a resolution asking for the number of citizens arrested by military authority and the number still under arrest. They wanted to know how long the prisoners had been confined and what measures had been taken to secure a speedy and impartial trial for them. Secretary of War Randolph replied to the president's request for information on the matter thus:

it is impossible to ascertain how many citizens have been arrested by military authority. . . . these arrests are usually made by the Army in the country which [is] for the time being the theatre of military operation, . . . the persons arrested are often discharged in a short time without being turned over to the authorities . . . an officer here and one at Salisbury North Carolina are employed in investigating the cases of persons under arrest and . . . they are discharged when it is ascertained that it is compatible with the public safety.[12]

This negative response apparently staved off congressional curiosity until the habeas corpus legislation was near expiring in early 1863. Such elastic qualifiers as "usually" and "often" would not have satisfied a determined Congress, and the absence of discussion of western prisoners or prisons revealed the blindness of Richmond authorities to the war in the West.

Congress subsequently demanded a listing of prisoners in Richmond and Salisbury, and the War Department complied conscientiously. However, prison officials had not taken Baxter's advice to keep separate lists of prisoners of war and civilian prisoners. The War Department had no idea how many prisoners there were and no way of finding out without sending in officials to take an inventory of prisoners. This they did for the report to Congress. The publication of the resulting report on those prisoners in early 1863 led congressmen inclined to criticize the system to demand information about those among the three-hundred-odd prisoners on the lists who were their constituents, but the reports did not provoke a more general hue and cry for outraged liberty. Authority to suspend the writ of habeas corpus was discontinued, but this action was apparently unrelated to the report of prisoners.

When Congressman Baldwin, a sharp critic of the system who had introduced the resolution demanding an accounting of prisoners, inquired in March 1863 about his constituents whose names were printed on the list, the War Department asked Baxter to reply. Baldwin had seen from the published report that by the War Department's own admission men were held as "Union men" or even with "no charges preferred," and he did "not understand how these men are retained in custody in view of your directions 'to discharge those against whom no well-grounded cause of suspicion exists of having violated a law or done an act hostile or injurious to the confederate states' or of the rule declared by you that 'none are retained unless there be a cause of suspicion, supported by testimony rendering it probable that the discharge of the prisoners would be prejudicial to the public interest.'"[13]

Baxter responded first by pointing out that a large portion of Virginia was "in the possession of the enemy, and there the Authority of the laws and constitutions both of Va and the Confederate states, is, for a time suspended." "Many crimes are committed against our citizens in that region," Baxter said, "which for want of evidence cannot be tried elsewhere, even if there were legal jurisdiction to try the offenders elsewhere. . . . Criminals from that region whose release would be dangerous to the security of our friends, must be held . . . especially . . . those who . . . refuse to take the oath."

"It is impossible to administer justice in the regular course" in many counties,

Baxter said, as courts simply were not open. "A third class of cases," Baxter went on, "is the class of persons removed by military authorities from the theatre of army operations. . . . The security of our armies requires a large discretion should be rested in our generals over such cases." Finally, there was "a fourth class of cases by persons arrested in districts or counties not disturbed by the operations of the enemy. In these cases arrests and trials of citizens should always be made by the laws of the county," but "even here," he pointed out, "If a statute could be passed in reference to this class of cases it would furnish a guide for their disposal."[14]

Secretary of War Seddon relied on Baxter to answer a similar inquiry and explained that "Baxter, a lawyer of high repute, [was] charged with the duty of inquiring into the cases of prisoners in the military prison and of either discharging them or handing them over to their proper tribunals for trial." In fact, discharge or surrender to state authorities did not exhaust Baxter's options; he often recommended further imprisonment in Castle Thunder. Seddon must have known that, because Baxter sent his reports to Seddon. The War Department engaged in minor deceptions like these and perhaps in some self-deception about the work of the commissioners.[15]

Baxter's work continued steadily through the period after February 1863 when Jefferson Davis had no authority to suspend the writ of habeas corpus, and he reported on Virginians, North Carolinians, and Tennesseans, along with deserters, enemy aliens, and prisoners previously examined. Twenty-three reports survive from the period 23 February to 15 October 1863—about three a month. The government continued to appoint commissioners to examine political prisoners all over the Confederacy throughout the period as well, apparently without statutory authority. M. J. Saffold's original appointment as commissioner in Alabama, for example, came on 23 February 1863, after the expiration of Davis's authority to suspend the writ of habeas corpus and of the law creating the commissioners.[16]

Congressmen knew that civilians still languished in military prisons despite the security of the writ of habeas corpus in 1863. Henry Foote, who was chair of the House Committee on Illegal Searches and Seizures and an old nemesis of Jefferson Davis's, asked Richmond prison keeper John H. Winder on 21 December 1863 "to lay before them a *catalogue* of the *names* of all prisoners now in custody" under Winder's authority who were "charged with criminal offences—citizens of the Confederate States of America."[17] The secretary of war ordered the list made. Foote still had received nothing by 15 January 1864 and reminded the War Department of the "urgent and pressing character" of the request.[18] Five days later, B. R. Wellford Jr. noted that Winder had sent his list in to the congressional committee, showing "prisoners now in custody &c &c—with specification of offences with which they are charged—date of commencement of imprisonment—place where apprehended &c &c." Wellford needed further information from Baxter and said, "It is desirable to attend to it at once," adding ominously, "Foote is Chm of the Committee."[19] Foote's list was never published, and he apparently did not find on it adequate ammunition to convince his colleagues to halt a new bill to authorize the suspension of the writ of habeas corpus.

The habeas corpus suspension bill of February 1864 established or reestablished the commissioners, and the perennially awkward subject of their payment came up in the Senate in May. The pay proposal evolved into a proposal to confer certain powers on the commissioners as well. A full discussion in the House on 6 June 1864 resulted in the statement that the commissioners would be "clothed with the judicial powers vested in the District Courts." A. H. Garland of Arkansas, who had himself offered the act authorizing suspension of the writ of habeas corpus and thus creating the commissioners anew, said, "if this office of commissioners was to be established he would vote to pay them. . . . In the first place he will inquire of the chairman of the committee [Ways and Means, because it was a funding bill], (Mr. Lyons), whether these commissioners had entered upon their duties yet?" Lyons "believed" two were at work already. Then Henry Foote chimed in and "said he had expected this apparition would come up; he had been looking for a bill of this character, and he now greeted it most cordially. As the disembodied ghost of the dead *habeas corpus,* he would combat it to the last."[20]

Foote's cynicism should not set the tone of interpretation entirely, though there was room for cynicism; Lyons, a former commissioner himself, must have known they had been at work for years. To a degree, the commissioner system did in fact bear witness to the vaunted constitutionalism, legalism, and love of white liberty present in southern political culture. It is significant that the War Department and the president repeatedly disallowed the institution of trials by military commission. Though the commissioners provided a substitute for or halfway house to such a system, the War Department never considered making the commissioners who investigated civilian cases "officers" of the army, as the language of the statute of 13 October 1862 might have allowed. They carefully chose civilians who were able lawyers, some of whom proved to be sticklers for legality.

Confederate officials from their perspective doubtless saw the commissioner system as a protection of civil liberties, but from the perspective of history the system looks rather different. Ultimately commissioners provided a military substitute for real justice.[21]

The significance of the habeas corpus commissioners has been heretofore lost to history. Only the diligent student of the Confederate judiciary William M. Robinson Jr., writing around the time of World War II, got wind of their existence, and he tended to take an indulgent view of their work, for the habeas corpus commissioners did not square with his basic assumption that "The Confederate people by nature were lovers of Constitutional forms."[21] His treatment of the subject in the section of his book on the habeas corpus suspension act of 15 February 1864 is symptomatic. The act expired on 1 August 1864 and with it, presumably, the authorization of office for habeas corpus commissioners to review cases arising under it. Robinson had a different view: "Upon the expiration of the Habeas Corpus Act, some of the commissioners were continued by the War Department as special commissioners to complete the investigation of the cases of persons remaining in the military prisons within their areas."[23]

The theory is plausible but unsupported by any surviving document. No statute authorized continuance in office for any purpose. No "special" status was attached to the appointment of commissioners who continued work past the expiration of the statute authorizing their office.[24]

Freedom of Speech

If we believe their self-conception, the habeas corpus commissioners freed the innocent and dispatched the potentially criminal to court. In fact, that is not all they did. They caused many prisoners to be held indefinitely, and they dealt routinely with political freedoms within a framework of military imperatives different from an ordinary system of justice. The rest of this chapter and the three chapters following deal with their work.

The record offers abundant evidence to counter a long-standing myth of Confederate history. Noel Fisher, for example, says that in East Tennessee Confederate leaders "all drew a line between dissenting actions and dissenting beliefs, punishing the one but tolerating the other." William Robinson, noting that "numerous arrests were made . . . on charges of treason and on suspicion of aiding and abetting the enemy," specified that prisoners were "taken in an act of disloyalty, or suspected of such" and were accused of "treason and war crimes and suspicious conduct." In all of those statements, which for Robinson defined the parameters of Confederate internal security policies, he said nothing of "dissenting beliefs," as though they were not a matter of concern in making arrests. More than fifty years separate Fisher's and Robinson's historical judgments, in which time no new research altered the conclusion that the Confederacy by distinguishing between thought and action provided "a marked contrast to Federal policies," as Noel Fisher expressed it.[25]

Yet a phrase commonly appearing next to the name of a civilian prisoner in Confederate records was "Union man." The beliefs of such prisoners obviously mattered. There was never a moment in Confederate history when pro-Union opinions could be held without fear of government restraint. Naturally, such opinions were more dangerous near the borders and the active military fronts than in the interior, but nowhere were dissenting beliefs secure.

At first, commissioners opposed arresting citizens merely for expressing opinions. James Lyons, for example, reported 12 December 1861 on "a violent Whig and Union man" named Daniel Hand, a native of Connecticut who had lived in the South for over forty years. Hand "went to the utmost length of his party—was in the habit of talking freely, and very openly, and was initially against secession . . . and sometimes even expressing opinions unfavorable to the institution of slavery." But, Lyons countered, "he is not charged with any act or fact, constituting a crime under our Laws, and is not liable to be punished for the absurd opinions which he has entertained or the folly of expressing them." He urged Hand's release from prison.

Lyons adopted a stern tone seldom found in War Department bureaucrats later in the war. When he examined Edward Johnson, a fifty-seven-year-old farmer from Fairfax County, Virginia, who owned sixteen slaves and was "always a Democrat and secessionist," Lyons declared his arrest "inexcusable folly, or wanton outrage." Johnson had been in Confederate camps near Bull Run, but "a man found within the lines of a Camp," Lyons pointed out, "is liable to arrest, it is true unless he has a passport," but it was wrong to send every such man all the way to Richmond.[26]

Sydney S. Baxter made similar judgments at first. After examining a Kentuckian named John Dells in 1861, Baxter concluded that "While Dells entertains very objectionable political opinions I can find no evidence which would authorise him to be tried in either a civil or military court. He has committed no overt act of hostility."[27]

Lyons, however, asked to be relieved of duty that December, and Baxter would gradually change his mind. What proved significant about these early investigations was that they included as relevant data in their considerations the political opinions of the prisoners. That information would always remain relevant. The commissioners might recommend the prisoners' release once they got to Richmond, but the only way to stop arrests for opinion's sake was to lay down rules in general orders to be applied at the point of contact with civilians. That was never done.

In a substantial number of cases, over 13 percent, political opinion was the key to the prisoner's arrest. Since southern society tended to localism—with its scattered pattern of settlement, poor transportation network, and traditions of strong local government—the standard of allowable expression in the Confederacy varied. Authorities as different as mayors and major generals sent in prisoners accused of sedition. Some areas had self-styled committees of public safety involved in local security matters. In 1863 a committee in Columbus, Georgia, preferred charges against a man named Chapman, a teacher at the principal academy in their town, for writing two letters to New York abolitionists. General W. H. C. Whiting, commanding at the blockade-running haven of Wilmington, North Carolina, could inspect mail leaving the Confederacy, and he had seen Chapman's letters and sent them to the committee. The fifty-two-year-old teacher wound up in jail in Montgomery, Alabama, in August 1863 after being arrested by the commandant of the Confederate post in Columbus.[28]

A committee of public safety in Pirote, Alabama, recommended early in 1863 that Henry H. Cowdry be sent beyond the lines as disloyal, to be hanged if he returned. A "reliable man" had informed the committee on oath that Cowdry had said, when his wife wanted a black woman whipped, that the slave had as much right to whip his wife. On another occasion Cowdry had said that if he were a black man whipped for stealing a cow, he would poison the person who whipped him. Cowdry also blamed the war on the South. By the time the case reached Richmond, B. R. Wellford believed the prisoner had suffered punishment well beyond the severity of his offense. A letter written on his behalf noted the prisoner was a lifelong Democrat. But Cowdry, who had been born in New York, was held in prison in Richmond as an alien enemy for at least a year.[29]

Normally, prisoners held for sedition had been arrested by local authorities or by Confederate soldiers in disputed areas of the country and sent to Richmond or Salisbury, where commissioners made what sense they could of the evidence sent with the prisoners, interrogated the prisoners, and sometimes themselves initiated inquiries in the area where the arrest had taken place. The evidence was rarely strong, even when some was properly submitted—as was seldom the case. John C. Gilliland, of Greenbrier County, Virginia, for example, was arrested for "using grossly seditious language." Gilliland was a farmer and a "negro and horse trader" who had voted against Virginia's secession. Sydney Baxter examined the prisoner in March 1862. When he looked at the accompanying affidavit from one Mary Peters, he noted: "The testimony of Mrs. Peters clearly [shows] Gilliland was guilty of using seditious language and conduct. But she proves no act of communication with the enemy and no threat to communicate with them. I think this man ought to be brought to trial for sedition, but the proper place for his trial under the law of Virginia is Greenbrier County."[30] As Greenbrier County was not then under Confederate control, Baxter recommended the prisoner be held pending trial. The practical effect of this recommendation was to hold the prisoner for an indefinite period.

Mary Peters's affidavit survives to permit a glimpse at what Baxter deemed "clear" evidence of sedition. She told the local justice of the peace that Gilliland in conversation "said that the south had no right to invade the Kanawha valley because it gave a majority to the Union. He said that Virginia ought not to have seceded and if called upon, to have raised arms in favor of the North, and to have helped to whipped south Carolina back into the union. He said that Gen Floyd had stolen arms from the North and that the South had no right to any of them at all. Said that the North would go all over Virginia and that the South could not keep them from it, and that he would rather see the Yankees come in than to have the toothache."[30] Instead of presenting "clear" evidence of sedition, this affidavit seems quite problematic. The semiliterate record of Mrs. Peters's testimony affords a reader no confidence that the War Department possessed in the affidavit a transcription of exactly what she said, let alone exactly what Gilliland said.

Interpreting this prisoner's purported words seems no easy matter. The Yankees might be better than a toothache, but how good was that in the Kanawha Valley in the days of primitive dentistry? Perhaps Virginia should not have seceded and should have fought South Carolina, but prisoner Gilliland had not stated what Virginia ought to have done *after secession was a fact* or what he personally would do for the cause here and now. That the Confederacy should not "invade" Kanawha was the most obviously disloyal sentiment expressed in the affidavit, but the notion that local majority sentiment should prevail came uncomfortably close to applying secessionist argument to smaller geographical units, regions rather than states.

We are allowed an unusual glance at the War Department's state of mind in the notes of the interrogation and the affidavits surviving from these well-preserved cases from western Virginia. In the same month as the Gilliland case, Baxter found that the language used by another prisoner, Newton Mann, was "seditious but not so glaring as . . . the other prisoners." Mann had said "that every man that voted for Secession ought to go and be killed," and that "their was not one dozen men in Greenbrier County in favor of the Southern Confederacy."[32] What made Gilliland's "toothache" speech more "glaring" in its sedition than Mann's remarks about the proper fate of secessionists is by no means clear.

Joel Mayhue, of Pittsylvania County, Virginia, an illiterate plantation overseer given to talking "freely," told a neighbor, an old enemy, in the summer of 1863 that "if the enemy . . . should come through this county he would join them as quick as snapp his fingers." Mayhue admitted making the statement but said he did so to exasperate the neighbor, and letters from his employer, proving among other things that Mayhue was "a good disciplinarian among negroes, except sometimes too passionate," led Commissioner Isaac H. Carrington to recommend the prisoner's discharge.[33]

Robert Tyson, also a Virginian, was arrested at Gold Mine Ford in March 1862 in part because he appeared to be escaping the Confederacy and in part because he had cursed the rebels, saying "Damn them they will soon be starved out."[34] Dr. Charles A. Thatcher, of Greenbrier County, had run into trouble with the Confederate army earlier, but in March 1862 he landed in military prison in Richmond for disloyalty and for being an avowed Unionist. This reputation rested on his having predicted a dire future of the Confederacy, according to affidavits gathered by the provost marshal in Lewisburg. In a private conversation he had envisioned military defeat, with the enemy overrunning Georgia, Alabama, Mississippi, Tennessee, and Kentucky. Then Richmond would be surrounded and the South subjugated. He said he supported southern independence but regarded the cause as hopeless.[35]

As late as August 1864 Carrington, now provost marshal in Richmond, was still struggling with the problem of seditious utterances. John Miller, from Henry County, Virginia, was arrested for saying that he wished the Yankees would invade the county, that he would not help the southern cause, and that he wished "every secessionist was hung." Carrington decided that no case could be made in court "for the utterance of the Treasonable language imputed to this prisoner," but that it was "inexpedient to allow men who utter such sentiments to go at large during the present crisis."[36]

The War Department stood as a greater threat to private expression than to public expressions in the press. Freedom of the press in the Confederacy has long been a prominent exhibit of those who emphasize its relative constitutional freedom in comparison to the North.[37] The substantial press freedom, however, was as much a tribute to a long tradition of self-censorship as to consistent respect for constitutional liberty.

What the South had done for a generation to silence criticism of slavery had lasting effects on journalism.[38] The internalization of this rather restrictive southern patriotism can be seen in the case of Frank Smyth, a correspondent for the *Petersburg Express,* who was arrested by militia when he went to Winchester, Virginia, on business for the newspaper. Thrown in jail "with criminals and slaves" in Winchester, Smyth appealed his case to the secretary of war, saying, "I know it becomes every patriot to use every means in his power to cause to be apprehended persons who are not sound on the cause of Southern Independence." He pointed out that he had said nothing about his own case in print for fear the North would use it to their advantage against the South. When a commissioner investigated the case, he found no cause to detain Smyth, but the secretary of war checked with editors from the *Dispatch* and *Whig* in Richmond, mentioned as references by Smyth. They reported him "inquisitive" and "indiscreet" but by way of mitigation also "timorous," an adjective that might well be applied to the whole of the press corps in the Confederacy.[39]

The foreign press did not necessarily know the unwritten rules of regional self-censorship and could fail to demonstrate the appropriate timorousness. One foreign reporter, Gabriel Cueto, who worked for a Scottish newspaper, was arrested in 1862 for using "stern abolition language." Sydney Baxter said simply, "If Mr Cueto is an active abolitionist I cannot see how he can be permitted to go at large in the South." The British consul eventually inquired after Cueto and agreed to transport him out of the Confederacy if released from prison.[40]

We can get a notion of the short fuse some Confederates had in regard to the press from a complex case that arose in 1864 in the state with the most developed political opposition in the Confederacy, North Carolina. A bookseller and newspaper vendor named T. S. Whitaker was arrested there on the orders of General W. H. C. Whiting, who was among the most callous of Confederate generals in regard to civil liberties. By 1864 political opposition forces in North Carolina regarded Whiting as "an unprincipled tyrant."[41]

Whitaker sold newspapers in the camps of the Confederate army, but he could do so only because he was exempted from military service as a Wilmington fireman. Such exemptions were a sore subject with Confederate mobilization officers, who regarded city fire brigades as havens for draft dodgers.

Whitaker was selling newspapers in the season of the hottest election in all of Confederate history, Zebulon Vance versus William W. Holden for North Carolina governor. Holden was widely regarded as a peace candidate, and his movement was much feared by Confederate authorities in Richmond and elsewhere. Whitaker was arrested for selling the 12 July 1864 "extra" issue of Holden's *Raleigh Standard* in Camp Holmes. Because General Whiting regarded this issue of the *Standard* as a treasonable document, he had Whitaker imprisoned in Camp Holmes and sought to revoke his exemption as a fireman so he could be sent to the field as a conscript. Peter Mallett, the local conscript officer and veteran of many a scrape with North Carolina officials over mobilization in the fractious state, could not see his way clear to revoke Whitaker's exemption unless the *Standard* were pronounced treasonous by higher authorities.

Ultimately Governor Vance gained Whitaker's release, but the case affords important evidence of surveillance (apparently informal in this instance) of the election polls to monitor opinion of potential dissenters. Lieutenant Hardy B. Welles was able to testify in Whitaker's favor that the vendor had not himself voted for Holden. "I know Whitaker did not *vote* for Holden," he reported, "as I made it my business to be at the polls and watched him particularly. He voted . . . for Vance."[42]

In many instances arrests for sedition might be attributed to the overzealousness of officers in the field.[43] But the commissioners often sustained their judgments by keeping the victims in prison for a time. Daniel F. Dulaney of Fairfax County, Virginia, arrested late in 1863 for uttering disloyal sentiments and for accepting office under the Unionist government of Virginia, apparently admitted both offenses, and Carrington carefully spelled out rulings on both. In regard to uttering disloyal sentiments, Carrington noted, "For this offence, under the precedents established in similar cases, the Prisoner may be confined as a traitorous citizen—It is not an offence for which he may be tried." The other offence, holding office in a rival government, constituted treason, Carrington noted, as it was an overt act and violated Virginia law; however, there was no Confederate law against it. Carrington recommended that the prisoner, a twenty-seven-year veteran of the U.S. Navy, now old and in failing health, be held as a "political prisoner" until asked for by the state authorities. As witnesses were usually unobtainable from areas of western Virginia under Union control, this meant effectively imprisonment for the duration of the war.[44]

What the Commissioners Did Day to Day

William D. Hennen was the commissioner for southwestern Virginia and East Tennessee after July 1863, at a time when no statutory authority existed for such commissioners.[45] In 1864 he held the position under the Habeas Corpus Act of 15 February, but he continued in office as late as 7 November 1864, more than three months after the expiration of statutory authority.[46]

Hennen functioned ultimately as a mobilization officer. He did not primarily seek justice, retribution, national security, or domestic peace. He sought manpower. The commonest solution to a problem of conflict between civilian rights and Confederate military authority was neither to keep the civilian in prison nor to give him his liberty but, if of proper age, to turn him over to the enrolling officer. The official policy was enunciated by the War Department's most accomplished lawyer, Assistant Secretary of War John A. Campbell, in a letter written 19 June 1863 to Alabama's habeas corpus commissioner, M. J. Saffold: "The Department does not desire to initiate prosecutions for political offenses and is satisfied, as a general rule, to restrain the capacity for mischief of disloyal citizens. If nothing better can be done, they must be confined, but a far preferable disposition, when it can be made, is to place them in a situation to render service to the country by useful labor, under the eye of some officer of the Government who can guard against communication with the enemy."[47]

William Gallycan, of Knox County, Tennessee, whom Hennen investigated in Dandridge, was discharged from prison and turned over to the enrolling officer even though he was an avowed Union man.[48] Only those prisoners still refusing service because of Union feeling were kept in prison (with some exceptions). For those able-bodied prisoners of conscription age and eligible for military service, announcement of the change in their feelings of political loyalty usually would suffice for release from prison—into the waiting hands of the enrolling officer and military discipline. Standard practice was to send those of doubtful loyalty to a regiment from their state stationed far from that state (and from opportunity to desert).[49]

Military manpower demands were so great that Hennen allowed even some accused of serious crimes to go into Confederate ranks. For example, Robert

Ramsey was accused of murdering Richard Brown, of the First Tennessee Cavalry, in a night of drinking and visiting what they thought was a house of ill fame. When the mother of four daughters ordered the drunken soldiers out of the house, a struggle ensued, a pistol went off, and Brown died. Hennen decided that, in the first place, the crime was manslaughter, not murder. In the second place, there were no state authorities to whom Ramsey could be turned over for trial, so extensive was Federal control of Tennessee by that late date. Besides, Ramsey's crime was "not political," and he would "make a good soldier" (presumably Hennen referred to Ramsey's robust physical condition and not to his proven willingness to kill). Ramsey joined the Twelfth Tennessee Cavalry.[50]

Hennen was anything but softhearted. When confronted by Andrew Gray, a British immigrant resident more than two decades in America and now fifty-nine years old, Hennen noted that the man had been twice arrested as a suspicious character and possible spy. He was now old, squalid, and decrepit, without shoes and dressed in tatters, so revolting in personal hygiene that the Abingdon jailer kept him in a special tent in the jail yard in order not to bring pestilence to the jail. Gray wanted to be sent beyond the Union lines, but the local Confederate general did not want to risk that. Hennen decided on 8 July 1864 to recommend that Gray be discharged under threat that if he came before Hennen again he would be shot.[51]

Henry J. Leovy was commissioner for southwestern Virginia and for East Tennessee in 1864.[52] Months after the demise of the Habeas Corpus Act of 1864, Leovy was still at work in what he called "court" in Dublin, located on the eastern side of the Virginia mountains between Wytheville and Blacksburg. He decided the fate of at least twenty-two civilians between 12 October 1864 and 10 February 1865. He remained deferential to military authority. Leovy noted, when he recommended release of a prisoner named J. P. Lawrence, of Floyd County, Virginia, on taking the oath of allegiance and posting $5,000 bond, that the man had been arrested where bands of deserters commonly defied both civil and military authority and from which it was impossible to obtain evidence. He professed that he did not interfere with military arrests in such areas but that in this case an arresting officer recommended release on bond.[53]

It is clear from Leovy's record that when the writ of habeas corpus was not suspended, the rate of arrest slowed, though arrests of civilians never ceased. The writ could be a genuine impediment, especially if politicians were involved. Thus Leovy served for the War Department in the late autumn of 1864 as an investigator of the disloyal organization called the Heroes of America. On 4 November 1864 he reported to the secretary of war the following:

> We are ready to make arrests. I have the names of over 100 persons, and evidence against most of them, but we have thought it desirable to make the

arrests by military authority, and that cannot be done unless the writ of habeas corpus be suspended. We wish to know whether the President will apply to Congress for the suspension, and also concerning the probability of the compliance on the part of Congress. Mr. [Thomas S.] Bocock [the representative from the area] . . . appears to doubt that the legislation of Congress will reach the case of treasonable organizations. We had a consultation concerning these matters with Generals [John C.] Breckinridge and [John] Echols. They are prepared to do what we conclude is best. . . . It appears to me of the greatest importance that the writ should be suspended.[54]

Bocock thought that "the law as it now stands affords no adequate remedy for the evil; none but such as, if attempted to be applied, would by the very failure to suppress, stimulate the growth of the association. My opinion is clear that the only mode of successfully combating this alarming evil is by military authority, which can only be done upon legislation . . . relieving it of interference by . . . the writ of habeas corpus or otherwise, until the treason is effectually suppressed."[55]

Less than a week later, President Davis transmitted to both houses of Congress "a communication from the Secretary of War, showing that a dangerous conspiracy exists in some of the counties of Southwestern Virginia and in the neighboring portions of North Carolina and Tennessee, which it is found impracticable to suppress by the ordinary course of law." He recommended suspending the writ of habeas corpus.[56] Congress did not budge.

Two of the commissioners after James Lyons allowed their role as potential liberator to overshadow the needs of the War Department—Percy Walker and Peter Hamilton. Walker resigned as commissioner in Mobile in January 1863, partly because of poor health but also partly because of lack of cooperation from the army. The military authorities, Walker told the secretary of war, did not report civilian arrests to him and instead had citizens tried "by a tribunal consisting of the Provost Marshal and a so called Provost Judge." Unwilling "to prefer charges or make a formal complaint," Walker resigned, warning, however, that "some such officer as a commissioner is needed here to guard against illegal and prolonged detention of citizens by the military."[57]

Hamilton had an uneasy relationship with Richmond and interpreted military power over civilians narrowly. When finally his first case came to him, it raised questions and provoked criticism rather than offering opportunity for the exercise of extraordinary judicial power. James B. Miller, a hard-shell Baptist preacher, had sent a letter to the editor of a newspaper, advising others to abandon the Confederate cause, but the editor did not publish the letter. Hamilton asked the opinion of the secretary of war on the case, and he wrote the assistant secretary to ask him about the nature of the commissioner's duties. Miller's letter, Hamilton pointed out, "may be nothing but the expression of an opinion; and it is plain civil right that a citizen has to form and express his opinion upon all political matters." Hamilton went on:

> What are the duties of the Com[missione]r—shall he advise the discharge of the prisoner—because positive proof of a criminal act is not produced, or should he advise him to be held, because the case is suspicious and at this juncture the act proved may be injurious? Does the Com[missione]r simply act as an examining magistrate, to pass upon the probability of a crime legally declared, or does his duty call upon him to go further and consider the case in the aspect of a thing of dangerous tendency. . . . I can readily see the propriety of such discretionary power existing somewhere—tho such course of arbitrary power is foreign to our notions of the rights of the citizen—but it is exceedingly dangerous—This power has for some time been exercised by Military officers—and it may very well be that the suspension of the Hab. corp. & the mode of exoneration herein proposed will operate a less restraint upon the rights of the citizen, than practically existed in many cases before the law was passed.
>
> I am disposed to think great laxness has heretofore prevailed—men have been confined on vague charges and suspicions and been allowed to remain in custody from inattention and neglect.
>
> This morning four names were sent me for investigation—charged with being connected with deserters and tories in Miss. Upon calling for the proof against them—I find they were sent to this place by a provost Marshall in the interior with the simple statement above [that is, "connected with deserters and tories"] contained in the letter accompanying the men—I advised the Genl, there was nothing to investigate.[58]

Hamilton, having no idea what policy was, bombarded the department with questions, as he lacked proper instructions or printed legal decisions and statutes from which to decide. On 23 April 1864, he was confronted with the case of an alien in the hands of the local conscript officer. According to War Department instructions sent in a letter on 14 March 1864, Hamilton was also "to afford counsel to the Commandant of Conscripts, and the Enrolling officer in cases that may arise, in which the interposition of that writ . . . may be claimed." Hamilton noted, as commissioner, that "discretion to discharge appears to be final," but he did not have similar authority as counsel for the conscript officer. Secretary of War Seddon's view was that the department did not want to compel an alien to fight but that he might be claimed for local defense in case Mobile was in immediate peril. He thought Hamilton should examine cases and advise the enrolling officer but avoid litigation and do justice.[59]

Hamilton showed more interest in law than any other commissioner. American lawyers are generally interested in legal precedents and, in new areas of legal practice, in their creation and accumulation.[60] Most Confederate habeas corpus commissioners did not appear particularly interested in legal precendents. They likely regarded the situation on the frontiers of a desperate war as an anomaly of little future importance.

However, their behavior was lawyerly in another way. They practiced the attorney skills of witness examination, verification of testimony, weighing of affidavits, and character study. Litigators, especially circuit-riding lawyers bereft of libraries and short on book learning in law, prided themselves on these human relations skills and felt comfortable deciding whether their fellow men were sincere or insincere, cowardly or brave, on the strength of answers to questions rather than other evidence.[61] In other words, the commissioners emphasized the side of legal work that resembled what would be called personnel management today. And that, more or less, is how the habeas corpus commissioner system worked: as a personnel office for the War Department, disciplining difficult people with the ultimate goal of salvaging as many of them as possible for service to the state.

Why Their Work Has Been Forgotten

After the war was over, leaders of the defeated white South circled the wagons to resist Reconstruction, impose white racial solidarity, and rehabilitate the Democratic party. Suspension of the writ of habeas corpus became a major initiative of the hated administration of President Ulysses S. Grant to enforce Reconstruction, and conservative white southern politicians were not eager to be reminded that Jefferson Davis himself had suspended the writ of habeas corpus, that other white southern politicians and lawyers had administered a program for political prisoners, and that the Confederate Congress by omission or commission had sanctioned it all.

The case of Jabez L. M. Curry is instructive. One of the habeas corpus commissioners during the war, Curry chose to leave no mention of his work as commissioner in the history books. A Democratic politician and member of the Confederate House, Curry accepted appointment on 28 March 1864 as commissioner to serve with Joseph E. Johnston's army, then campaigning in Georgia. Curry had lost his bid for reelection to the Congress in August 1863, and he took the new job despite his knowledge of the obvious political difficulties of administering a system of political prisoners in Georgia, a state that had developed considerable political resistance to the Richmond government:

> The execution of the act will be attended with some difficulty, owing to the opposition of Governor [Joseph E.] Brown, the Vice-President [Alexander H. Stephens, also a Georgian], and other prominent men in Georgia. My aim shall

be to avoid all collision with State authorities, and so to use my office as to prevent discord and promote harmony. An early occasion will doubtless be seized to test the constitutionality of the act before the Georgia courts. If Judge Campbell, who drafted the bill that passed the House (as I understood), could find time to write and publish an editorial in the Sentinel explaining the law and replying to some of Governor Brown's objections, good would be accomplished. The message of the President not being published, nothing has appeared in the newspapers defensive of the law, while scores of malcontents have done what they could to excite odium against the law, the president, and yourself.[62]

When General Johnston's army began retreating before William T. Sherman's advance, Curry had little to do and attached himself as a volunteer aide to Johnston's staff.[63] With the expiration of the Habeas Corpus Act in August, Curry's duties expired, but he had made an easy and natural transition from commissioner to staff officer in the realm of quasi-military offices.

Many years later, Curry, by that time a famous southern educator and intellectual, wrote a *Civil History of the Government of the Confederate States.* The only mention of the suspension of habeas corpus and imposition of martial law in the book came in Curry's discussion of *the Lincoln administration.* In other words, the only suspension of the writ of habeas corpus he remembered in the book was Abraham Lincoln's:

> By a presidential proclamation, martial law was declared and the *habeas corpus* was suspended over the whole United States, without regard to the existence of active military hostilities in particular localities.
>
> The friends of the President, however, did not regard this as a rightful exercise of executive power, for Congress afterwards authorized the President to suspend, and then endeavored by strained inference to concentrate the power upon itself. Functions belonging to the judiciary were transferred to military tribunals, and citizens not connected with the army were tried by military commissions.[64]

"These excesses of tyranny," Curry concluded, "did not end with the war."[65] The "tyranny" of Reconstruction was the only tyranny Curry remembered; he could not recall his own service to tyranny.

PART THREE

DISSENT

FRANK L. OWSLEY'S *State Rights in the Confederacy*, published in 1925, was perhaps the earliest and most influential interpretation of Confederate history to emphasize internal dissent as a cause of defeat. An unintended consequence of Owsley's identification of states' rights as the most debilitating internal problem was the marginalization of dissent in East Tennessee and western Virginia. States' rights made no sense as an explanation of these dissenters, for they hated their own state governments as much as the Confederate government. The most virulent and effective dissent in the Confederacy did not follow state lines or invoke state sovereignty. It cut across state lines and invoked the Union. Owsley's thesis thrust North Carolina and Georgia into the limelight of a newly exciting internal Confederate history but consigned East Tennessee and western Virginia to shadow.

There they have languished ever since, while the grand tradition of narrative history writing about the Confederacy has substantially ignored them. In the case of East Tennessee, the historians have unconsciously followed the lead of Jefferson Davis. Although, like Abraham Lincoln, Davis had to send messages regularly to his Congress, informing the legislators of the state of the nation, he never in these documents mentioned East Tennessee. He did not tell the rest of the Confederate people how troublesome that section had become or inform them that it required ten thousand Confederate troops to occupy and pacify the region. Davis and other loyal Confederates acted at times as though East Tennessee did not exist. It was the Confederacy's madman in the attic.

Historians neglected western Virginia for other reasons. Statehood for West Virginia shifted that region out of Confederate history in 1863. The willingness of Confederate historians to let Northerners rather than Southerners tell West Virginia's story nevertheless seems somewhat surprising, for it might have proved quite an embarrassment to the Union to stress the hypocrisy of recognizing the secession of West Virginia from Virginia in the midst of a war against secession. A close examination of the troubled society in that area might have made reassuring reading for some Southerners.

After the Civil War, however, the demands to create a myth of historic unity in Confederate history, as a means of circling the southern wagons of white unity against Reconstruction and racial equality, were great. They proved powerful enough to overcome Alexander H. Stephens's seemingly inexhaustible interest in proving southern constitutional arguments correct and his glee in exposing the constitutional hypocrisy of the northern states. Despite numerous references to Virginia in his *Constitutional View of the Late War between the States,* completed in 1870, Stephens nowhere mentioned West Virginia in the two-volume work.

Jefferson Davis, though he continued his silence on East Tennessee after the war, could not resist comment on western Virginia and offered the readers of *The Rise and Fall of the Confederate Government* six pages on the "perversion of true republican principles" there. Davis focused on the abstract constitutional questions involved in West Virginia statehood. He summed up United States approval of West Virginia's secession as a matter of "whose ox it was that was gored by the bull."[1] He showed little interest in analyzing or describing the extreme social disorder in the seceding counties or others contiguous to them in Virginia, briefly attributing the antisecessionist movement in western Virginia to the "contiguity of the northwestern counties of the State to Ohio and Pennsylvania."

Historians writing one-volume narrative histories of the Confederacy have for the most part observed Stephens's policy of silence on western Virginia, and like Davis they have mostly ignored the problems in East Tennessee. Thus Charles P. Roland's compact book *The Confederacy,* though it contains a chapter entitled "A Divided South and Total War," mentions neither East Tennessee nor western Virginia.[2] Frank Vandiver's epic history of the Confederacy likewise contains no mention of West Virginia or East Tennessee.[3] The volume on the Confederate States of America written for the banner New American Nation series gives western Virginia a paragraph but has no index entry for East Tennessee or the region's famous political martyr, William G. "Parson" Brownlow.[4] The fullest treatment of the areas in modern narrative histories comes in Clement Eaton's *History of the Southern Confederacy.* Eaton gave West Virginia two paragraphs and East Tennessee three. Yet the revolt in East Tennessee in November 1861 was the largest internal uprising against Confederate authority during the Civil War.[5]

Although essentially ignored in the grander narratives, these dissenting regions receive considerable attention from local histories and specialized studies. In the twentieth century, those who have considered the problem of dissent in upland regions of the Confederacy have fallen into two camps. One interpretation denigrates the motives of the dissenters. Thus J. Mills Thornton III speculates that most Alabama yeomen of the upland Confederacy at first became loyal Confederates and did not have their loyalty "challenged" until 1863, when conscription and military defeats caused them to rethink the wisdom of seceding from the old Union.[6]

The more favorable modern view celebrates resistance in the Confederacy's upland regions as essentially a social class movement. Thus Eric Foner, in his landmark history of Reconstruction, says, "It was in the secession crisis and Civil

War that large numbers of upcountry yeomen discovered themselves as a political class." East Tennessee became "the most conspicuous example of discontent within the Confederacy." Foner makes a point of downplaying nationalism and loyalty to the Union, however, in dealing with most Confederate dissenters. "It was not simply devotion to the Union," he says, "but the impact of the war and the consequences of Confederate policies, that awakened peace sentiment and social conflict." "Poverty descended upon thousands of upcountry families," and "initial enthusiasm for the war was succeeded by disillusionment, draft evasion, and eventually outright resistance to Confederate authority—a civil war within the Civil War."[7] An emphasis on material factors of economic deprivation seems to be a hallmark of the social class interpretation of upland dissent. Paul Escott, for example, declared, "Ideology meant less . . . to the common people of the Confederacy. Their prime need was immediate economic assistance, and they did not hesitate to seek or accept it whenever it was offered."[8]

In a way, emphasis on material factors constitutes a denigration of the motives of the Confederate dissenters, making their motives entirely matters of class hatred without qualities of selflessness or idealism. Nevertheless, the historians who champion such views have not thought them discreditable to the dissenters. However, these historians carefully distance themselves from the dissenters. Foner, for example, notes that the white yeomen retained their aversion to African Americans.[9]

There is some validity in all these views. Marginalization itself embodies the truth that the most remarkable characteristic of the Confederacy was its completeness of mobilization and extreme military sacrifice, not the extent or effectiveness of dissent from the cause.[10] Likewise, conscription forced decisions on many reluctant uplanders that they would not otherwise have made. And the politicians of the region had long played on the enmity of upland yeomen against lowland planters, causing some of the rough farmers to internalize class hatred of the rich.

But all three views seem flawed as well, when seen from the perspective of the political prisoner in the Confederacy. Chapters 6 and 7 reevaluate the attempts to quash dissent in East Tennessee, western Virginia, and North Carolina. Chapter 8 examines social groups victimized by internal security measures.

6

THE POLITICS OF PASTORALISM IN EAST TENNESSEE

EAST TENNESSEE CANNOT GET ITS NOSE into the stable of thoroughbred subjects in Confederate history despite considerable regional literature written on the subject. This chapter joins other recent attempts to gain for East Tennessee its rightful place in Confederate narrative.[1] East Tennessee certainly holds the most important place in the history of civil liberty in the Confederacy: the region's residents made up over 16.5 percent of the Confederacy's known civilian prisoners.[2]

Historians are divided on the significance of the events there. Noel Fisher, for example, says that "Confederate officers . . . display[ed] a remarkable restraint in East Tennessee."

> [General Felix] Zollicoffer, [General Edmund] Kirby Smith, and [General Samuel] Jones all drew a line between dissenting actions and dissenting beliefs, punishing the one but tolerating the other. . . . This restraint held up under the greatest stresses. Even in the days following the uprising [in East Tennessee in late 1861], Brig. Gen. William H. Carroll and Secretary of War Judah P. Benjamin made clear that mere Unionist beliefs were not a sufficient cause for arrest. Officers in the field, of course, frequently failed to observe these restrictions, and department commanders did not sufficiently enforce discipline among their men. Nonetheless, this belief in restraint and this continued respect for constitutional protections were a marked contrast to Federal policies in East Tennessee. Northern officers freely arrested secessionists for disloyal statements or even supposed sentiments, and they detained a far greater percentage of the enemy population than their Confederate counterparts.[3]

Charles F. Bryan Jr. makes the opposite point: "Ironically, the policies adopted by the Confederate authorities in dealing with East Tennessee 'Tories' were similar to those used when their enemy occupied the South. Loyalty oaths, mass arrests of people on suspicion of treason, reconstruction of civil government, and at times, harsh treatment of civilians were no less hallmarks of the Confederate military occupation of East Tennessee than they were of Union occupation of the South."[4]

These positions characterize the poles of Confederate historiography on the question, or what might be called the histories from the top down. The view from the local scene, the question of what motivated the East Tennesseans to resist, or the historiography from the bottom up, has been characterized in the introduction to this section of the book. Thornton points to conscription and defeatism as motivating upland dissent, to which others would add "hunger and hardship."[5] Hunger and hardship, on the other hand, provide the central focus of the social class interpretations of upland dissent. Examination of evidence heretofore unknown to historians of East Tennessee, records of 660 political prisoners from the area, should help resolve these conflicting interpretations.

The thirty Tennessee counties extending eastward from a diagonal line running along the Cumberland crest had a distinct identity based on low slaveholding and inferior wealth in comparison with the rest of the state.[6] The term *mountain whites,* widely used in the nineteenth century to describe the area's inhabitants, seems misleading. Oliver Temple, an early historian of the region and a political leader there during the Civil War era, was at some pains to point out that they were not really "mountain" people. Probably 80 percent of them lived in the valley between the Cumberland and Allegheny Mountains, he insisted. The idea that these people were lazy, ignorant, immoral, barefoot, whiskey-drinking mountaineer woodchoppers, trappers, herdsmen, root grubbers, and rail-splitters was much resented by those among them who were hardworking, literate, and God-fearing Methodist farmers raising hay and hogs for market. William G. Brownlow, a journalist and political leader from Knoxville, identified East Tennessee as "a *valley* three hundred miles in length, and varying in width from fifty to seventy-five miles."[7] "We have no interests in common with these Cotton States," Brownlow said early in 1861. "We are a grain-growing and stock-raising people, and we can conduct a cheap Government, and live independent, inhabiting the Switzerland of America."[8]

The mountains may have isolated the East Tennesseans physically, but they did not do so politically, for the nineteenth-century American party system, the wonder of the world then and now for its ability to mobilize and energize voters, penetrated nearly every corner of America's diverse and heroic geography. East Tennessee may have been "backward" in some ways, but politically it was and had long been in the vanguard, the scene of strenuous political campaigns, the home of enthusiastic voters, and the nursery of able politicians. Voter turnout in Tennessee hit 90 percent in the election of 1840 and was normally over 80 percent after 1852, with partisan divisions stable in shape though hot in temperature.[9]

Politics in East Tennessee were particularly intense in the period 1860–61. East Tennesseans had undergone one of the most prolonged periods of political education in American history. Oliver Temple said that he campaigned for eight months solid from November 1860 to June 1861. After the conclusion of the strenuous presidential canvass, campaigning resumed in December for February elections to a secession convention. That was followed by an East Tennessee convention to consider secession from the state, followed by a canvass for June elections to reconsider secession of Tennessee after the outbreak of war. The East Tennessee convention met again to propose statehood to the Tennessee legislature, and the traditional elections for Congress were held the following August. November saw elections for the Confederate legislature. By that time political consciousness had been raised to the level of active rebellion in East Tennessee.

The quality of political leadership in the region happened to be exceptional. A future president of the United States, Andrew Johnson, and a future governor of Tennessee, William Brownlow, led the fight against secession. David T. Patterson, Johnson, and Brownlow later became U.S. senators. Horace Maynard served seven terms in Congress, and Thomas A. R. Nelson also provided able congressional leadership.[10]

The leadership, the prolonged canvass, and the crucial issues combined to give East Tennessee's Unionist counties, according to voting analyst Daniel Crofts, "the highest turnout rate in the state" in the 9 February 1861 election for delegates to a secession convention.[11] This is doubly amazing because what Crofts called the ossified voting patterns of the 1850s were shattered early in 1861, with a reversal in voting so dramatic as to suggest that the elimination of political party opposition in most East Tennessee counties was the telling result of the election. "That the Union party would gain a decided victory at the polls in East Tennessee on the 9th of February was a foregone conclusion," recalled Temple, "and yet none expected it to be as overwhelming as it proved to be." In Sevier County, for example, perhaps only 1 person out of the 1,302 voting cast his ballot for a secession candidate.[12]

Diminished party competitiveness often causes lowered turnout, but apparently such was not the case in politically charged East Tennessee. The region maintained high turnout throughout the crucial period. Altogether, 41,874 voters went to the polls for the presidential election of 1860 in the twenty-eight counties for which statistics are available; the Constitutional Union ticket headed by John Bell took about 51 percent of the vote, the southern Democratic ticket about 46 percent, and the northern Democrats about 3 percent. This compares to a total vote of 39,771 in 1856. In February 1861, the number of voters was 40,369, of whom only 7,069 were pro-secession convention voters. In the June secession vote, the total of voters was 47,370, with only 14,617 voting for secession from the United States.[13]

Confederate officials could read election results, too, and their initial policy toward East Tennessee was conciliatory. Under Jefferson Davis's cautious guidance Confederate authorities worked to prevent the creation of political martyrs.[14] The East Tennesseans rose anyhow, on 8 November 1861, when Unionists, encouraged by Federal army agents, burned five railroad bridges and attempted to burn four others. A feeble general uprising followed.

Colonel W. B. Wood, on the scene in Knoxville, declared martial law, "as there was a large majority of the people sympathizing with the enemy and communicating with them by the unfrequented mountain paths."[15] When General Felix Zollicoffer heard Wood's news, he congratulated him for making arrests and said: "Their leaders should be seized and held as prisoners. The leniency shown them has been unavailing."[16] Perhaps some four hundred arrests resulted from this November outbreak alone, but most of the prisoners were eventually sent to Tuscaloosa, and those prison records have never been located.[17]

A brief period of uncertainty as to what to do with the prisoners followed.[18] After thinking things over, Secretary of War Judah Benjamin finally wrote Colonel Wood this order:

> First. All such as can be identified as having been engaged in bridge-burning are to be tried summarily and by drum-head court-martial and if found guilty executed on the spot by hanging. It would be well to leave their bodies hanging in the vicinity of the burned bridges.
>
> Second. All such as have not been so engaged are to be treated as prisoners of war and sent with an armed guard to Tuscaloosa Ala., there to be kept imprisoned at the depot selected by the Government for prisoners of war. . . . In no case is one of the men known to have been up in arms against the Government to be released on any pledge or oath of allegiance. The time for such measures is past. They are all to be held as prisoners of war and held in jail till the end of the war.[19]

Four men were hanged as a result of the order. One of the dozen woodcut illustrations in Brownlow's popular volume of wartime reminiscences published in 1862 depicted the hanging of two of the prisoners. From the rear platform of a railroad car, a Southerner whacks one of the corpses with his cane, as women look on and another citizen holds up an infant to observe the spectacle.[20]

The provocation given by East Tennessee was enough to change Confederate policy. Benjamin had been striking the usual libertarian posture less than a month before he endorsed the imprisonment of hundreds of Confederate citizens in Tennessee. "No lawgiver of these Confederate States ever dreamed of conferring on any public functionary the power of holding our own citizens in jail on suspicion," he said on 26 October, disclaiming any desire to "imitate the loathsome practices" of the North.[21]

Only a week before Benjamin's order, Jefferson Davis, too, had stressed the "radical incompatibility" between the Confederacy and the Union in their outlooks on civil liberties: in the Union, he asserted, "justice and law [were] trampled under the armed heel of military authority, and upright men . . . dragged to distant dungeons upon the mere edict of a despot."[22] Thirteen days later, when

Davis was informed of the arrest of the upright opposition newspaper editor Brownlow, he referred the letter to the secretary of war without comment.[23] The *behavior* of the Confederate leadership changed for good at this point but not their avowed *policies* announced to the public and to the world. On those, East Tennessee never had any effect.

The date of the uprising alone is enough to call into question all general theories of upland discontent in the Confederacy. The East Tennesseans took action; their revolt did not wait until the conscription law outraged their sense of individual liberty. It did not wait until the twenty-slave law aroused their class jealousies. It occurred in the heyday of Confederate optimism, as the gray-clad armies went into winter quarters after winning the first battle of the war at Bull Run; thus Confederate military defeats were not yet turning opportunists northward. It did not wait until economic hardships, a stringent blockade, or impressment of supplies hurt their pocketbooks.

What accounts for the uprising is the paradox of East Tennessee politics: this region, regarded by most as "backward" economically and culturally, was in fact advanced politically, with very high voter participation and the regular production of political leaders of exceptional caliber. These American voters and politicians were not at all isolated politically; they were connected to the most advanced party system in the world. Penetrating the "backwoods" with a pungent message of nationalism and Union, the political system, after a year of ceaseless canvassing and organizing, raised the mass of East Tennesseans to an active hatred of the Confederacy, lifted them above neutrality, and drove many to armed and open revolt with no material provocation. In East Tennessee the connection between antisecessionist politics and dissent was direct. George DeLaVergne, for example, an East Tennessee Unionist, recalled in answering a postwar questionnaire that he cast his "first ballot for the State to remain in the Union; after this I was treated as an outlaw and was obliged to go north."[24]

Who Were the East Tennesseans?

The political cause of the revolt has been obscured in part by the cultural image of the East Tennesseans. Sympathetic observers at the time were almost as much at fault for this as hostile ones. Thus H. Casey Young, writing to General William H. Carroll, then commanding Confederate forces in East Tennessee, to convince him that the extent of the revolt had been exaggerated, said that "every jail in the eastern end of the State was filled with poor, ignorant and for the most part harmless men who had been guilty of no crime save that of lending a too credulous ear to the corrupt demagogues whose counsels have led them astray"; they were but "poor victims of designing leaders."[25] The obverse of this Confederate view was that of Oliver Temple, whose stress on the quality of the region's political leadership was a way of saying positively what Young said negatively.

After the revolt, the contempt of the pacifying officers in East Tennessee, no longer restrained by Jefferson Davis but instead encouraged by Judah Benjamin's outburst, knew few boundaries. Confederate Colonel Danville Leadbetter, a Maine-born West Point–trained engineer who married a Southerner, reported in December on hanging two of the bridge burners per Benjamin's order. "The women," Leadbetter commented, "in some cases were greatly alarmed throwing themselves on the ground and wailing like savages. Indeed the population is savage."[26]

It hardly seems possible that these modern voters could accurately be depicted as savages or as poor, ignorant, and credulous dupes of designing demagogues. Let us turn to the prison records of the 660 East Tennessee political prisoners for a better portrait.[27] Although we cannot presume the guilt of the parties arrested, the information recorded in interrogations does offer revealing testimony about resisters, many of whom confessed.

The greatest concentration of arrests (186 of 660) occurred in Greene County and the circle of counties surrounding it. Next came the area around Chattanooga, where vast military operations swept up some of the civilian populace. Finally, there were minor concentrations in counties bordering Kentucky, where gaps in the mountains lured East Tennesseans attempting to get north.[28] Naturally, the people were overwhelmingly engaged in agricultural and rural rather than industrial and urban occupations. The most systematic series of records, summaries of investigations of prisoners undertaken by the War Department for reporting to Congress in 1863, includes 73 East Tennesseans among the total of 303 (24 percent).[29] Among these, 74 percent listed farming as at least one of their occupations. There were seven blacksmiths, one of whom, a man named George M. Billingsley from Claiborne County, was said to own $20,000 in property near Cumberland Gap. He insisted he was a good southern man wrongfully arrested.[30]

There were also five carpenters, a distiller, a teacher/preacher, a ferryman, a trader/farmer, a shoemaker/farmer, and a printer/shoemaker. Accounts both sympathetic and hostile emphasized the poverty of the East Tennesseans, and they were obviously poorer on average than western and middle Tennesseans, but the arrest records fit a varied and middling sociology. These were surely not the poorest of a poor region. There were men of property and status among them, including one carpenter who was also a school commissioner.

Much of the suffering came not from the poverty endemic to the region but, later in the war, as a result of supplying armies operating in the region. Likewise, the abandonment of farms by men conscripted or escaping conscription caused stress on the women, children, and elders left behind.[31]

If the distiller listed among the prisoners conjures up the familiar image of backwoods whiskey purveyors, it is striking that this is the only occupation that does remind us of the mountaineer stereotype. Absent among the prisoners were the other occupations peculiar to poor mountain people: woodchoppers, rail-splitters, root grubbers, trappers, shepherds, and herdsmen. The prisoners were valley people, as Brownlow and Temple described them. Brownlow pointed to the region's commercial products:

> East Tennessee is not a cotton-growing country, but is favorable alone to grazing; and great numbers of livestock—horses, mules, cattle, hogs, and sheep—are exported from thence to the Atlantic States. Indian corn and wheat are the great staples. Besides these, rye, oats, buckwheat, potatoes, (sweet and Irish,) wool, flax, and hay, are produced in great abundance. Apples and peaches, pears and plums, grow to great perfection. Maple-sugar is made of a fine quality, also superior butter and cheese. It is, in one word, the Switzerland of America.[32]

The advent shortly before the war of the East Tennessee and Virginia and the East Tennessee and Georgia Rail Roads, connecting the valley to the plantation regimes of Virginia and the lower South, brought a gradual transition from crops that could be fed to hogs and carried to market on the hoof or that could be turned into alcohol to be transported. Wheat (hay) was drawing even with corn as the region's main crop.[33]

Of the 60 other East Tennessee prisoners who were identified by occupation, 27, or just 45 percent, were farmers. The remaining prisoners tended to be of relatively high status: 3 legislators, 2 former legislators (1 of these a doctor and the other a lawyer), and 1 judge gave politicians 10 percent representation. There were 5 lawyers, 3 preachers, 2 teachers, 1 newspaper editor, 1 manager of a cotton factory, 1 tannery owner, 1 saddler, 1 miller, and 1 printer. Some were well-off economically: the saddler owned 3 slaves, and a farmer named Dixon Chitty was described as owning "much land" and 16 slaves. Another farmer owned 370 acres, and still another prisoner had a government contract to manufacture iron. The lowest end of the social order, as evidenced by occupation, was not conspicuously represented: there was 1 convict (recently released from prison, where he served a term for a "crime against nature") and 1 woodchopper. In these less well kept records the tendency was to note only exceptional higher-status occupations.

Some 75 percent of those prisoners listed in the 1863 report to Congress for whom information is available were family men, most with a wife and children at home. But nothing is reported in a majority of cases, and this often meant the men were unmarried, for these were often the men described as young or in their teens.[34] Some had large numbers of children, suggestive of a subsistence economy before birth rates fall, but the youth of many of the prisoners prevents any conclusive surmises from the incomplete figures. Brownlow's observations and the railroad links, on the other hand, suggest a population orienting toward the market after years of economic, but not political, isolation.

The leaders of the Unionists from these upland regions were themselves contemptuous of *mountain* people. Theodore F. Lang, for example, a West Virginia Federal officer and chronicler of Unionism there, described mountaineers thus: "The improvident mountaineers are not referred to here as having furnished any considerable part of the population whose methods and aims in life contributed to the advancement and elevation of the State. On the contrary, their life work was little above the savage who inhabited these same hills when the country was yet a 'howling wilderness.'" Lang said they produced corn and potatoes; hunted game and fished; and exchanged fur, ginseng, and other roots for clothing, coffee, sugar, "and, of course, whiskey."[35]

Oliver Temple dealt with mountain men in his narrative in a patronizing way. Benjamin Tolliver Staples, of Morgan County, for example, was a farmer, stockman, surveyor, and court clerk of no schooling who was arrested after the bridge burning in 1861. When released, he fled to Kentucky, became a Union soldier, and was killed by Confederate guerrilla Champ Ferguson. Temple described Staples as a "mountain man" of influence on the Cumberland plateau. He defended such people as "in the main lawabiding," not given to feuding as they were in Kentucky and West Virginia, and living where intoxication and illicit distilling were "not prevalent."[36]

Records kept by the habeas corpus commissioner for East Tennessee in 1863 and 1864 confirm the nature of the pastoral revolt. Of the 58 prisoners, 39 were identified by occupation, and 26 (67 percent) of those listed farming as at least one occupation. There were also a lawyer, an impoverished preacher, a wheelwright, a farm laborer, a shoemaker, an unemployed marble cutter, a saddler, 2 millwrights, a blacksmith, a carpenter, and a county tax official. Older family men predominated, as most young men had been drafted or had fled. Of 32 identified by family status, 28 had a wife or children. The average number of children per household was almost 5. For heads of household aged forty-five years or older, the average was 6 children, and 5 men had 9 or more living children.

Of the 33 cases in this group for which the circumstances of arrest seem clear, 28 arrests occurred away from home—on the road or in the woods. In other words, few were denounced by secret affidavits and taken from their homes; this was an active population of discontents. The judgment is confirmed by the East Tennessee cases on the congressional report: of 73 on that list, 23 percent had

been arrested on their way to Kentucky, and no other cause came near match-
ing that figure. The authorities obviously waited in most cases until the people
made some move.

Blackman Jones, James McCloud, James Prophet, A. P. Rawlings, William
Sims, and M. C. Watson, for example, were Sevier County men captured in the
woods without arms in February 1864. Confederate officials suspected them of
being bushwhackers. The prisoners ranged in age from nineteen to forty-five,
and all but one were married with children. They told commissioner William D.
Hennen that there had been a rumor that southern soldiers were killing everyone, sparing no man. They took to the woods to hide. A man named James M.
Sharp wrote a letter in their behalf to the commandant of Confederate forces at
Dandridge explaining that "They like most other Union Men fled at the approach
of your Army through the Mistaken notion that all Union Men were to be very
harshly dealt with." In the interrogations, two of the men admitted voting for
the Union in the 1861 elections, one said he did not vote, and the others did not
say. None said that he supported the Union now. Thus suspicious circumstance—
hiding in the woods—combined with Unionist sentiment, expressed in voting
three years earlier, to make these men political prisoners.[37]

Ordinary as most East Tennessee prisoners were, a political explanation—that
frequent identification as "Union men"—is superior to the increasingly popular
class explanation. East Tennessee political leaders did make appeals to social class,
but such were already a part of the political repertoire of East Tennessee's politicians before the war began. They were present in the rhetoric of a Democrat like
Andrew Johnson and an old Whig like "Parson" Brownlow. Brownlow wrote in
an editorial as early as 29 September 1860: "But this is really nothing to what
awaits us, if a 'Southern Confederacy' shall be established. The wealth and aristocracy of the 'eight cotton states' will be represented in the Confederacy and
will control it, and the right of voting will be limited to those who own slaves.
The Government will be that of a 'Slave Oligarchy' and none but the owners of
slave property will be allowed to vote."[38] As early as 22 December Brownlow had
perfected an antiaristocratic appeal that uncannily prefigured the anticonscrip-
tion arguments of later war years: "The honest yeomanry of these border States,
whose families live by their hard licks, four-fifths of whom own no negroes and
never expect to own any, are to be drafted,—forced to leave their wives and children to toil and suffer, while they fight for the purse-proud aristocrats of the Cotton States, whose pecuniary abilities will enable them to hire substitutes!"[39]
Oliver Temple, a moderate, recalled: "The people of East Tennessee knew that
secession meant a change in the form of government. They were told by some
of the leaders of the movement that slavery was to be the chief corner-stone of
the new government. This new government was to constitute a splendid aristocracy of slaveholders. The people knew that this meant degraded white labor."[40]

The area was relatively poor, but surely it is naive to think it was not itself divided within by class differences, yet the revolt, like the radically changed voting pattern of the recent elections, was marked by surprising unanimity. As much as possible, Brownlow, for example, made it seem as though aristocracy was a problem external to Tennessee, a trait of cotton states juxtaposed to Tennessean unity.

The Union appeal was the great common denominator and umbrella of all appeals to the voters. Whatever the exact social content, the intensity of belief was remarkable. The acts of political independence and self-sacrificing courage performed in Confederate military prisons for its sake have been completely overlooked by Civil War historians. Operating under the familiar guiding principle that the Confederacy was desperate for manpower, Confederate authorities worked to get prisoners who were able-bodied Southerners into military service. As early as 21 December 1861, Brownlow, himself a prisoner by then, noted from his Knoxville cell: "Took out five of the prisoners . . . , liberated them by their agreeing to go into the Rebel army. Their dread of [going to military prison in] Tuscaloosa induced them to go into service. They have offered this chance to all, and only sent off those who stubbornly refused."[41]

There was little mystery about the system, and prisoners found that they could get out of prison if they would go into the army. The Confederate army, with its uncertain supplies, high casualty rates, and enforced reenlistments, hardly offered an attractive fate, but a nineteenth-century military prison was likely worse, and many were the pleas for release on the grounds that prison life had ruined health.[42] Among the 73 East Tennesseans reported to Congress in 1863, the fate of 48 is known. Over a third (18) chose to take the oath of allegiance to the Confederacy. But a full third (16) chose not to compromise their beliefs and so suffered continued imprisonment. They included these men, in prison in the East in February 1863:

1. David Payne, a farmer, thirty-four, from Blount County, who wished to go north. At first authorities vowed to hold him for the war, but when they discovered he was crippled in his arms, they decided to exchange him for a citizen prisoner in northern hands.

2. Ebenezer Stockbridge, a native of Maine and a teacher and preacher, who was arrested for saying that he did not regard the Confederate government as legitimate. Officials decided to classify him an alien enemy despite his residence in Tennessee since 1838 and to exchange him for a citizen prisoner.

3. Lewis M. Beard, age sixty-seven, who owned a farm with a wife and grandchildren at home. Although he said he had tried to dissuade his son from U.S. service, he was retained, having been imprisoned the previous November.

4. John L. Brown, a twenty-five-year-old distiller from Campbell County, who had a brother in the Union army and tried to join it himself. In prison since November, he had no dependents.

5. Thomas Caton, a forty-three-year-old blacksmith from Cocke County, with a wife and nine children, who allegedly aided "stampeders" to Kentucky. He had voted for the Union and was refusing cooperation after some five months in prison.

6. Elijah Fortner, twenty-three, a farmer from Claiborne County with no dependents. He was in prison with no papers indicating the nature of his crime. He said he was "arrested as a Union man" in August 1862 and clung to his convictions, refusing to take the oath or serve.

7. Andrew J. Johnson, the nephew of the politician, who was a carpenter with no family and as devoted a Unionist as his namesake. He wanted to be sent north. Richmond investigators could find no papers in his case and decided to exchange him for a southern civilian.

8. David H. Kelly, a young man accused of being a member of the Second Tennessee Infantry (U.S.), who was nevertheless held as a civilian awaiting Tennessee trial.

9. David Ledger, a married twenty-year-old who had been in prison a little under six months. He was said to have been associated with a band of marauders.

10. David Miller, twenty-six, who was accused of going to Kentucky to enlist (he said he went for salt). He wanted to be sent north.

11. Alexander Thornhill, a young farmer with no wife or children to worry about, who said he preferred to lose his property in Tennessee and move north if the Confederacy were successfully established. Nearly nine months in prison had not changed his mind.

12. Alden Tucker, a young farmer who was being held for trial in Tennessee.

13. Albert Shanks, a Union man and farmer who was being held for trial in Tennessee.

14. Emerson Walker, eighteen, a farmer who told interrogators he wanted the Union restored.

15. Horry Walker, a Hawkins County carpenter caught going to Kentucky to avoid conscription, who, even after eleven months in prison, said he wished to be sent north.

16. Solomon Fortner, a thirty-six-year-old Claiborne County farmer with a wife and four children, who had spent over six months in prison.[43]

Some prisoners, after an initial refusal to cooperate, changed their minds. Thomas Mercer, of Greene County, for example, had allegedly been on his way to Kentucky to enlist in the Union army; after over four months in prison, the young farmer decided to join the Confederate army. Elijah McGuire, forty, a ferryman, changed his mind between Christmas and mid-February and decided he was no longer a Union man. Nathaniel Williams, a Carter County blacksmith and the son of a Union man, changed his mind in a little over a month. When William Kenny, only seventeen, changed his mind after nearly six months in prison, he was sent to live with his uncle, vouched for as a true southern man by Tennessee senator Landon C. Haynes.[44]

Parson Brownlow noted in his prison diary early in the war that prisoners were brought in for "talking Union talk."[45] East Tennesseans apparently kept talking that way throughout the war, despite a loss of political leadership. Brownlow, imprisoned in 1861, made his way north in 1862. Thomas A. R. Nelson was arrested heading north in 1861 and struck a deal with his captors, exchanging political silence for physical release. Andrew Johnson remained north at first and then came to the western part of the state as military governor. Nathaniel G. Taylor of Carter County agitated in the North for relief for East Tennessee. Levi Pickens died in prison. Daniel Ellis, a Carter County farmer and wagon maker turned Union guide, made a penetrating point when he commented on the desperate situation in the region late in the summer of 1863: "The leading Union men were now all gone; and there being scarcely none to urge the common masses to hold on to their love for the Union, I thought that they deserved the utmost praise for adhering so steadfastly to their principles."[46]

Isolation and ignorance do not explain these acts of heroism. Neither do precapitalist traits.[47] These were not men of education and worldly sophistication, it is true, and their expressions of political beliefs fell short of systematic propositions of reasoned political science. The usual expression came in the phrase that they opposed secession for attempting to destroy the best form of government ever devised by man. Union guide Daniel Ellis bitterly hated Jefferson Davis and the Confederacy. He recalled in his memoirs after the war that he and his like-minded neighbors were opposed to a Confederacy "supplanting and annihilating the best form of government which has ever been devised by the wisdom of men upon the whole face of the earth."[48]

The East Tennesseans' political beliefs may have gone little beyond the level of slogan. Beyond that it is difficult to go, and I have not found it possible, despite my belief that nationalism always has specific social content, to reduce the Unionism of East Tennessee's dissenters to any particular social program or ideal. Noel Fisher probably accurately identifies Unionism in East Tennessee as a "mass movement that reflected republican fears of a slaveholder's aristocracy."[49] Any student of history longs for more but for the most part must rest content with knowledge of the *intensity* of the political beliefs when uttered in a prison and in certain knowledge that the utterance would guarantee continued imprisonment.

The Problem of Conscription

Conscription in East Tennessee was by all accounts, sympathetic or not, important in creating discontent; Taylor, Temple, Ellis, and other partisans of the region freely admitted that it brought immigration to flood stage. But it did not necessarily signify in East Tennessee what it did elsewhere. In the first place, East Tennesseans did not always perceive conscription as a new and separate political issue apart from secession. We have already heard Brownlow's prescient prewar view of the issue, and others regarded it as the same old issue of planter tyranny now made inescapably pertinent. Ellis described "the great object" of the "chivalry" in seceding as the establishment of "an aristocratic government by abridging the political privileges of the poorer class of Southern citizens, and by enlarging those of the slaveholder and the landholder." It forced the sons of the yeomen to do what the planters' sons, with their twenty-slave exemptions and substitutes, did not have to do.[50]

Naturally, many Unionists preferred to wait for rescue by the Federal armies rather than to have to choose to fight for the hated Confederacy or to make the extremely perilous flight to Kentucky to join the U.S. Army. But they were no more neutral in feeling than were those slaves who preferred to wait to be rescued rather than hazard the breakout from the plantation. All such men could be consistent Unionists from the beginning.

Far from being a matter of cowardice and disloyalty, draft evasion in East Tennessee was for the most an expression of loyalty to the Union that required courage, enterprise, stamina, and a little money.

It was almost impossible to escape military service in East Tennessee. If the Confederates did not get the Unionists, probably the Federal soldiers would. The guides who could take Southerners on the dangerous and grueling journey through the mountains to Union lines all worked for Federal recruiters—except one, who carried enlistment papers with him and was always met by Federal soldiers upon arrival in Kentucky.[51]

Though called *stampeding,* escaping to Kentucky was not as disorganized and spontaneous as the term suggests. Guides made a living at it; safe houses along the way became well-known landmarks—the white Unionists' equivalent of the stations on the escaping slaves' Underground Railroad—and Federal authorities eagerly awaited arrivals. Escapees had to contact a guide and rendezvous with the group gathered for each exhausting and harrowing trek through the mountains. Their rewards of food and shelter on arrival came at a price, whether formally stated or not: enlistment in the U.S. Army. Thus draft evasion in East Tennessee amounted not to avoidance of military service but a choice of which military to serve. Some 42,000 Tennesseans served in the Federal forces, more than from any other Confederate state.[52]

Conclusion

Leniency clearly did not work, but Confederate attempts to keep East Tennessee under control resulted in a blackout of civil liberty equal in thoroughness to any imposed by the Lincoln administration in the North. The motives of the East Tennesseans have been underestimated. Regnant interpretations, both hostile and sympathetic, emphasize the material side of things and self-interest. Yet the most striking quality of East Tennessee resistance was its disinterested selfless-ness. Inured to economic hardship, the residents of this region took action before those hardships increased, before conscription forced difficult choices on the men, and before military defeats marked the Confederacy for failure.

Another striking quality is that disaffection was largely *unaffected* by eman-cipation policies in the North.[53] Here even their defenders have let the East Tennesseans down. Foner, for example, has been too willing to emphasize the allegiance of the rebellious uplanders to white supremacy. Yet available wartime evidence offers only the famous statement of one of the East Tennessee leaders, Thomas A. R. Nelson, who broke his silence on political issues to help the Con-federacy with a statement condemning emancipation in 1862. As for the follow-ers of such leaders, I was able to find only two East Tennesseans who played the race card to get out of prison. It was a sure way to reach the hearts of Con-federate interrogators. Even depraved Union deserters figured it out. Such men often said that they had enlisted in the North and then decided to desert to the South when they learned that the war was being fought for the black race.[54]

The East Tennessee prisoners who used the race issue were Charles W. Wise-man, twenty-two, and Edward Poor, twenty-four. They wrote Secretary of War Seddon on 23 January 1863, when news of the Emancipation Proclamation was fresh, to say that "in the earlier part of this war, they were disposed to uphold the Old Government, but . . . have never taken sides either pro or con. . . . Since the emancipation proclamation was issued by the Federal president, and orders issued by him upholding that proclamation they have and now do avow their loy-alty to the Gov'mt of the Confederate States." They promised to take the oath of allegiance and enlist.[55]

Tennessee was exempted from the Emancipation Proclamation, but most of the region's political leaders eventually came around to emancipation anyway. Brownlow endorsed emancipation though he accepted it haltingly.[56] The Rev-erend William B. Carter, of East Tennessee's Carter County, himself a slave-holder, stated at a Union rally in New York City in October 1862 that he regarded "the Union of these States as of infinitely more value than all the negroes in America, and Africa, and Europe," and that "if in the progress of this war it should become absolutely necessary . . . in order to save this Government that Slavery should die, . . . let it perish."[57] Andrew Johnson also endorsed emancipation. Moreover, when Lincoln invited the border states to endorse a plan of compensated emancipation in 1862, a majority of representatives rejected it, but a minority report supporting Lincoln's proposal was signed by Andrew J. Clements of Tennessee and endorsed by Horace Maynard.[58]

Finally, the profile of East Tennessee's political prisoners and the political geography of the region as described by participants suggest that another great interpretation of the Civil War must be in error—the one derived from Charles and Mary Beard. In that interpretation, the war is depicted as a conflict between an agrarian, traditional society on the one hand and an industrial, modern society on the other—or in more Marxian versions as a conflict between a modernizing free labor society in the North and an aristocratically precapitalist one in the South. Such theories have little validity for conflicts *within* the societies at war with each other. No group of white southerners longed more for northern victory than the East Tennesseans, and they were surely more agrarian than the average Confederates.

The most enthusiastic pro-Confederates among the East Tennesseans, by all accounts, were located in the towns along the railroad; they seem the most progressive economically, linked most closely to the metropolitan world and the market.[59] Town addresses and railroad occupations are as lacking among the East Tennessee political prisoners as mountain ones—more so, in fact; they are completely lacking. The farmers of the valley, though also linking themselves more to the market than ever through the new railroad, seemed backward to Confederate authorities. These authorities viewed the East Tennesseans with the contempt reserved by townsmen for agriculturists. If it makes any sense to divide East Tennesseans into modernizers and traditionalists, then the modernizers may well have been the supporters of secession, whereas the supporters of the Union were in fact adherents of a pastoral life in what one of their leaders called America's Switzerland.

7

PERSISTENT UNIONISM IN WESTERN VIRGINIA
AND NORTH CAROLINA

"You had a clear right to vote for the Union but when secession was established by the voice of the people you did ill to distract the country by angry words and insurrectionary tumult. In doing this you commit the highest crime known to the laws."[1] These words, meant to reassure East Tennesseans about votes cast against secession in the past, come from a proclamation issued after the hanging of two alleged saboteurs in 1861. Actually, the proclamation confirmed the existence of the Confederate authorities' suspicion that the antisecessionists of 1860–61 were not to be trusted. And during the war, with civil liberties often suspended in these doubtful areas, suspicion could quickly confer guilt.[2]

No doubt all Confederate officials shared the belief that citizens had a right to vote freely against secession before their states joined the Confederacy. Nevertheless, when habeas corpus commissioners asked prisoners about their political affiliation, when the commissioners noted it in their records, and when they weighed the significance of Unionism in determining the disposition of their cases, they drifted toward political repression. Such repression was a feature of Confederate practice in handling political prisoners that distinguished it from that of the Lincoln administration.

Unlike the Unionists of East Tennessee, those of western Virginia were successful in establishing a government separate from the secessionist government of their state. Despite this success in establishing a new government, a full narrative account of western Virginia history during the Civil War is difficult to find. Perhaps the nearest thing to it, Boyd B. Stutler's *West Virginia in the Civil War*, consists of newspaper articles gathered in book form and lacks systematic chronology, analysis of grand strategy, numbers engaged, and descriptions of the role of civilians and the economy.[3]

Historians have been preoccupied by the constitutional and political questions involved in the origins of West Virginia statehood and have not worked as hard on creating an image of life in western Virginia during the war nor a sense of developments over time.[4] For a look at daily life, in part, we can turn once again to the records of political prisoners from the state. They are best considered apart from other "Appalachian" Confederates because of significant economic and geographical differences. The Virginians shared a state border with the Tennesseans as well as qualities of low slaveholding, regionalism, and self-conscious political identity. But the railroad through the Cumberland Valley linked East Tennessee with the plantation regimes of the Tidewater and of the new cotton South, whereas the Baltimore and Ohio Railroad (B&O), running across northern Virginia from Baltimore to Wheeling and beyond to Pittsburgh, linked the farms and villages of western Virginia to Pennsylvania and the free states of the Old Northwest. As James McPherson points out, West Virginia was physically and economically closer to Pennsylvania than to the Virginia Tidewater, with Wheeling only sixty miles from Pittsburgh.[5]

Moreover the B&O ran eastward as well as westward, and the failure of the secession movement in Maryland proved a crucial development for western Virginia history.[6] The Lincoln administration's vigorous moves to occupy Baltimore in the earliest weeks of the war surely played a role in maintaining the loyalty of the northwestern counties of Virginia, dependent on the B&O with its terminus in Baltimore. That kept both ends of the road in Union hands and tied western Virginia's interests inexorably to the northern economy, society, and government.

Military force shaped West Virginia as well, as historian Richard O. Curry pointed out. The final fifty-county configuration included twenty-five counties that opposed secession from Virginia, and thus the campaigns of Generals George B. McClellan and William S. Rosecrans in western Virginia in the fall of 1861 proved crucial to creating the state.[7] No Union armies entered East Tennessee for two years after the war began.

Frequent collaboration with the enemy revealed the weakened claims of loyalty to Richmond in the Confederate-held counties near Union-controlled western Virginia. For example, James Cornan, of Nicholas County, who described himself as a Union man until secession, was arrested, apparently at home, because the enemy camped near his farm and he fed them corn. Cornan maintained that he could not resist the power of the Federals. Interrogators in Richmond ascertained that he had served in the militia and been honorably discharged. Thus his collaboration with the enemy combined with his Unionist political past was enough for a time to overcome his military service record as evidence of loyalty. He was ordered released on 16 January 1862.[8]

The Old World has long had the word *collaboration* to describe the actions of people disloyal to their government in contacts with an invading army, but it has never been applied to the American Civil War. Even a book with bleak assumptions about human motivation such as Michael Fellman's *Inside War: The Guerrilla Conflict in Missouri during the American Civil War* never employs the term, choosing instead "survival lies" and other terms more psychological than political.[9]

Persistent Unionism made collaboration likely, especially in the areas of the Upper South penetrated earliest by the Federals. The persistence of Unionism is apparent from defiant avowals of prisoners and from the rarity of occasions when political prisoners could claim the opposite—that they had voted *for* seces-sion—in order to gain favor with their jailers. Sydney S. Baxter, who interrogated many of the Virginians in Richmond's Eastern District Military Prison ("Castle Thunder"), usually wanted to know about previous voting behavior. From his interrogations and others as well, we can determine that of 337 political prison-ers from western Virginia (including southwest Virginia but not the Shenandoah Valley) for whom records survive by name, only 7 laid claim to having voted for secession or were said never to have been Union men. By contrast, some 81 were identified as "Union men." If we eliminate from the calculation prisoners for whom no information on cause of arrest is given (26) as well as records of per-sons for whom a Union vote was an impossibility (7 aliens, 3 women, 1 slave), then the 81 Union men represent 27 percent of the white male citizens from west-ern Virginia who were arrested.

Political behavior, especially in Virginia, where oral voting persisted, was not a matter the prisoner could hope to conceal. Records indicate that some pris-oners were arrested simply because of their previous votes against secession, and many more felt this was the case. J. W. Butler may have been Virginia's first lit-erally *political* prisoner. He was arrested on election day, 23 May 1861, in Loudoun County, Virginia. He voted against secession, and he was arrested and required to give bond to keep the peace for twelve months. A maker of quack medicines, Butler remained in prison a long time, while his wife and child were cut off behind enemy lines. He was still in prison in February 1863, when authorities rec-ommended sending the fifty-one-year-old north in exchange for a civilian pris-oner. Butler was not the only one. Samuel Gordon was also required by the Loudoun County Court in May 1861 to give security for good behavior and remained in jail almost a year later.[10]

Cain Morrall and his son John, who hailed from Seneca in Pendleton County, one of the three counties in the upper Shenandoah Valley included against majority will in West Virginia, were arrested by the Pendleton militia in 1861 and sent to military prison in Richmond. Both thought they had been arrested only because they had voted against Virginia's secession from the United States. Seneca had been a stronghold of sentiment against separating from the Union, with 47 voting for secession and 92 against the secession ordinance in 1861. At year's end, Confederate authorities recommended the discharge of the Morralls, on condition that they take the oath of allegiance to the Confederacy and be removed from the area of military operations.[11]

Some prisoners admitted their Union votes but professed changed loyalties since the election, "acquiescing" in secession from the United States or "going with" their state.[12] Others proved stubborn, refusing to disavow their Unionism even though it meant continued imprisonment. Like the Tennesseans, these pris-oners and their partisans knew that a claim to a secessionist voting record could

well be an aid to release. Thus when G. W. Thomas put in a good word for prisoner Thomas W. Goodman, from White Oak Swamp, near Richmond, Thomas
noted that Goodman was an inoffensive man of no influence, that he had a large
family to support, and that he was "always a states rights democrat."[13]

The ambiguity of the phrase *Union man,* of course, leaves room for its denot-
ing, not previous party adherence necessarily, but current emotional identification
with the enemy in the war. Nevertheless, there are several indications that the
phrase usually meant someone who had voted the Union ticket and now appeared
to persist in opposing the work of the secessionists. For example, African-American prisoners were almost never identified as Union men, though most of them
surely identified with the northern side during the war. They could not, however, have voted for a Union party in 1860–61. Likewise, no female prisoner was
identified as a Unionist.

Prisoners too young to vote might be identified as Union men, but they were
usually the sons of Union men.[14] Thus Hiram Atkin, age seventeen, the son of
Peter Atkin, age forty-five, was arrested in 1863 as a witness against his father,
who was accused of having stood guard over prisoners taken by Union men.
Peter was identified as "an avowed Union man," but Hiram was not. Baxter
interrogated Hiram but did not ask him whether he was a Union man because
a seventeen-year-old could not have voted.[15] More revealing is the record of
D. Harrison, of Cabell County, arrested in 1861: commissioner James Lyons noted
that he was a Union man but did not sympathize with the enemy.[16]

Collaboration boiled down to proximity to the enemy combined with the suspicion of the accuser. A Unionist vote in 1861 combined with residence in one
of the contested counties of western Virginia put a man at risk for military arrest
by Confederate authorities.

Western Virginians did not have to leave home to find trouble; trouble came
to them—in the form of Yankee invaders and Confederate scouts. Samuel Currence, for example, drove the stage between Beverly and Webster Counties. On
a trip during the summer of 1861, the stage ran afoul of Federal troops operating at Philippi. When he returned home after this unavoidable contact with the
enemy, he was arrested and held for a time in the Augusta County jail. A petition
sent to Jefferson Davis in Currence's behalf protested, "It is true he voted against
the Ordinance of secession as he thought every man had a right to do under the
law,—but he has done nothing against the State of Virginia, and was willing to
abide by the Majority of Virginia."[17]

A. G. White, of Cabell County, killed a cow for the enemy. He had been a
Union man but said he had not been since secession. He produced witnesses who
said that the enemy forced him to slaughter the animal. Commissioner Lyons
recommended his discharge on 12 December 1861.[18]

Examples like these suggest that a reputation for having supported the Union cause in the secession crisis could arouse suspicions in the field that did not seem as compelling in Richmond. But the commissioners in the capital, after all, apparently asked about the prisoners' political past and noted the information in their record; this information was not forced on them. Nor did commissioners disqualify arrests because of political prejudice, criticize local authorities or generals for such arrests, or publish rules to limit the political content of accusatory affidavits. Rather, the commissioners weighed the political evidence they received with the rest, and they created their own by interrogation.

As in East Tennessee, the prisoners from western Virginia did not consist mostly of "mountaineers" but of valley-dwelling farmers. Among the exceptional few mountain men imprisoned were John O'Brien and his son Miles, of Webster County. The father dug ginseng for a living and was described as an "ignorant" man who had spent his life in the woods hunting. But he held intense political views nevertheless. The report added that he seemed "very ignorant of what is going on in the settlements" but had "a great respect for the old Commonwealth of Virginia and great contempt and hatred for the attempted government at Wheeling." O'Brien did "not seem to know much of the difference between the United States and Confederate States," but he was willing to "take the oath of allegiance to the old State of Virginia and any government she belongs to." Son Miles was described as a cooper, farmer, and ginseng digger—and as "ignorant."[19]

Tolleson Stover, arrested for "disloyalty" in Raleigh County on 26 October 1861, was a farmer who had been "raised in the woods."[20] William Deekins, arrested two miles from his home in Fayette County by the Caskie Rangers, was heading toward Kanawha with a load of beeswax and ginseng, mountain products.[21]

With two claimants to legitimate government authority in Virginia and widespread guerrilla warfare, it was not easy to separate military from civilian prisoners. As late as 1864, Confederate authorities took prisoners like Calvin Boyd, age thirty-six, who had drilled as a militiaman for the pro-Union government of Edwards Pierpont in occupied Virginia and was surprised in arms with seventy-four others. He hailed from Upshur County and was given a chance to enlist in the Eighth Virginia (Confederate) Infantry. Boyd and eight other West Virginians arrested with him refused to serve, refused their weapons when issued, and insisted on being treated as prisoners of war. Confederate investigators in Richmond considered the "charge very serious," as the men were not in the service of the United States (the Confederacy did not recognize the Pierpont government). "They should be treated as banditti," said one. "They are guilty of treason, both against the Confederate States, & against the State of Va." Technically they were guilty also of mutiny and could be tried by a military or a civilian court. Yet there was undoubtedly a "question . . . as to . . . policy" in bringing them to trial. Ultimately, confinement in prison was recommended rather than pursuit of the more drastic charges that would invite retaliation from Federal officials and a degeneration of fighting conditions.[22]

The Case of W. E. Coffman

The counties neighboring Union-controlled western Virginia were unsettled and tense, and they bred the jitters and ferocity in the local warriors. In Rockbridge County, in the western Shenandoah Valley, for example, Confederate authorities narrowly avoided creating a martyr whose fame might have outstripped that of the bridge burners hanged on Benjamin's order. In December 1863 General John D. Imboden, commanding the Valley District, attempted to hang William E. Coffman, a civilian from Rockbridge County, after a court-martial found him guilty of communicating with the enemy. Imboden had entered the war by organizing a partisan ranger unit and would soon embark on a raid on the B&O. His was very much the western Virginia war of raids and partisans, though he had distinguished himself in the Gettysburg campaign of the previous summer and was regularly commissioned and in command of an important district.[23]

The military court, which met first on 2 November 1863 and then adjourned to 3 December, dealing with a number of cases in that period, had its doubts about trying a citizen under the Fifty-seventh Article of War, which stated that "whosoever" corresponded with or aided the enemy was subject to "court mar-tial and death." But Imboden had no doubts. A lawyer in the valley town of Staunton before the war, he declared his "opinion that violations of said article can only be punished by sentence of a court martial and not by a civil tribunal. The pronoun 'whosoever' was evidently intended to mean any one not with-out exception, who 'shall be convicted,'&c."

Judge James W. F. Allen of the Twelfth Virginia District Court disagreed and issued a writ of habeas corpus. Imboden then exemplified the rage of the west-ern warrior and defied the writ. Imboden said he held himself "responsible before the courts and country for . . . a righteious act" and expressed confidence that a "more unmitigated scoundrel was never hung."[24] He ordered the provost marshal holding Coffman to get on with the hanging on Imboden's responsi-bility, but the officer had already telegraphed Richmond, and the secretary of war told him to obey the writ of habeas corpus and appear in court with the pris-oner on the appointed day—several days after Coffman was supposed to hang. The Confederacy thereby was spared its Vallandigham-style martyr—or worse— by the promptness of a lowly provost marshal, by the close timing of the tele-graph, and perhaps by the circumstance that Congress had not authorized the suspension of the writ of habeas corpus for 1863.

In February 1864 Congress demanded the papers in the Coffman case from the president. Davis and the secretary of war sent what they could, explaining that the originals had been stolen from the provost marshal's office in Harrisonburg in late December. What the administration knew but did not report to Congress was as significant as what they sent. In the first place, the question of the application of the Fifty-seventh Article of War to civilians had already been settled—in an opinion of the acting attorney general, Wade Keys, written at the request of the secretary of war on 18 November 1863—at the time of the adjournment of the Coffman trial. In answer to the question whether the Fifty-seventh Article of War applied "to any but persons belonging to the Armies of the Confederate States," Keys had answered "at once in the negative."[25] The Articles of War applied only to people in the armed services.

The administration did not inform Congress of the attorney general's opinion—or that it came in answer to a question raised by the president of the very court-martial that tried Coffman! General George H. Smith's letter asking for the opinion had been endorsed by Imboden himself, saying, "I have in my guard house certain disloyal citizens of Virginia, charged with enticing soldiers to desert and piloting them to the enemy; and, also, furnishing the enemy with information of the position and movements of our troops in this District."[26] "Another class of cases I have," the general continued, "is that of members of an organized band of men who shoot our soldiers, and rob and murder our people, but are not Federal soldiers, nor in our Army." The attorney general said such men could not be tried by court-martial, and the president could have informed the Congress of the law.[27]

The Enforcers

Though a writ of habeas corpus saved Coffman, abuses of civil liberties were rife in western Virginia, and other officials operating in the theater were as ferocious as Imboden. There were notorious irregulars and partisans, including groups known even to War Department officials in Richmond for their bad reputations. Many of these groups had been organized under the Partisan Ranger Act of 1862, an attempt at mobilizing ill-disciplined men that proved so ill-advised that Congress revoked it in 1864.[28] The Moccasin Rangers and Vincent Witcher's irregular cavalry provide notorious examples from western Virginia. The rangers, who got their name from the Moccasin River rather than from the Indian footgear, regularly practiced entrapment. In an 1862 incident, for example, rangers posed as Federal cavalry and demanded food from Greenbrier County's William Cruickshanks and his son John. After William fed them—out of fear—they arrested him for disloyalty and sent him to Richmond with his son. Cruickshanks insisted he had "always advocated the southern cause."[29]

The rangers also sent to Richmond Samuel B. Cutlip and other men arrested in Greenbrier County. Sydney S. Baxter, in his report on the prisoners, explained that Virginia governor Letcher had told him that Confederate general Henry Heth "was under the necessity of disarming the moccasin rangers who arrested these Greenbrier men." That circumstance helped make Baxter sympathetic to the prisoners' plight, and he decided, "as they are poor men and their families destitute humanity suggests they should be permitted to go home and be subjected to the law there. To force them into the service here seems harsh."[30]

As for Vincent A. Witcher, Federal forces opposing him regarded his troops as "thugs" given to "murdering, plundering, and burning."[31] A delegate to the Virginia House from Cabell County wrote that "Captain Witcher's Company is one of independent scouts and are supposed to be indiscriminate in their arrests."[32] Witcher's career, like Imboden's after the Coffman trial, stands as a reminder that a reputation for insensitive treatment of civilians could seldom damage, let alone ruin, a career in the Confederate Army.

Promotions came steadily to Witcher. Once a captain of sixty-four mounted riflemen, he became a major by the summer of 1862 and lieutenant colonel of the Thirty-fourth Virginia Battalion in the Army of Western Virginia by spring.[33] He served with General J. E. B. Stuart and the regular cavalry of the Army of Northern Virginia in the Gettysburg campaign and was commended by Stuart.[34] That autumn he returned to East Tennessee and western Virginia. He made a successful expedition late in 1864. Federal forces reported that Witcher's raid robbed the people of West Virginia of horses, clothing, cattle, and money and laid waste to the country, making no distinction between Union men and secession sympathizers.[35] From the Confederate side, the expedition looked different, and Robert E. Lee reported to the secretary of war on 5 October 1864: "Lieutenant-Colonel Witcher has returned from his expedition to Western Virginia. He visited Bulltown, Jacksonville, Westover, Buckhannon, Walkersville, and Weston. Reports that he destroyed a million dollars worth of stores, captured 300 prisoners, with their horses and equipments, brought out 500 horses, and 200 beef-cattle, and sustained no loss."[36] Lee pronounced himself "very much pleased at Witcher's success."[37]

Examined closely, Lee's carefully drafted report complimented Witcher for doing what the Federal reports condemned. Lee's language made military actions, no matter how drastic and bloody, seem routine and civil: thus Witcher, in Lee's parlance, "visited" various villages in western Virginia (he did not "raid" them). Lee said of the horses and cattle that they were "brought out." He did not say that they were captured, as were the three hundred prisoners. That left room for the horses having come from the inhabitants and not from the Federal supply trains—which would be consistent with Federal allegations that

Witcher robbed Union and Confederate sympathizers alike. Witcher's raid occurred after the Confederate Congress rescinded the Partisan Ranger Act, and he was operating not as a partisan but under direct authority of Confederate high command and under the rules governing the Army of Northern Virginia.

Unsettled conditions made for mistakes and careless record keeping (phenomena hardly confined to western Virginia prisoners). Baxter, for example, determined that the arrest of Adam Bragg early in 1862 at Bragg's Mill in southwest Virginia, evidently the rendezvous of a home guard unit led by Bragg's brother, had been a "mistake," for he had not joined his brother's unit.[38] The following are notations in the records from western Virginia indicating problematic procedures in the field: "No papers on file," "No charge," "No evidence," "Doesn't know why arrested," "County never disturbed by the enemy—commissioner thinks he should not have been arrested without affidavits" [Hale], "arrested on mere suspicion; waited long enough for evidence" [Weddell]. Yet the Richmond bureaucracy could add its own careless errors to the abuses, as these further notations from the western Virginia records indicate: "Arrested two days before Rich Mountain battle in our camp as spy. Forgotten about" [Smith], "Examined before but his name was badly written in my reports and was read Storms" [Stover], "It is hardly possible this man could have been here so long without charges" [Jackson], and "The papers I cannot find."[39] Over 13 percent, 45 of 337 records from western Virginia, are tainted by these flaws identified by Confederate authorities themselves. Like the East Tennessee records, most of these lack mention of the issue of emancipation.

The Peculiar Population of the Poquosin

General John Bankhead Magruder, who rode roughshod over civilian rights throughout his Civil War career, encountered an intractable group of Virginians early in 1861 before his transfer to Texas. The "peculiar population of the Poquosin," as Magruder described them, lived in an area of southeastern Virginia identifiable to this day as a "subregion" of the South. *Poquosin,* according to environmental historian Jack Temple Kirby, means "high swampland," and the name has become attached to the area between the James River in Virginia and the Albemarle River in North Carolina, the most prominent feature of which is the Great Dismal Swamp.

Until the twentieth century, Kirby tells us, the area was notable for its "barely commercial" culture, "close to subsistence." Hog runners, shingle cutters, escaping slaves, and agriculturists who burned woodlands for fields and then moved on lived near great plantations, one of which was owned by the famous secessionist ideologue Edmund Ruffin. What Kirby did not notice was that, like most

Americans at the time, the white males among these people, though maintaining a "hinterland" culture different from the "cosmopolitan" culture of Ruffin and the planters, also nurtured a political identity. Southampton County, for example, on the western margin of the subregion, saw an 86 percent voter turnout in the election of 1860.[40]

When war came to Virginia, the local political identity of the Poquosin came into conflict with the national aspirations of the Confederate States of America. General Magruder had heard that the people there voted against secession. A portion "of the poorer classes" of those who lived "on the Poquosin and Buck Rivers, . . . pursued the business of fishing and oystering." The people "were in the habit of trading at Fortress Monroe and with Northerners almost exclusively." When Magruder called out the local militia, thus taking the humble fishermen away from their trade, he deemed them so impoverished that he fed their families on government rations. The militiamen subsequently became convinced that they need serve only six months and went home—four deserted to the enemy.

Several inhabitants complained to Richmond that they had been illegally removed from their homes and made prisoners at West Point, Virginia, and Magruder explained to the War Department that when he marched through the region he "found small white flags at most of their doors proclaiming neutrality." They lighted their homes at night, he said, to warn the enemy when the Confederates were coming. Magruder rented wagons and moved the Poquosin people with their furniture to West Point, accounting for all their crops and cattle and partly paying for them. He fed the citizens rations as prisoners of war.[41]

The numbers involved in the depopulation and the final resolution of the controversy are not known, in part because Federal forces soon operated freely in the area. But this evacuation of a region was a significant event in the history of civil liberty in the Confederacy. Again the old Beardian version of the Civil War does not fit, as these Unionists did not represent the commercial future of the Union. Moreover, the Poquosin people defy the usual pattern of Confederate political geography, which pits upland Unionists against lowland planters.

The most serious problems of resistance to Confederate nationalism were rooted in regionalism, on high ground or low. They were exacerbated by persistent Unionism implanted by the prewar political system, which created intense political identification almost everywhere. In 1860, as Magruder seems to have known, Nansemond, Norfolk, and Princess Anne Counties, part of the Poquosin region, had all voted for the Union ticket headed by John Bell.[42]

Yet, East or West, only the political system penetrated all the South efficiently. Even the Tidewater of Virginia, the oldest of English settlements in the South, still contained pockets of population not really integrated into the culture of the state. As historian Eugene Genovese has noted, "nonplantation areas found themselves developing as enclaves more or less detached from the mainstream of southern society."[43]

In Europe such differences from the cosmopolitan culture of the capital were likely to breed political ignorance and indifference in the peasant countryside.[44] But in America geographical isolation did not necessarily breed pre-political indifference. Intense identification with republicanism and the most efficient system of popular party politics in the world led even rural and isolated groups to vote and to develop partisan identities. "Those nonslaveholders who lived as farmers and herdsmen in the up country and well back of the plantation districts had only minimal contact with the great planters and created a world of their own," wrote Genovese. He did not say that these worlds were reflected in political participation and identity—and he might have added to his groups living "back of the plantation districts" the shingle gatherers and fishermen of the coastal lowlands.

The peoples of the swamplands of southeastern Virginia shared with those of the uplands of western Virginia low slaveholding, political identity, and a regionalism only being recognized in history books now. Otherwise they were unlike. Kirby emphasizes the distinctive burn-and-move agriculture of the Poquosin, a contrast with the permanent field agriculture of the uplands. Fishing and oystering were distinctive, too. These lowlands reached all the way south to Wilmington, North Carolina, and this region proved as troublesome to the Confederacy's internal security as the uplands did. The fall of much of the region to Federal naval invasions early on kept its story, and that of the Poquosin in particular, from the standard works of Confederate history, but a look at North Carolina's political prisoners should go a long way to arousing an awareness of the distinct political geography of the coastal lowlands.

North Carolina

In a way, the arrest records for North Carolina are disappointing; only two hundred have been located for this study. Few of these refer to men from upland areas, where resistance to the Confederacy was strong, and probably those records went elsewhere and were lost. The historian is left primarily with records from the eastern counties vulnerable to Federal penetration from the sea and up the rivers. These records have the virtue, however, of revising the standard image of Confederate political geography.

The surviving evidence, disappointingly thin and regionally skewed as it is, resembles the Virginia case. Of two hundred North Carolina political prisoners, only two were identified as *not* being Union men. Some twenty-six were positively identified as Union men, and most of those were arrested *as* Union men. The region from which most records survive was substantially a part of the Poquosin subregion. Washington County, a troublesome lowland area neighboring the Great Dismal Swamp, has already been the subject of a book, Wayne K. Durrill's *War of Another Kind: A Southern Community in the Great Rebellion.*

Northerners had penetrated the region before the war to extract a living from the swamps and shores, and they would penetrate it militarily once war began. Some of these people of northern origin were still in the neighborhood when war came. J. M. Morehead of Greensboro warned the secretary of war about them as early as 26 August 1861:

> I have no doubt the exterior coast of NC will be the scene of many marauding parties of the Enemy this winter—
>
> The North, through their shingle-getters—timber-getters—oyster men & fishermen &c who have spent their winters in our waters, in large numbers— are well posted up as to our whole coast—& know when they can damage us most—
>
> We must meet them at every point—[45]

Brunswick County, to the west of Wilmington, contained the great Green Swamp and Lake Wacamaw. The region came to Commissioner Baxter's attention in the cases of two alien enemies who tried to maintain a lumber business for a company owned jointly by Northerners and Southerners. The arrangement came to grief in late 1862 because one of the principals, Gideon S. Bolton of Maine, grew homesick and attempted to reach the Federal blockading fleet to go home. Confederate pickets arrested him. Suspicions grew fevered when the Confederates discovered that Bolton and Clement Richardson ran a little post office set up for the use of the Green Swamp Land Company. The idea that these men of Yankee origins could send clandestine communications via the Confederate mail to accomplices anywhere in the Confederacy was frightening.

Baxter gathered evidence on the case and summarized it for the secretary of war. To set the scene, Baxter noted: "The country is swampy inhabited by Timber getters—and Fishermen & Hunters and on the ocean[,] Wreckers [who made their living off salvage washed up on the beaches from shipwrecks] and Beachmen. This is precisely the character of the population most injurious to us in North Carolina. There is no road through the swamp in the direction of the Ocean—but it is traversed by paths known to the Timber getters and hunters— Through this swamp secret and stealthy communication may be kept up with the enemy on the ocean"[46] One North Carolina native, part of the Green Swamp Company, agreed that "Most of the country is swamp and but little known, the population is sparce and ignorant."[47] Brunswick County, where the Green Swamp timbermen, fishermen, and wreckers lived, voted Constitutional Union in 1860. In fact, the swampy areas of eastern North Carolina voted Constitutional

Union, often by large margins, as in Camden, Pasquotank, and Washington Counties. Only New Hanover County, the site of Wilmington, voted Breckinridge Democratic (by a wide margin).[48] Bearing out Baxter's suspicions was prisoner David Stowe, from Hatteras, North Carolina, identified as a wrecker and Union man who took the oath of allegiance to the United States as soon as Federal forces took Hatteras.[49]

These Unionist lowland margins in the East proved to be areas of concentrated dissent, as did the western uplands.[50] The North Carolina portion of the lowland region was more flavored by the presence of Quakers, who naturally did not fit in well in the Confederacy. Thus the North Carolina records reveal the presence of the most anomalous of white Confederate citizens, the southern antislavery advocate Thomas Kennedy, for example, farmed in Kinston, Wayne County, where he was arrested, entrapped by a Confederate lieutenant posing as a Yankee to elicit his opinions, on 20 December 1862. Kennedy was sixty-six years old and had emancipated some sixty slaves thirty years earlier. He was opposed to slavery on principle, though he hastened to add that he did not sympathize with abolitionists. Kennedy did not believe North Carolina had a right to secede, considered himself a U.S. citizen, and refused to take the oath of allegiance to the Confederacy. These opinions, freely expressed in Salisbury Prison, made likely his continued imprisonment and hardship for his wife, niece, and four children still at home. War Department lawyer B. R. Wellford Jr. remarked after investigation that Kennedy was honest but "out of place in these circumstances."[51]

Class conflict is perhaps the regnant theme in histories of Civil War North Carolina.[52] Political prisoners lend some support to the idea. One of the North Carolina political prisoners forthrightly set his class interest against the Confederacy: John Buck complained that the chances of a poor man in the South were not good.[53] Many of the prisoners—surely most—were men of very modest means. Amariah B. Allen, for example, was a farmer on twenty-five acres. Arrested 30 October 1862, he remained a prisoner in August of the next year, confined as a traitorous citizen because he was an avowed Union man, had taken the U.S. oath, refused the Confederate oath, and would not serve in the armed forces though he was under forty.[54]

Jesse W. Davis, of Washington County, farmed on forty acres and fished as well to make ends meet for his wife and eight children.[55] Edward Williams, who wanted to be sent north, was sixty-four, had a wife and seven children, and said he had no money.[56] Edward B. Hopkins, arrested 1 June 1863, was poor and had to work for the Yankees or starve, he said. They forced him to take the oath of allegiance to the United States for the work. He was forty-seven and ill and had a wife and five children at home. Confederate authorities believed his story and released him on oath as a "true southern man" in unfortunate circumstances.[57]

To read the statements by and about the political prisoners might at first cause us to emphasize the social class and even class consciousness of the prisoners. But, as a control, we must read as well the many other letters written to the War Department, from patriotic Confederate citizens, likewise complaining of economic hardship and bitterly denouncing speculators as the impediment to victory. Then we would know to weigh the economic evidence carefully, keeping in mind how often it is not present in the prisoners' records.

The same approach is necessary in evaluating the impact of northern policies on slavery. Emancipation politics in the North had but little effect on North Carolina's prisoners, whatever their social class. Only two prisoners, excluding a Presbyterian minister named Sinclair (discussed below), mentioned emancipation as a factor in their loyalties. One was a British-born deserter from the U.S. Army named George Morley, who said he determined to leave the army when he "found that the war was being prosecuted for the negro."[58] The second, Jeptha A. Ward of Chowan County, a twenty-eight-year-old merchant, explained his neutrality in the war by saying that he did not like either emancipation or conscription.[59]

There were, after all, many poor men who were also "true southern men," and the records of North Carolina's political prisoners are more useful for suggesting the importance of other factors, among them religion. With North Carolina's Quakers, religion in several instances completely overrode social class—as in the already mentioned case of the wealthy prisoner Thomas Kennedy. Likewise Calvin G. Perkins, a thirty-six-year-old Quaker merchant from Goldsboro, in Wayne County, arrested 10 April 1862, was described as having a good deal of property. When the Federal forces came to New Bern, Perkins was making salt and was cut off from home. Under the circumstances he took the neutrality oath to the United States. Later, Confederate authorities arrested him. When a Quaker lawyer sued out a writ of habeas corpus for Perkins, the judge delayed the hearing, giving the Confederates more time to find reason for the arrest. After the passage of ten days, President Davis suspended the writ of habeas corpus, and the judge said the matter was settled. Perkins later defiantly told his jailers that arrest and imprisonment led him to believe he was ill-treated and made him more a Union man than ever.[60]

The presence of Quaker meetings expanded the spectrum of permissible religious opinion in the area, and two other religious dissenters show up in the records as well. One was an itinerant preacher named Isom Wood, arrested 4 April 1862 for treasonable conduct and inciting slaves to insurrection. He held strong antislavery convictions and had been repudiated by the Baptists for preaching without a license. Wood opposed slavery on principle, he said, because it violated the Bible's golden rule.[61] James Sinclair, a Presbyterian minister, was described as an "enemy to the government and institutions of the South." He had served as a chaplain of Confederate forces at Bull Run and then applied for a pass to leave the Confederacy. He read Lincoln's Emancipation Proclamation in the meantime and decided to remain in the South. Sinclair's opinions clearly stopped short of the heresy of antislavery, but they were obviously somehow heterodox, and opposing the "institutions of the South" was usually a code for opposition to slavery.[62]

Some other men of property, status, and influence became political prisoners. In particular, W. C. Loftin, of Craven County, arrested on Christmas Eve 1862, was a sixty-year-old farmer described as a "man of property" who had once run for Congress. He admitted going to New Bern to obtain protection for his property from the Union military governor Edward Stanly, but Stanly would not consent unless Loftin took the loyalty oath to the United States. Loftin refused and returned, empty-handed. He said he was loyal to the Confederacy though originally a Union man. Loftin was arrested in part because he had influence over poor men in the area. He denied treasonable communication with the enemy but admitted he had given false information to Confederate authorities about enemy movements—through ignorance, he maintained. Wellford recommended his parole once Loftin took the oath after about five weeks in custody.[63] Seventy-four-year-old John Medlin Sr., of Union County, was described as having at least $100,000 worth of property and working "more than 50 negroes on his farm." He was arrested for trying to protect his son, a deserter who, in company with other Confederate deserters, was being pursued by Confederate authorities, one of whom was killed during the chase. Medlin was released on $10,000 bond.[64] Finally, ownership of three to four thousand acres did not prevent the arrest of Michael Tighlman on the day after Christmas in 1862. The Yankees had first carried Tighlman to New Bern, and he was denounced for arrest, apparently, because people erroneously thought he went voluntarily with the enemy.[65]

Tighlman was mistakenly arrested, if his story could be believed; these men were exceptions anyhow, but wealth is always an exception. No single reason can account for the varieties of people in the South who ran afoul of the Confederate nation, but belief in the political idea of the Union was a frequently cited cause in the records.

Constitutional historians Harold M. Hyman and William E. Wiecek have pointed out that the excesses of the Red Scare and of McCarthyism in the twentieth century "have left a tenacious suspicion that all efforts by government to protect itself against internal enemies are partisan, unnecessary, and hazardous to a fragile democracy."[66] Though the Confederate measures taken for internal security, when noticed at all, have been assumed to be necessary and, if anything, too mild, there is evidence of political repression. The evidence is best for East Tennessee and western Virginia, but the North Carolina records do not defy the pattern of persistent Unionism and the suspicions it aroused.

The element of party oppression is generally lacking in the northern records of civilian prisoners. Northern interrogators rarely identified a prisoner as a Democratic party adherent or voter. Confederate interrogators, on the other hand, wanted to know about the prisoners' prior political affiliations. It was unfortunate that during the secession crisis the opposition parties in the southern states often took the name of Union parties, for during the war being a "Union man" had a sinister meaning. In the North, by contrast, Democrats were members of an opposition party often suspected by Republicans of harboring disloyal people, but their very name did not denote cleavage to the enemy or to the enemy's principles. Thus, despite the lack of a two-party system in the Confederacy, internal security nevertheless placed a heavy burden on those who had once opposed secession at the polls.

8

A PROVINCIAL SOCIETY AT WAR
CIVIL LIBERTIES IN "THE OTHER CONFEDERACY"

THE PATTERN OF SCATTERED SETTLEMENT, consequent rural isolation, and poor transportation bred a provincial society, suspicious of outsiders and hostile even to people from other southern states. The Mississippi lawyer Hawkins, who was so troubled by Earl Van Dorn's martial law, complained of its enforcement by "a man imported—a stranger—from Tennessee." In normal times of peace, the "other Southerners," as Carl Degler dubbed the region's subcultures, could sometimes exist with minimal contact with the dominant society. But a war for national existence, marked by extreme mobilization for military service, served to bring the "other Southerners" into contact with the "true southern men."[1]

A Native American Encounter

The customary ploy of the weaker power in contests for supremacy on the North American continent was to attempt to win the support of the Indians by making a more generous policy toward them than did the stronger party. That policy explained the French relationship with the Indians before the Revolution, and it lay at the heart of the Confederacy's promise never to trouble or molest the Five Civilized Tribes.[2] Actual encounters with Indians, as opposed to avowals made in treaties and policy statements, were another matter.

During the summer campaigns of 1862 in Virginia, Federal soldiers came to a town of Pamunkey Indians, who eked out a living from farming, hunting, and fishing. The soldiers stole horses and hogs and forced some of the Indians into service as guides or as pilots on the rivers. Afterward Confederate forces regained control of the area and arrested some of the Indians and sent them as civilian prisoners to Richmond. When Sydney Baxter reviewed their cases, he demonstrated the paternalism of racism in the old southern elite, and he also revealed the tendency to racial thinking beyond the bounds of slavery apologetics.

Baxter was inclined to discharge the Pamunkeys as an act of mercy. In part, he based his decision on their testimony that they had been forced into guiding the Federal forces. Although he was willing to take that part of their story on faith, he found much of their testimony otherwise dubious and declared some of their explanations of escape from Yankee control as "improbable tales." Baxter's willingness to show leniency stemmed ultimately from his contempt for these people. "Their grade of intelligence is not above that of ordinary negros," he reported. "If restored to freedom they are incapable of doing harm except as pilots on the river, and even in that capacity I think they would do the enemy more harm than service." Yet he was able to make individual judgments, too. He noted that at least two of the prisoners had been arrested "for the faults of their tribe" and not from personal guilt.[3]

I found no prison records from the western departments where most Indians were located, but it is possible to imagine what such records held from examining a letter by Texas's John R. Baylor, defending a controversial order he gave in Arizona Territory in 1862: "If objection is made to that part of my order making the children of the [Apache] Indians *slaves,* I have only to say that the reasons for making slaves of savage Africans applies to savage Indians, and in my opinion, is the very *method* of *civilizing them.*"[4]

African-American Southerners

In the best of times, slaves in the South lived in conditions resembling house arrest, and free blacks, in conditions analogous to parole. The Civil War made these living conditions even worse for some African Americans. Though planters and their kin complained of the relative freedoms enjoyed by slaves during the war when so few white men lived on the plantations to maintain order, in fact the demands from Richmond and other governments for labor on fortifications in the straitened circumstances of the Confederacy overrode those effects for conscripted slave laborers. Moreover, the belief that African Americans posed a security threat heightened white suspicions of the race.

Some African Americans, free and slave, did in fact endanger the Confederacy's national security, as the letters and papers of Confederate and Union officials alike show. The Federal army's basic strategic disadvantage—operating where the enemy knew the country and they did not—was compensated for mainly by the information courageously supplied by the Confederacy's black people. Confederate States Attorney P. H. Aylett, for example, attempting to prosecute a free black man who served as a guide to Federal forces in the disastrous Kilpatrick-Dahlgren raid on Richmond in 1864, stated, "It is a matter of notoriety in the sections of the Confederacy where raids are frequent that the guides of the enemy are nearly always free negroes and slaves."[5] Both sides knew this, though whites on both sides tended to forget later—the Confederates in their Lost Cause mythology of the faithful slave and the Yankees in their ungrateful racist dismissal of the "reliable contrabands" (with the term *reliable* being used ironically).[6]

The famous northern artist-correspondent Edwin Forbes recalled:

The knowledge of the intricate wood-paths and river-fords which the colored people had gained in stolen night visits about the country, aided greatly in simplifying the movements of the Union army. When an important movement was contemplated, the commanding officer would send for some negro in the neighborhood, and if, after close questioning the man was evidently familiar with the surrounding country, his services would be secured. When the column moved he would take position beside the commanding officer at the head, and guide the column through swamps and woods that were apparently impassable, with the intelligence of an Indian hunter.[7]

Guiding the enemy in country was not all glory, however. During the Kilpatrick-Dahlgren raid of 29 February–1 March 1864, for example, the hapless Federal soldiers killed and captured were not the only victims. Confederates interrogating some of the captured Union cavalrymen discovered that one black guide, a slave who had gone north through the lines with an escaped Union officer from Libby Prison, was assigned to the forces by General George G. Meade, commander of the Army of the Potomac. A captured cavalryman named Martin E. Hogan, of Company C, Third Indiana Cavalry, said that the slave "was looked on by the Genl as reliable." The slave had maintained that he lived near Dover Mills and knew a ford across the James River near that point. There proved to be no such thing and never had been, as a local citizen later informed the cavalrymen. The Federal soldiers hanged the slave from a tree limb by the side of the road.[8]

Another guide for the Union raid, Thomas Heath, a free man of color from Goochland Court House, received more lenient treatment when captured by the Confederates, despite his apparent treason. With only one witness to his alleged crime, Heath could not be prosecuted (the Confederate Constitution, like the U.S. Constitution on which it was modeled, required two witnesses to treason), but the Confederate States attorney decided Heath could be held in prison because the writ of habeas corpus was suspended at the time.[9]

Slaves and free black people alike proved troublesome to the Confederacy, as the records of military arrests of civilians show. Among the 4,108 civilian prisoners, at least 345 (about 8 percent) were African American. They are surely underreported. All the available names of black prisoners appear in records from Richmond, where record keeping was superior. Most of the names come from one set of registers of prisoners received at Castle Thunder from 25 February 1863 to 14 June 1864.[10] Similar prison admittance records do not exist for other prisons or periods. It did not occur to local officials to report them to the central authorities, as whites considered their liberties of little consequence, whereas the noisy professions of concern for constitutional liberty and southern rights made even the most impetuous military men tread a little softly around white civilian rights.

Carelessness about black freedom marked the Confederate military from top to bottom. Thus when D. G. Cooper sent in civilian prisoners from Brandon to Meridian, Mississippi, in September 1863, his covering letter stated: "I send you by train this evening Five Prisoners—Sent to these head quarters by Jacksons

Cavalry—Two negroes & 3 Confederate citizens. The names of the latter are as follows."[11] Three prisoners are named, along with the allegation against them, trading with the enemy. No names and no charges were provided for the anonymous African Americans to be received by the commander in Meridian. When the Confederate Congress demanded an accounting of political prisoners early in 1863, the War Department complied fully with the request—that is, in so far as white prisoners were concerned. No African-American prisoners were reported, though they were surely present. War Department officials employed to investigate the cases of civilians in military custody rarely examined black prisoners. Therefore the African-American prison records are spare.

Despite their normal lack of freedom in the Confederacy, African Americans had their few freedoms diminished still more during the war if they lived near the lines or possible points of enemy contact.[12] Though the army's ranks were filled with southern poor nonslaveholding whites, the soldiers seemed generally complicit with the slave regime. At times they apprehended runaway slaves, and military prisons apparently held the slaves until they were reclaimed by their masters. The records describe slaves as "delivered" to their masters—an extraordinary service, if the phrasing can be taken literally, in the transportation-strapped Confederacy. In at least one telling instance, a slave was deposited for safe keeping for two nights in the Castle Thunder military prison.[13]

Although slaves and free blacks represented genuine security threats, not all cases of arrest had to do with national security. Henry Williams, for example, was an eighteen-year-old free black well-digger who was arrested in January 1863, apparently at the instigation of a mail contractor. Williams had been hired out by his grandmother to work for the contractor but had not been paid, and when she took Williams away the contractor had him arrested.[14]

Of the 345 black prisoners identified for this study, 63 were of undetermined status; of the remaining 282 prisoners, 170 (over 60 percent) were identified as slaves. Of these, 11 were captured with the enemy army, likely recaptured from Yankees trying to carry them to freedom. Two more black prisoners had apparently become Federal soldiers and had been captured, but it is not clear why or for how long they were held as civilians. Twenty-six others were taken on their way to or from the enemy lines. Mosby's rangers brought in 8 other African Americans enumerated in the records. Nine more were held on specific charges, some as serious as informing the enemy about Confederate troops. But most appear to have been runaway slaves. Fourteen were specifically identified as "runaway" slaves. Two were slaves whose masters had been captured by the enemy, and another was a hired-out hospital worker who left his post. Others, typically, were identified simply as slaves and the property of an individual named, and there was often some notation of delivery to the owner: 121 of the 170 African-American prisoners fall into this broad category.

Despite evidence that the army helped recover slaves, the army and the planters actually had divergent interests. This was made apparent in a sensational instance when General Samuel Jones, then commanding the Department of Alabama and West Florida, attempted to try several slaves in a military court and to execute some of them.

For the army, slaves loomed mainly as a security risk (and as labor for work on fortifications). For the planter, they were a valuable economic asset. The divergent viewpoints came into conflict in Pensacola in the spring of 1862 when Confederate soldiers apprehended seven slaves attempting to escape to the enemy. Customarily, escaping slaves were returned by the state to their masters' own private discipline. But in such a case as this, the state had a larger interest, or so thought General Jones. As he told the adjutant general of the Confederacy, "Stringent measures should be resorted to both at Pensacola and other places to prevent negroes from conveying information to the enemy. If when detected in the act of escaping to the enemy they are suffered to go at large with only the punishment of the lash, many will escape and convey information to the enemy who would be deterred from attempting it if a few were punished with death for attempting it."[15] Colonel Thomas M. Jones conducted the court, he reported, "not as a regular Court Martial, but rather as an 'Investigating Committee' to determine whether these slaves could be held longer as property without danger to the public, or whether they should be destroyed. Consequently the proceedings are not altogether as regular as they would have been under ordinary circumstances."[16] The colonel spoke of the slaves as though they constituted an infected herd of livestock. The owners of the slaves, William Jackson Morton and R. L. Campbell, protested mightily. Morton ridiculed the general for "playing the Autocrat of Pensacola." "I suppose," he told a friend, "you have seen or heard of his 'pronunciamento' about hanging all the world and the rest of mankind here, and hereabouts, his errecting a gallows in the Public square for the purpose and all such Tomfooolery; there it stood at this day in front of the City Hall and Catholic Church."[17]

Eventually the War Department requested the trial record. The court had tried the slaves under the Fifty-seventh Article of War. They sentenced two to death and four others to be flogged four mornings in succession as many as fifty times. But the Articles of War, in the estimation of many lawyers, applied only to members of the armed services. Even extending the articles to citizens under martial law in Pensacola still left slaves out of their jurisdiction, some said, since slaves were not citizens. Besides, the fifty-seventh article did not forbid *attempting* to correspond with the enemy or to give them intelligence. The military court justified its action under "military necessity."[18]

No black prisoner was ever identified, as so many white ones were, as a

"Union man." Surely the reason for that was that virtually *all* African Americans were in fact supporters of the Union and *were assumed to be by their captors, who knew there was little point in asking.* Moreover, in its narrowly political meaning, "Union man" was applicable only to voters. White Southerners knew or suspected, though they did not often admit it at the time or afterward, that black people were in their hearts disloyal to the Confederacy and desired Union victory over their masters and white fellow Southerners. In the summer of 1864, Secretary of War James A. Seddon rejected a request to exempt free blacks in Culpeper County from impressment to work on Confederate fortifications so that they could cut and haul wood in Culpeper by saying, "The free negroes are not such faithful friends I fear as to make them reliable in a County so likely to be visited by the enemy."[19] Only 1 of the 345 black prisoners was arrested for "disloyalty"—yet in a sense almost all of them were.[20]

Likewise, there exists not a single indication that the oath of allegiance to the Confederacy was ever thought efficacious as a sign of African-American loyalty. Even whites of the most dubious loyalty, formerly professed Union men or desperate Federal deserters, could gain release from prison upon taking the oath, especially if they were released to join the Confederate army. For most of the war African Americans were not allowed to join the army, and thus the Confederates could not be assured that their released prisoners were under firm military discipline outside prison. Racial prejudice meant that the oath of even a free black man was suspect. But, in part, Confederate authorities surely knew that almost no African American, free or slave, was genuinely loyal to the Confederacy.

Though most of the African Americans were likely Unionists, the records offer little proof of their readiness for what many on both sides in the war predicted, "servile insurrection." Not a single slave prisoner was armed when arrested or was carrying poison; not even knives are mentioned in the records. Not one prisoner was arrested for plotting insurrection or for hiding arms or maps. A meager half-dozen were termed "dangerous," two had made threats, and one was allegedly a member of a home guard unit (presumably pro-Union) with white officers. There was never even the loosest allegation of attempts at organizing or gathering or training for rebellion or sabotage.

A revealing incident involving the arrest of free African Americans came on the Gettysburg campaign in 1863. The prisoners—at least sixteen free African Americans from Pennsylvania—were sent back or brought back with the retreating army after the campaign and imprisoned in Castle Thunder. Their apprehension by invading Confederates proved deeply revealing of southern racial prejudice, for Confederate soldiers did not retain white Pennsylvania civilian prisoners. The arrests of free African Americans also offered compelling evidence of the validity of the fears of antislavery reformers that the prewar fugitive slave laws were invitations to kidnapping in the North, for these arrests constituted nothing less than kidnapping.

They also call into question the vaunted gentleness of the Confederate army while operating in enemy territory. Robert E. Lee issued General Orders Number Seventy-three on 27 June 1863 to maintain "the yet unsullied reputation of the army" and to remind his soldiers that "the duties exacted of us by civilization and Christianity are not less obligatory in the country of the enemy than in our own." Rape, plunder, and destruction were thus kept to a minimum, suggests Lee's worshipful biographer Douglas Southall Freeman, and the orders, though obviously useful as propaganda in playing on the northern peace movement, were "drafted in sincerity and . . . enforced with vigor."[21]

Enforcement must have been selective, however, and where free blacks in the North were concerned, enforcement appears to have been quite lax. Free black men, women, and children as young as two years of age were taken by Confederate troops. Edwin Coddington, a northern historian of the Gettysburg campaign, takes a more antisouthern view of the practices of Lee's army in Pennsylvania and specifically denounces the kidnapping of African Americans, which he attributes mostly to "semi-independent" cavalry commands.

But Coddington does not quite get the story right, either. The Pennsylvania free African Americans were not "sent South into slavery."[22] The record suggests, rather, that Confederate troops had them placed in Richmond military prisons as civilian political prisoners. Then they were returned north by flag of truce boat after negotiations with clergymen from the Mercersburg theological school in Pennsylvania.[23]

Poor White Southerners, Religious Minorities, the Insane, and the Ignorant

Much has been written about the factor of guilt over slavery as a cause of Confederate defeat.[24] Nothing in all the records consulted for this book would support such a view, but southern leaders did sometimes reveal their tacit agreement with critiques of slave society that emphasized its ill effects on poor white people. By pitying white Southerners who resisted the Confederacy or got in its way, some leaders may have unconsciously revealed guilt over the adverse consequences of a plantation society for its nonplanting members. If they did not thus betray guilt, they surely showed tacit awareness that slave society failed many of its white citizens and left them in apparent ignorance and cultural backwardness.

Such judgments made about other Southerners often misinterpreted their real political or religious motives for not cooperating with the Confederate war effort, as often was the case in East Tennessee. But the fact of the interpretation is nevertheless significant. It proves the extent of the southern leadership's tacit acknowledgment of the poor whites' critique of slave society for absorbing resources that a free society would apply to capital improvements in infrastructure and education.

The poor were often victims of military arrest. The authorities were not necessarily prejudiced against the poor and may have felt pity for them in many instances, but poverty drove men to acts that put them in danger of arrest. Desperation for work might lead them to attempt to leave the Confederacy or even to work as employees of the enemy in or near occupied areas. The need for salt or other critical supplies could drive them to attempt to find it in forbidden places. In some well-documented cases—and doubtless in others where sentiments were left unspoken—poverty led some to an ideology of opposition to the Confederate state as a nation run by and for the planter class.

Among the poor white prisoners were some pathetic cases. James or Joseph Cavanaugh (or Brunagh), identified as an Italian despite his name, was arrested near Winchester, Virginia, in March 1863. He was described as "an unfortunate," having no trade and traveling around Tennessee with an organ grinder box.[25] Levi Bennett, of Norfolk, Virginia, had been master of a steamer when the war began, but the blockade ended most seafaring work, and the Confederate navy rejected him because of defective hearing. Destitute and in need of a job to support his family, he agreed to work as a pilot for a Union vessel in May 1863. He was arrested in North Carolina and languished in prison for eight months (the final disposition of his case is unknown).[26] A citizen named Fedler, who was a share farmer in Henrico County, Virginia, also found his family starving, and northern men would not let him purchase food unless he took the oath of allegiance. Taking the oath might constitute treason unless it was taken under duress, but Sydney Baxter was willing to interpret the plight of the prisoner's hungry family as duress enough for this "very ignorant feeble obscure person." Baxter discharged Fedler from military prison but took the case to a grand jury.[27]

Several of the prisoners proved to be mentally ill. In fact, the condition was often enough encountered that standard procedures called for a medical examination of such persons (there was, of course, a risk that genuine saboteurs, spies, and traitors might feign insanity after being captured). The practical but somewhat cruel resolution of mental cases was to export the problem to the North if possible. Thus Allen Leonard, a Philadelphian arrested at West Point, Virginia, on 2 June 1862, was imprisoned for expressing strong desire for Union victory and on suspicion of trying to get to the enemy's lines near the Seven Pines battlefield. He had been held on a previous arrest for four months. On the second occasion, Leonard was declared a "lunatic," and despite his having lived in the South for seven years, he was held for exchange with the North as an enemy alien.[28]

Some of these unfortunates were shuttled back and forth between the cruel nations. Auguste Sheran, a beggar with one arm, came to Richmond from Baltimore in a Federal flag-of-truce boat. He said he wanted to return to the North, and Confederate authorities after his arrest willingly sent the Sardinian back by flag of truce in January 1863.[29]

Another sad case was Edward Barnes, a Canadian who was ill treated about equally by North and South. He was arrested in Pocahontas County, Virginia, on 20 November 1861—perhaps on suspicion of spying. Confederate pickets took Barnes, apparently on an open road; he had left his previous employment as a farm laborer and was heading to the Mississippi River to chop wood for steamers. Though he was initially examined by Baxter, the War Department lost the report, and Barnes was not examined again until B. R. Wellford Jr. went to Salisbury to prepare the report to Congress on civilians in military custody early in 1863.

Barnes had been in prison some fifteen months by then. Wellford, determining that Barnes was a British subject, recommended that he be given to the British consul to send north. Nothing happened, and in August, Barnes was still a Confederate prisoner. He was described by this time as "almost literally naked." Sometime thereafter, Barnes was apparently sent by flag-of-truce boat north, only to be arrested there on 20 October 1864. "This man appears to be idiotic," noted investigating authorities of the United States War Department.[30] Similarly, a man named Rush, described as a cattle driver who could not speak English, was declared idiotic: he had been sent north by flag-of-truce boat three times.[31]

The Confederacy had no monopoly on illiterates, but they had their share. Benjamin Carney, a laborer arrested at the Orange and Alexandria bridge over the Rappahannock, allegedly making his way to the Yankees, was described as an illiterate with no property. After four months in Castle Thunder, he was sent to the army as a conscript.[32] Robert Morton, a sixteen-year-old from Monroe County, Tennessee, was released because he was "too ignorant to do harm."[33] Daniel Wolff, arrested as a Union man in Wyoming County, Virginia, in the winter of 1863–64, denied the allegation. The War Department examiner noted that he was "very much disfigured by cross eyes" and "exceedingly simple." There were no papers on file in his case, but Wolff was sent to the enrolling officer to be put in a regiment remote from his home.[34]

Felix Hinkle, a sixty-two-year-old man from Hardy County, Virginia, who apparently was arrested for contact with Unionist or Federal forces, denied ever having been in the camps of the pro-Union home guards. He was a Union man but had acquiesced in secession and was a little confused. "The old man," reported commissioner Baxter, "thought he and many of his neighbors voted for Lincoln and Everett but does not know. Does not remember the names of the candidates. Says he voted the Union ticket." When Baxter consulted a local notable on Hinkle, he learned that the man was honest and had "certainly voted for Bell and Everett." The informant added that there were many Union men in Hinkle's neighborhood, but that they had remained quiet and were gradually coming around to support of the Confederacy.[35]

Descriptions of prisoners come from the notes of their interrogators and rarely from the prisoners' own hands. They are rarely systematic enough to derive reliable statistics on the literacy of the civilian prisoners taken: we are allowed only occasional glimpses of well-described prisoners. It is worth noting that the authorities themselves repeatedly and unconsciously admitted their society's failures in their attitudes toward lower-class Confederate citizens, especially those from nonplantation districts. In lieu of statistics, incidents interpreted as mass panic in the Confederacy offer an interesting contrast with the North.

The most astonishing example, not paralleled in the home-front experience of the North, was the great Shenandoah Valley panic of 1862. When the governor of Virginia proclaimed the draft of the state militia in March, "a wild and almost frantic panic arose, in several neighborhoods" of the Shenandoah Valley, said Sydney Baxter. More than seventy men who fled for the far western counties of the state were captured. "The impression seems to have gone abroad," Baxter explained, "that the valley of Virginia was to be abandoned to the Yankees, and all the male citizens between 16 and 60 were to be drafted and taken East of the Blue Ridge to defend that portion of the State."

The willingness to interpret the movement of the Shenandoans as ignorant panic led to lenient treatment of them, but the authorities at first misinterpreted and underestimated political and social forces underlying the citizens' dislike of Confederate mobilization. Baxter was willing to believe, as were many southern leaders otherwise defensive about their society, that great masses of their people were as stupid as sheep. Reporting on the cases of thirty-one prisoners from Rockingham and Augusta Counties, Baxter explained to the War Department that none of the men who fled were really attached to the northern cause or unfaithful to the South. Afterward, they were ashamed of their panic, he said. Many of the prisoners, he pointed out, were mere boys eighteen to twenty-one years of age, and all of the prisoners were ignorant of public matters—simply ignorant country youths. All were now willing to volunteer and "should be placed in Regiments in which they will as far as possible be exempt from demoralizing influences." On 13 May they were ordered released to volunteer.[36]

Pacifist Religious Minorities

Investigating authorities also determined that nearly half of the prisoners from the Shenandoah Valley had fled not from ignorance but from firm conviction. These were the Dunkards and Mennonites of Augusta and Rockingham Counties. "One of the tenets of those churches," Baxter explained, "is that the law of God forbids shedding human blood in battle and this doctrine is uniformly taught to all their people." He did not doubt the sincerity of "their declaration that they left home to avoid the draft of the militia and under the belief that by the draft they would be placed in a situation in which they would be compelled to violate their consciences."

He was able to ascertain evidence of their loyalty to the Confederacy. Some of the men had attempted to procure substitutes. Others did what they could to encourage volunteering. Some furnished horses for cavalry. "All of them," Baxter concluded, "are friendly to the South and they express a willingness to contribute all their property if necessary to establish our liberties. I am informed a law will probably pass exempting these persons from military duty on payment of a pecuniary compensation. Those . . . unable to make the payment will cheerfully go into service as teamsters or in any employment in which they are not required to shed blood." With this solution on the legislative horizon, Baxter recommended the release of all the religious prisoners on taking the oath of allegiance to the Confederacy.[37]

The peculiar turn taken in the valley panic incident serves as a reminder that religious minorities occasionally suffered at the hands of Confederate authorities, though legislation allowing them alternatives to conscription and a generally sympathetic attitude in the Protestant South—among persons like Baxter—kept interference with religion from being a major feature of the system. Yet the extreme consciousness of numbers inferior to those of the North, as the Mennonite historian Samuel Horst points out, at times drove Confederates to oppress these minorities. Mennonites such as John Kline, Jacob Wine, Henry May, Joseph Beery, Solomon Beery, and Henry Beery were arrested in 1863, some of them more than once, on charges of aiding desertion.[38]

The relative ease with which the communities of religious minorities met the exemption requirements of Confederate conscription (a $500 commutation fee, essentially) is proof that these minorities were not motivated by social class but by religious belief and the influence that belief had on their political views. In the end, the Mennonites and Dunkards suffered their greatest economic hardships and were substantially driven out of the Shenandoah Valley by the Federal invasion led by Phillip H. Sheridan in 1864, the point of which was to destroy food and farms in the valley as sources of supply for Confederate armies.[39]

The revelation of religious motivations among half the valley prisoners, however, serves to point up the willingness of Confederate authorities to believe that their society harbored great ignorance and unsophistication about public matters. They jumped to the conclusion that ignorance was the problem, when in fact many were obviously motivated by religious conviction. Political ignorance, innocence, or indifference was rarely the problem, either. On the contrary, persons arrested often held political views critical of secession or the Confederacy.

The valley panic was but the most spectacular incident. The "stampedes" from East Tennessee to Kentucky to avoid Confederate conscription and control likewise revealed—mainly in the nomenclature applied—the widespread willingness to regard large segments of southern society as ludicrously ignorant. What can be said conclusively about the "panics" and "stampedes" is that the readiness of the Confederate authorities to attribute mass behavior to the ignorance of its people provided unconscious indictment of their society for consistent underinvestment in education and economic development.

Foreigners and the Problem of Alien Enemies

The decade preceding the Civil War was marked by the emergence of the greatest anti-immigrant and anti-Catholic movements in all of American history. A nativist Protestant party in politics arose and came close to gaining a firm place in the nation's system of political parties. The American (Know-Nothing) party enjoyed considerable sway in the southern states before the war, especially in the upper South. Their sentiments did not go away when war came to the overwhelmingly Protestant and heavily native-born South. If the pattern of isolated rural settlement did not give rise to urban anti-immigrant and anti-Catholic movements that were as sweeping in nature as the one in the North in the mid-1850s, it did make for a provincial society.

Moreover, conservative Southerners sometimes feared the radical political ideals held by refugees from European revolutionary movements. Jefferson Davis, who as a Democrat before the war had tangled with Know-Nothing opposition, provoked a spirited response when he expressed mild "sympathy" for foreign veterans of European independence movements who recognized "the same cause as vindicated by the Confederate States of America."[40] Confederate Secretary of War Leroy Pope Walker, a former Whig who had not dallied with the Know-Nothings, countered with the opinion that any brigade composed of foreign-born men ought especially to have a native-born officer "when it is considered that most of the modern 'Refugees' from Europe, following to this Country Kossuth and Garibaldi, entertain 'Red-Republican' sentiments that closely accord with those entertained by 'Black-Republicans,' and constituting the life & death issue existing between the North and the South."[41]

Suspicion of foreigners tainted many Confederates and caused considerable harassment of foreigners. Before proceeding to the evidence of victimization of foreign-born civilians, it is important to clarify the problem of alien enemies in the Civil War. The North had available the Alien Enemies Act still on the books from the Federalist era. It proved of little use to them, however, because the enemies that the Lincoln administration felt the need to restrain were not aliens—or rather, the administration claimed they were not aliens. The Lincoln government could not use the law for their most pressing and obvious security problems during the Civil War, because the whole point of the war for the North was that Southerners were not aliens but Americans. Therefore the military prisons of the North swelled with southern-born citizens and southern residents from occupied areas who came to be described in history as "political prisoners." For the Confederates, there was no ideological or constitutional problem with defining people from the North who happened to be in the Confederacy as alien enemies. From the southern perspective, the whole point of the war was to prove that the South was indeed a separate nation from the United States.

The Alien Enemies Act of the Confederate States of America, approved 8 August 1861, proclaimed "all natives, citizens, denizens or subjects of the hostile nation or government, being males of fourteen years of age and upward, who shall be within the Confederate States and not citizens thereof . . . liable to be apprehended, restrained or secured and removed as alien enemies." The act did not apply to U.S. citizens residing in the Confederacy who intended to become citizens of the Confederate States or to citizens of Delaware, Maryland, Kentucky, Missouri, the District of Columbia, the territories of Arizona and New Mexico, or the Indian territory south of Kansas—as long as they could not be charged with actual hostility to the Confederacy or other crimes against the public safety and would acknowledge the authority of the new government.

After passage of the act, the president was to issue a proclamation to U.S. citizens within the Confederacy directing them to depart within forty days or be declared alien enemies. Courts were charged with examining any alleged alien enemies and deporting them or otherwise restraining them thereafter. Davis issued the prescribed proclamation on 14 August 1861.[42]

Though not much admired, such acts are common in modern nations at war. What is remarkable about the Confederacy's act is not so much its existence, therefore, as its exemption from criticism and, except in one case, from comment in history books written since the Civil War. The four-volume *Encyclopedia of the Confederacy* has no entry for the Alien Enemies Act, and Wilfred Buck Yearns's *Confederate Congress* does not discuss the passage of this bill. It is not mentioned in Emory M. Thomas's basic history, *The Confederate Nation, 1861–1865,* nor does it figure in the roll-call analysis on which *The Anatomy of the Confederate Congress* is based.[43]

William M. Robinson's *Justice in Grey* mentions the act but gives it essentially a barrister's interpretation, from the standpoint of determining who was eligible to sue in Confederate courts. Otherwise Robinson regards it not as a sinister measure but as one allowing the gentle Confederate administration to deal leniently with disloyal people: "A native taken in an act of disloyalty, or suspected of such, was generally regarded as an alien enemy on the theory that upon the dissolution of the Old Union every citizen had the right to determine whether he would remain a citizen of the United States or go with his State to the new Confederacy."[44]

In fact, the act was *never* applied as Robinson said it was— to expel native-born Southerners rather than to imprison or otherwise punish them for disloyalty. The act's principal effects went well beyond the pettifogging question of who could sue in Confederate courts. Moreover, the timing of the act seems significant. It was passed in the flush of victory, after Generals P. G. T. Beauregard and Joseph Johnston threw back in confused disorder the Federal forces at First Bull Run, and not in the anxieties of defeat. It revealed confidence in refusing to count as aliens the citizens of such border states as Maryland, Kentucky, and Missouri, which many thought likely to secede after Confederate military success. And it revealed an aggressive willingness to build a nation without help from any lukewarm or reluctant people. The act was intended to expel people who were not, in the phrase then commonly in use, "true southern men."

Nearly as many political prisoners proved to be alien enemies as Union men— 10.9 percent. Some were arrested because of their northern birth alone. A few of the enemy aliens were unlucky Yankees: merchants who set up shop in captured territory that was later recaptured, incautious newspaper reporters, or sutlers and their employees who got too close to the battlefield. Most enemy alien prisoners were southerners who after arrest and interrogation were found to have been born in the North, and classifying them as alien enemies offered a category of offense against the state and a pretense for holding them.

The legality of such summary declarations of alien status is not at all clear. William M. Robinson argued that "the act contemplated summary expulsion of alien enemies," but "the courts allowed jury determination of disputed citizenship or friendly intentions."[45] But the act of Congress called for the president to prescribe regulations for apprehending alien enemies who did not voluntarily depart after the initial proclamation of warning. In four regulations issued on 14 August 1861, Davis specified district attorneys, marshals, and other officers of the Confederate States as the enforcers and clearly contemplated orders from courts expelling the aliens or ordering their confinement. Military authority was mentioned only in the instance of aliens who were expelled and then returned to the Confederate States; they were to be treated as spies or prisoners of war. In fact, the habeas corpus commissioners made most of the determinations of authority. The act and the regulations published pursuant to it did not contemplate military arrest or military determination of alien enemy status.[46]

The law was not applied to real foreigners—Europeans resident in the South, for example—because, though alien, they were not enemies of the Confederacy.[47] Nevertheless, conscription posed special problems for aliens. Aliens did not have to serve, as was the conventional practice under international law, but they did have to register with the provost marshal and procure exemption papers from an official representative of their native government. Lists of foreigners were created after the imposition of conscription in April 1862, and in Richmond alone in 1862 and 1863, 1,078 resident foreigners registered. The ledgers contain a physical description of the individual, his signature, and the name of the consul whose protection he claimed.[48]

Frustration with the majority tyranny of the South showed itself in the case of Adam Scharrer, a Bavarian immigrant in Danville, Virginia. His seditious sentiment was not pro-Union. Enraged at taunts that all foreigners ought to be in the army, Scharrer declared in a fit of passion that he would never serve and "he wished some foreign power would come and crush" the Confederacy. The Danville mayor apparently sent him in to Richmond in August 1863. Investigation determined that Scharrer was of conscript age and could offer no evidence that he intended to return to Europe. Therefore, since he was a domiciled alien his case could be resolved by sending him to the conscript bureau.[49]

Foreign residents ran increasing risk of being conscripted anyway and were subjected to insults from native whites for their exemption from service. James Magee, the acting British consul in Mobile, Alabama, thus wrote the secretary of war on 10 September 1862, "I am inundated with letters from various interior places in the States of Florida, Alabama, & Mississippi from British Subjects to whom I have *under your own oath* given protection, complaining that their conscripting officers would in no wise recognise said protection and insist on their going into the service."[50] Similar complaints came from other parts of the Confederacy. A French official reported in 1863 that most Frenchmen in San Antonio, Texas, had been arrested, taken from their homes, and imprisoned if they refused enrollment in the armed services.[51] From Savannah, Georgia, the British consul, who was named Fullerton, told the secretary of war, "Col Weems, the enrolling officer for this State, is arresting British Subjects indiscriminately even those having exemptions from his predecessor based on certificates of nationality issued by me." Colonel Weems interpreted the law, Fullerton reported, to mean that foreigners who had lived in the country one or two years must be considered domiciled, and he acted accordingly. Fullerton assured the War Department that he did not issue protection papers to foreigners who had illegally exercised the franchise in the United States or the Confederate States or who had declared their intention to become citizens of their new country.

The British consul in Richmond complained of the same Confederate practices.[52] Suspicion of foreigners reached the top of the Confederate government. Thus S. G. French wrote the secretary of war from Petersburg, Virginia, early in the spring of 1863 complaining that

a great many foreign subjects who have "protection papers," also a considerable number of deserters from the enemy [are] running at large. Can these foreign subjects be reached under the proclamation of the president granting all
of them forty days to leave the country or take the oath of allegiance? If not
then would it not be well to cause these two classes of people to be removed
say fifty miles from our lines and from any tidewater communications either
by act of congress [or] by orders from the War Department?

I am sure they have it in their power to work evil here in our midst—They
can live as well in the interior as here.

Jefferson Davis endorsed this letter: "There is propriety in having sufficient guarantee of the good conduct of such persons or their arrest &c."[53]

Former Know-Nothings in the Confederacy maintained a steady distrust of
foreigners. Some still dreamed of systematic exclusion of them from politics.
Thus Augustus S. Merrimon, a Union Whig from Buncombe County, North Carolina, was thinking ahead to the aftermath of Confederate victory when he
drafted "Memoranda: A Desirable System of Governmental Policy for the Confederate States" on 20 December 1861. Along with reviving traditionally Whig-
gish programs like internal improvements and a protective tariff, Merrimon
thought that "Foreigners should *not hold office,* nor be allowed to *vote* until they
have resided in the Gov. *at least twenty one years.*"[54]

Under the conditions of conscription, desperate manpower needs, and provincial suspicion, foreigners in the Confederacy were protected not by the law but
by the consuls. These resident foreign officials issued protection papers, called
the attention of the War Department to abuses, and gained release of foreigners from military custody—under ultimate threat of foreign government force.
British subjects went from feeling unwelcome to being downright insecure when,
in October 1863, the Davis administration expelled British consuls from southern cities. With no official representatives left in the Confederacy, English residents in the South could no longer obtain protection papers. Given the practices
revealed by the protests of the consuls before they departed, it is difficult to
believe that the law would protect the foreigners from the conscription officers.

The sense one gleans from the day-to-day documents, from first to last, is the
fragility of the tolerance of foreigners in the Confederacy. Symptomatic of the
occasionally perilous status of foreign-born citizens in the Confederacy was one
of the very first acts undertaken by the provost guard when martial law was proclaimed in Richmond. On 6 March 1862 authorities raided the German Turner
hall, arresting several citizens and discovering that there were Union flags folded
in the cupboards and a goddess of liberty holding a Union shield painted on the
wall.[55] Thus in 1864 the experienced and paternalistic Sydney Baxter and the sea-
soned Isaac Carrington dealt with the cases of three Irishmen, Edward Murphy,

John Fogarty, and James Burgess, who were arrested by Confederate pickets as they apparently attempted to go north. The prisoners maintained that they were looking for work on Virginia farms. Two had been workers at the Tredegar iron factory in Richmond.

Baxter got his back up over this case and sought the severest punishment—trials for treason. "Many foreigners," he protested, "reside here and make their living and some of them fortunes out of our people. They generally hold foreign protection papers [as the three Irishmen did in this case], and when their services are needed for the defence of the city refuse them, and when the enemy approach the city in defiance of the authorities they go over to them." Why the poor factory workers Fogarty, Murphy, and Burgess should take the blame for profiteering foreigners was by no means clear. Baxter made a long and tortuous argument that going to the enemy was treason, in part because affording mechanical aid to war production (the detainees were mechanics) could hurt the Confederacy badly. Carrington, at this late date, remarkably enough, asked whether the men could be tried by court-martial. B. R. Wellford prevailed, however, and allowed the men to be set free to work at the Tredegar company.[56]

Whatever the status of southern rights for "true southern men," by the end of the war the civil liberties of those Southerners on the margins of the society were definitely deteriorating.

PART FOUR

JEFFERSON DAVIS AND HISTORY

JEFFERSON DAVIS KEPT HIS EYE ON Abraham Lincoln and read his public papers closely. The Confederate president seized an early opportunity to comment on Lincoln's first extended statement on the war, his message of 4 July 1861 to a special session of Congress. Sixteen days later Davis offered his own annual message to the Confederate Congress, in which he called attention to Lincoln's

> assertion . . . that the Executive possesses the power of suspending the writ of *habeas corpus,* and of delegating that power to military commanders, at his discretion, and . . . [to] the additional statement of opinion in the same paper, that it is proper, in order to execute the laws, that "some single law, made in such extreme tenderness of the citizen's liberty, that practically it relieves more of the guilty than the innocent, should, to a very limited extent, be violated."
>
> We may well rejoice that we have forever severed our connection with a government that thus tramples on all the principles of constitutional liberty, and with a people in whose presence such avowals could be hazarded.[1]

There was room in Davis's message to talk about Lincoln and to boast of citizens' liberties in the South because the Confederate president had decided to quit talking about slavery. That had been the staple of his old stump-speaking days in Mississippi and of his career as a spokesman in the U.S. Senate for the planters.[2] But Davis had chosen not to mention slavery in his inaugural address as president of the provisional Confederate States of America back in February. As historian William E. Dodd noted, that was "an omission he had hardly ever made since he entered public life in 1844."[3]

Slavery had become a potentially divisive subject that might remind white yeomen of their differences with planters when their help was sorely needed to fill Confederate ranks. For the time being, talk of sacred civil liberties filled the Confederate void. But it was mostly that—talk. Action was another matter, as the previous chapters of this book show. Military arrests of civilians posed problems for the Confederate president almost from the start of the war. Less than a month after his message to Congress denouncing Lincoln's suspension of the writ of habeas corpus, Davis was negotiating personally with a political prisoner, Thomas A. R. Nelson of East Tennessee, for an agreement to end his criticism of the Confederate government in exchange for discharge from military arrest.[4]

Davis, like Lincoln, never dreamed what war would bring. Months earlier, in January 1861, when he was still a U.S. Senator, Davis had denounced the actions of the federal government in the Sumter crisis by asking, "What power has the President to use the Army and Navy except to execute process? Are we to have drum-head courts substituted for those which the Constitution and laws provide? Are we to have sergeants sent over the land instead of civil magistrates?"[5] Of course, "sergeants" had apprehended Nelson, and before the year was out, Davis's secretary of war, Judah P. Benjamin, would explicitly institute drumhead trials for other citizens of East Tennessee.

Jefferson Davis's letter to political prisoner Thomas Nelson is printed in the standard ten-volume edition of Davis's collected works—only four pages away from the document in which Davis denounced Lincoln as one who "tramples on all principles of constitutional liberty." That this anomaly should have gone without comment from the editor of the volumes, Dunbar Rowland, seems remarkable, especially because Rowland chose to entitle the work *Jefferson Davis, Constitutionalist*. Rowland might better have employed for his compilation of Davis's papers the more customary and less celebratory title for such volumes: "The Complete Works of" or "The Collected Works of."

But Mississippi historian Rowland felt compelled, as has often been the case with authors writing on Davis, not only to present him to the reading public but also to justify him at the same time. And Rowland chose the customary justification for those wishing to put Davis in the best light: constitutional rectitude. Davis saw himself in that light in retirement after the war. The interpretation echoes in historical works on the Confederacy to this day. Even Davis's critics continue to give it grudging acknowledgment. Thus Paul D. Escott concluded, "At no time did he abandon his claim to be a defender of states' rights and individual liberties, and indeed in these areas his record was much better than that of his northern counterpart." The modern edition of the *Papers of Jefferson Davis,* though representing a new age in editorial technique, follows on this subject perilously close intellectually to the Rowland-"Constitutionalist" tradition. Thus the editors are careful to inform us that "Davis was authorized to suspend the writ of habeas corpus only three times during the war. . . . He was very conservative in employing the power and in declaring martial law, actions so inimical to state rights."[6]

That old interpretation of steady constitutional rectitude was more an article of faith than a product of scholarship. Not a single book or article on the subject of Jefferson Davis and the constitution was published until 1996.[7] The subject deserves more than the attention of one journal article and thus chapter 9 of this book provides an exploration of Jefferson Davis's conception of the Confederate Constitution and his powers under it.

9

JEFFERSON DAVIS AND THE WRIT
OF HABEAS CORPUS

For the first eighteen months of the Civil War, Abraham Lincoln and Jefferson Davis faced the same problem of grand strategy: attempting to assure the adherence of the border slave states to their cause. Although it is rarely mentioned among the factors that might have brought victory for the Confederacy—European diplomatic intervention, a fluke northern battlefield disaster, or simply outlasting the North's political will to fight are the usual possibilities enumerated—the first and best strategy was to lure all the slave states to the southern side. Abraham Lincoln knew this would mean southern victory, and to his credit as a geopolitical thinker, Jefferson Davis also realized it and pursued the strategy with a vengeance.

We unfortunately often lose sight of the high political drama surrounding the attempts to secure the border slave states. No one does a better job of reminding us of the importance of the border area early in the war than historian James M. McPherson. Modern Americans have emblazoned on their memories the salient fact that eleven states seceded from the Union and formed the Confederacy, and to this day those states are regarded as forming a distinct region of the country. But in 1861 Americans had no idea how many states would secede. They had no way of knowing when the wave of secession, which commenced 20 December 1860 with South Carolina's secession ordinance, would end. As it turned out, one wave ended by 1 February 1861 after Mississippi, Alabama, Florida, Georgia, Louisiana, and Texas quickly followed South Carolina's lead. At that point a majority of slave states—eight—*remained in the Union,* and American politicians focused on getting or keeping them on their side.

The states remaining in the Union included Virginia, Tennessee, Arkansas, North Carolina, Missouri, Maryland, Kentucky, and Delaware. They contained, as McPherson reminds us, "more than half of [the South's] . . . population, two-thirds of its white population, three-quarters of its industrial capacity, half of its horses and mules, three-fifths of its livestock and food crops." The states also contained key cities—Baltimore, St. Louis, Louisville, Richmond, Nashville, and Memphis.[1] After President Lincoln responded to the attack on Fort Sumter in April 1861 with a proclamation calling for 75,000 men to put down the insurrection, Virginia, Arkansas, Tennessee, and North Carolina joined the Confederacy.

Four slave states remained in the Union. Delaware, with a negligible slave population, was never in doubt and was very small anyway, but enlisting Maryland, Missouri, and Kentucky became the focus of most politicians, North and South. Davis never had to explain his policy, but Lincoln did so explicitly in September 1861 when he revoked a proclamation issued by General John C. Fremont that would have freed the slaves of rebels in Missouri. Lincoln, fearing that meddling with slave property in Missouri would drive Kentucky to secede, commented, "I think to lose Kentucky is nearly the same as to lose the whole game. Kentucky gone, we can not hold Missouri, nor, as I think, Maryland. These all against us, and the job on our hands is too large for us. We should as well consent to separation at once, including the surrender of this capitol."[2]

Davis, too, recognized the importance of the border states, and both presidents reacted rationally to the problem. But because the southern and northern situations were slightly different, the two presidents pursued precisely opposite policies to reach the same goal. The critical difference lay in what might be called political inertia. Lincoln had an advantage with those states that had not yet seceded. His job was to keep them in. Davis's problem was more difficult: he had to lure them over to his side. Davis became a salesman; Lincoln became a warden or truant officer.

This situation explains something that has long mystified biographers of Lincoln, and it explains what has long seemed an important difference between Lincoln and Davis. Lincoln biographers have been at a loss to explain his early and easy embrace of the suspension of the writ of habeas corpus. Lincoln, however, recognized the realities of power and instituted policies permitting military arrests of civilians that ostensibly made it easier to suppress any movement that might take Missouri, Maryland, or Kentucky out of the Union. His policy on domestic civil liberties was at first mainly a function of his border state policy. Thus Lincoln shielded public opinion in Kentucky by revoking emancipation in Missouri on 3 September 1861, even as he allowed martial law to be declared in Missouri. He made his move in Maryland less than two weeks later, with a series of arrests on 13-16 September in which Federal forces imprisoned secessionist members of the Maryland legislature and certain allegedly disloyal Baltimore officials.

Jefferson Davis's policy on domestic civil liberties was likewise a border state strategy. But Davis enjoyed a less powerful position in each of the states in question and opted for a pose of dedication to civil liberty as a way of *attracting* these states to his side. For over a year he tried to sell the border on the virtues of membership in the Confederacy by stressing the freedoms they would enjoy there.

Historians have mistaken the policy difference between Lincoln and Davis on civil liberties for a deeper difference of political philosophy. They have judged Davis more reluctant because of habitual and consistent constitutional scruples to curtail civil liberties and to take actions like those Lincoln took in Maryland and Missouri. In truth, Davis's initial reluctance was temporary and situational.

The resulting southern policy, however, was well suited to the early days of the Confederacy. For one thing, it helped fire Confederates with zeal against their national enemy, depicted as a ruthless despotism. More important, Davis hoped it would expose the United States in world opinion as a tyrannical and oppressive country. This foreign policy component of the strategy dovetailed with the Confederate strategy of gaining European recognition or intervention. Thus on 11 November 1861 Secretary of State Robert M. T. Hunter sent a letter of instruction to Henry Hotze, who would become the Confederacy's agent in London. Hunter explicitly and carefully laid out the Confederate policy line and included this order: "You will keep constantly before the public view in Great Britain, the tyranny of the Lincoln Government, its utter disregard of the personal rights of its citizens, and its other notorious violations of law."[3]

Hunter's instructions closely paralleled the case Davis was making in his public papers in 1861, and the policy definitely scored some points with European powers. The British representative in Washington, Lord Lyons, had long since denounced the "monstrous" military arrests of civilians in the North in communiqués to his superiors in London. Americans, Lyons observed acidly, seemed to favor "placing their own lives and liberties, . . . without any reserve, into the hands of the officers of the army." Northerners appeared to be "recklessly applauding the suspension, without law, of all their liberties." The Lincoln government, he reported, "sends any one it pleases to a Fortress—and orders the Commandant to decline to make any return to a Writ of Habeas Corpus."[4]

Confederates took heart early in 1862 when Blackwood's, the distinguished British periodical, featured an article by James Ferguson, who had visited America the previous autumn. Ferguson noted: "For this war, the North is content to see extinguished that freedom which was her boast. . . . So far, in this war in the boasted seat of freedom and independence, a secret police, nightly arrests, without cause assigned, suspension of writs of habeas corpus, warnings, suspension and suppression of newspapers, are common and acknowledged." Conversely, the British traveler observed about the other side, "in the presence of actual war, beleaguered, threatened with the fate of conquered nations, the Government has had recourse to no exceptional proceedings . . . the liberty of individuals is respected . . . the press is free . . . newspapers publish without molestation the sharpest diatribes on the authorities and on the conduct of the war."[5]

J. H. Dillon, who had a regular correspondence with the northern Democratic financier and manager S. L. M. Barlow, epitomized some conservative British opinion. He told Barlow on 27 September 1862 that "it is quite impossible to estimate the injury which the cause of the North has sustained by the arbitrary despotism of the Lincoln administration. . . . if recognition should take place, it will be chiefly owing to the practical abrogation of the constitution by the Lincoln

admin." Davis had found a vulnerable spot in the Union's armor.[6] Thus with
some success, Davis identified "constitutional liberty" as the nation's goal for the
first year of the Confederacy's existence, as historian Paul D. Escott has pointed
out. But it is crucial to understand that the ideology served strategic purposes,
and those purposes explain the operative content of Davis's public papers, many
of which otherwise appear bland and platitudinous. A prime example is his message to Congress of 18 November 1861. The date happened to fall only ten days
after the bridge-burning revolt in East Tennessee, but the address contains no
hint of that trouble or of the draconian measures taken to counteract it by the
Davis administration, because Davis had at the moment greater reason than ever
to emphasize the liberty theme abroad.

It was notorious that the North was involved in a deep diplomatic crisis with
Great Britain. An overzealous United States naval captain had removed two
Confederate diplomatic representatives heading for Europe from a British mail
steamer called the *Trent* and had made them political prisoners. With England
watching America closely, Davis needed more than ever to convey the image of
the Union as a tyrannical power that disregarded law and rights.

Davis boasted in his message that recent Confederate military victories
"proved that numbers cease to avail when directed against a people fighting for
the sacred right of self-government and the privileges of freemen." He denounced
the violation of the laws of nations in the *Trent* affair and was careful also to
describe the principles of the Lincoln administration at home: "When [the citizens of the Confederacy] . . . see a President making war without the assent of
Congress; when they behold judges threatened because they maintain the writ
of *habeas corpus* so sacred to freemen; when they see justice and law trampled
under the armed heel of military authority, and upright men and innocent
women dragged to distant dungeons upon the mere edict of a despot; . . . they
believe that there must be some radical incompatibility between a people and
themselves."[7] Davis began to refer to the conflict regularly as "this war for constitutional liberty and State rights."[8]

By the time Davis delivered his inaugural address as president under the permanent constitution, on 22 February 1862, East Tennessee prisoners "dragged to
distant dungeons" in Tuscaloosa or even hanged publicly had become bywords
in Union propaganda. In the speech, Davis chose nevertheless to maintain the
theme of civil liberty—for the sake of luring those slave states, like Maryland,
that remained outside the confederation. He could now borrow rhetoric developed by the political opposition in the North, which complained bitterly of Lincoln's "bastilles":

> The confidence of the most hopeful among us must have been destroyed by
> the disregard they [the enemy] have recently exhibited for all the time-honored

bulwarks of civil and religious liberty. Bastiles filled with prisoners, arrested without civil process or indictment duly found; the writ of *habeas corpus* suspended by Executive mandate; a State Legislature controlled by the imprisonment of members whose avowed principles suggested to the Federal Executive that here might be another added to the list of seceded States; elections held under threats of a military power; civil officers, peaceful citizens, and gentlewomen incarcerated for opinion's sake—proclaimed the incapacity of our late associates to administer a Government as free, liberal, and humane as that established for our common use.

For proof of the sincerity of our purpose to maintain our ancient institutions, we may point to the Constitution of the Confederacy and the laws enacted under it, as well as to the fact that through all the necessities of an unequal struggle there has been no act on our part to impair personal liberty or the freedom of speech, or thought, or of the press. The courts have been open, the judicial functions fully executed, and every right of the peaceful citizen maintained as securely as if a war of invasion had not disturbed the land.[9]

What Davis said was untrue, of course, but East Tennessee and western Virginia constituted special cases somehow filed in another compartment of his mind.

Davis's blind spot for the Appalachian troubles was not the most remarkable feature of the inaugural address. Delivered on 22 February 1862, it preceded by only five days Davis's own suspension of the writ of habeas corpus after signing a congressional act giving him the power. From Dodd to Escott, all the careful and objective historians writing on Jefferson Davis have noticed this awkward juxtaposition. Davis, ever careful in crafting his papers, did not state, as he had on the preceding 18 November, that the writ of habeas corpus was "sacred to freemen." Now he said that the problem in the North was suspension "by Executive mandate." The writ of habeas corpus had lost its "sacred" status in the Confederacy.

New Directions

With the authorization by the Confederate Congress to suspend the writ of habeas corpus, the problem of public appeal was greatly complicated for Davis. We have already seen that Davis did not hesitate a moment to embrace the unfamiliar power granted him by Congress. He needed no period of adjustment to this unaccustomed authority. He issued a martial law proclamation the same day he signed the legislation. Davis obviously had more than an inkling by now that he would have to use Lincoln's methods to hold on to what the Confederacy already had.

It was not always obvious precisely what Davis's policy was. The absence of political parties and the six-year interval between presidential elections stipulated in the Confederate Constitution afforded him the luxury of silence on policy. Like the Confederate people themselves, historians today must infer Davis's policy from his actions. Often it must be inferred as much from what he did not say as from what he did say.

The best evidence for the critical shift in thinking on civil liberties in 1862 came in a September incident. With Confederate armies poised to invade Maryland and Kentucky, Robert E. Lee, marching into Maryland, needed a proclamation explaining to the local populace why the Confederate army was invading the state. Davis was preparing one, apparently, but Lee was already across the border. He turned to Colonel Charles Marshall, a member of his staff and a Marylander, for help, and together they produced a proclamation that capitalized on Maryland's status in Confederate mythology as a state martyred to Lincoln's despotism:

> The people of the Confederate States have long watched with the deepest sympathy the wrongs and outrages that have been inflicted upon the citizens of a commonwealth allied to the States of the South by the strongest social, political and commercial ties. They have seen with profound indignation their sister State deprived of every right and reduced to the condition of a conquered province. Under the pretence of supporting the Constitution, but in violation of its most valuable provisions, your citizens have been arrested and imprisoned upon no charge and contrary to all forms of law. The faithful and manly protest against this outrage made by the venerable and illustrious Marylander, to whom in better days no citizen appealed for right in vain, was treated with scorn and contempt; the government of your chief city has been usurped by armed strangers; your legislature has been dissolved by the unlawful arrest of its members; freedom of the press and of speech has been suppressed; words have been declared offences by an arbitrary decree of the Federal Executive, and citizens ordered to be tried by a military commission for what they dare to speak. . . . our army has come . . . to assist you . . . in regaining the rights of which you have been despoiled.[10]

Robert E. Lee was no politician, but he had so often heard the rhetoric coming out of Richmond as to be able to produce on the spur of the moment the quintessential document in the Confederacy's border state gambit.

But in 1862, Davis conspicuously had nothing to do with Lee's proclamation to Maryland, which was issued on 8 September. Davis's proposed proclamation, which the president apparently wrote on the 12th, is known from a letterbook copy and not from the original Davis sent to Lee (which has never been located). This circumstance somewhat complicates the episode.

The letterbook copy has a blank for inserting the name of the state to which Davis's proclamation is addressed, and in the version known from the standard edition of Davis's works, the letter is so worded that it could go to Lee, to General Braxton Bragg in Tennessee, or to General Edmund Kirby Smith in Kentucky. They were all planning campaigns in states where the border state appeal, used by Lee, might have been tried anyway. However, a signed copy of the Davis proclamation with the blank filled in for *Pennsylvania* has also been located. The proclamation meant for Kirby Smith, Bragg, and Lee actually made sense only for Pennsylvania because Davis's proclamation explained the reasons for "invading" enemy territory and described peace terms they might expect from the Confederacy. Kentucky was legally a Confederate state, and Marylanders were not considered alien enemies within Confederate states. Davis would not likely have ignored these constitutional points.[11]

Davis must have meant for the proclamation to be applied with minor alterations to each of the local situations faced by the invading Confederate armies, and it seems clear that the usual border state rhetoric about despotism and about men and women being dragged to distant dungeons could have been applied anywhere. Davis's draft proclamation, never issued, had none of that in it. Instead Davis dwelt on other issues. He denied any designs of "conquest" and pleaded "self-defence" as the Confederacy's sole reason to wage war. He described prewar attempts to negotiate for peace that had been rebuffed by the Lincoln administration. Northerners were assured that the Confederacy had always been and remained willing to allow free navigation of the Mississippi River when the war was over. Davis explained that the relentless and ruthless war made on the Confederacy now required the Confederacy, in turn, to make war in the enemy's territory, and he reminded the people of any occupied state that they could take the opportunity to make a separate peace.[12]

What is most remarkable about Davis's draft proclamation is what he excluded from it. The Confederate president made no mention of civil liberties. References to civil liberties were by now such standard catchwords for border state appeals that they came automatically to any Confederate's mind when the subject of the border states came up. Indeed, the Confederate army bands struck up "Maryland, My Maryland" upon entering the state—the song written during the Civil War with its first line describing Abraham Lincoln's policies thus: "The despot's heel is on thy shore, Maryland, my Maryland." The judicial decision condemning Lincoln's suspension of habeas corpus, *Ex parte Merryman*, written by Chief Justice Roger B. Taney, the "venerable and illustrious Marylander" mentioned in Lee's proclamation, was published in pamphlet form in the Confederacy in both Mississippi and New Orleans in 1861.

The appeal reached a popular audience. In a tableau formed at a fashionable Richmond Christmas party thrown at a house on Church Hill in 1861, a woman posed as Maryland "in chains, forced to the earth by the bayonet of a Federal sol-dier." And about seven months before the invasion of Maryland, one observer could say, "All Richmond is singing that beautiful and pathetic ballad, 'Mary-land—My Maryland.' It has taken the place of 'Dixie' with the piano-playing young ladies, the whistling street boys, the negro minstrel troups and the mili-tary bands." South Carolina planters summering at "The Barrows" in the first days of September 1862, as Lee's army entered Maryland, enjoyed the last scene of their *tableaux vivants* representing "The Confederacy." Kentucky and Mary-land were both bound. Kentucky was struggling to be free and was still erect, but Maryland was prostrate, and her hands were in chains.[13]

Yet Jefferson Davis did not embrace the border state civil liberties gambit in his proclamation. Many years later, after the war, Davis again took up the sub-ject of the invasion of Maryland in his memoir, *The Rise and Fall of the Confeder-ate Government*. Describing the opening moves of Lee's invasion of Maryland, Davis paused to explain, "At this time the letter, from which the following extract is made, was addressed by me to General R. E. Lee, commanding our forces in Maryland." What followed in Davis's memoir was the introductory paragraph of Davis's draft proclamation for Lee, Kirby Smith, and Bragg from his letter-book: "It is deemed proper that you should, in accordance with established usage, announce, by proclamation, to the people of Maryland, the motives and purposes of your presence among them at the head of an invading army; and you are instructed in such proclamation to make known, etc."[14] Davis then added in his later memoir, "In obedience to instructions, General Lee issued the fol-lowing address," and Davis then quoted the Lee-Marshall Maryland-in-chains letter at length.

Jefferson Davis's "etc." preceding Lee's letter was misleading, for what fol-lowed in the letterbook proclamation as opposed to the later memoir was Davis's own suggested proclamation *not mentioning the issue of civil liberties in the North*. When Davis wrote *The Rise and Fall of the Confederate Government*, fifteen years after the war was over, he was busy constructing a political myth of constitu-tionalism buttressed with historical references, and the idea of Union tyranny over Maryland fit that new philosophy. He then subtly appropriated Lee's work as his own. In other words, by 1881 Davis wished he had said to Marylanders in 1862 what Lee in fact did say to them in 1862—so Davis made it look as though he had.

But in reality, back in the autumn of 1862, Jefferson Davis had been jettison-ing the civil liberties theme. The failures of Confederate forces in Maryland at Antietam and in Kentucky at Perryville in 1862 confirmed the wisdom of aban-doning civil liberty in hopes of holding on to what the Confederates had. Mary-land and Kentucky did not rise in the Confederates' behalf when the gray armies arrived. Not long thereafter the foreign-policy component of the border state appeal to civil liberty also proved bankrupt, and it would not much matter whether European powers regarded the North as despotic or not. The eleven beleaguered Confederate States were on their own in a hostile world.

Recognizing the cross-purposes revealed in the Davis proclamation and the Lee proclamation is vital to understanding the policy issues that drove Jefferson Davis to alter his ideological appeals. At this fortuitous crossroad in Davis's thinking, historian Paul D. Escott's path-breaking interpretation of Davis takes a wrong turn. Escott declares Davis's Maryland-invasion letter a return "to the ideology used in the first year of the contest," stressing again "that the Confederacy had no aggressive designs and was fighting only in self-defence and for the right of self-government."[15] When Davis's proclamation is contrasted with the one Lee wrote for Maryland, however, one realizes immediately that Davis's proclamation was not a return but a new departure, an abandonment of the rhetoric of civil liberty and the cult of habeas corpus. Underlying that was the turn toward authoritarian measures for holding his own and the abandonment of hope that the border states would come to the rescue of the Confederacy. There was no real hope of appealing to the border states any longer, and liberty was the best policy only while the border states remained in doubt.

1863 as Ideological Crossroads

For 1863 especially we must infer Jefferson Davis's thinking on the subject of constitutional liberty as much from what he omitted to say as from what he did say. This was a period of change and vacillation—exemplified in his dealings with Arkansas in late 1862 and early 1863. On 21 October 1862 Davis cautioned General Theophilus Holmes to "dispose with the machinery of a military police over the people [of Arkansas]." Martial law had "been the subject of many complaints." Holmes was military commander of a "wide territory." He had "few trained officers and many untried agents," and abuses were likely where Holmes could not exercise close control of his subordinates. In such a situation Davis could readily believe there was just cause for the complaints he heard about civil liberties.[16]

In November 1862 Davis urged Holmes to rid Arkansas of the detested martial law measures associated with Holmes's predecessor, the remarkable Thomas C. Hindman. As late as 28 January 1863, Davis responded to Holmes's own request to impose martial law to end extortion, the economic hardships caused by it, and the consequent desertions from the army by lecturing him on "the relation of supply and demand." He also explained to Holmes that "A people called upon to sacrifice everything in resistance to usurpation and oppression should always have before them unmistakeable evidence of a strict regard for their rights on the part of those who invoke their assistance." These are the sorts of ringing affirmations of civil liberty in the face of threatened national disaster that stir the hearts of persons convinced of the Confederacy's dedication to southern rights.

That same day, however, Jefferson Davis received a telegram from Holmes describing Arkansas and Indian Territory as overrun with deserters, disloyal persons, and invaders, and describing his inability to enforce conscription. The next day, 29 January 1863, Davis reversed course and ordered the suspension of the writ of habeas corpus in Arkansas and Indian Territory. This occurred less than two weeks before his authority to suspend the writ of habeas corpus was to expire and on the very day Arkansas's congressional delegation visited his office to complain about previous impositions of martial law in their state.[17]

Davis might have abandoned the appeal to liberty in general sooner and more emphatically were it not for an accident of timing: the Confederate off-year elections for Congress came in 1863, and Congress decided in February to leave Davis without the power to suspend the writ of habeas corpus through the rest of the year. There was little point in justifying the authority he did not have.

Still, the summer of 1863 provided occasion for articulating new ideas that he had likely been formulating for some time. A particularly critical period in his thinking came in July. The loss of Vicksburg and Port Hudson, effectively isolating the trans-Mississippi West, caused Davis to write several letters to western commanders about what they should do now that they were substantially independent of Richmond's control. Suddenly the policies of Thomas C. Hindman were pertinent.

Davis spelled out the problems for Edmund Kirby Smith and Theophilus Holmes. Kirby Smith, for example, had "not merely a military, but also a political problem involved" in his command. The idea that the trans-Mississippi might secede from the Confederacy was in the air. Besides, the general had to see to his own supplies; he could not hope for supply from the East. What Davis left undescribed was the political adaptations that would be necessary to bring about government production of essential supplies for the western departments, and he did not say what would be necessary to meet political threats of secession within the western Confederacy. But surely increased government power was a likely answer for both problems.

The president described the fundamental problem to Robert E. Lee: "The trans-Mississippi Department must now become mainly self sustaining, and will require the exercise of extraordinary powers by the commander, but how far this may extend without involving opposition it is difficult to foresee. To secure efficiency there must be greater promptitude than is attainable if papers are to be sent here by present available routes, yet this war can only be successfully prosecuted while we have the cordial support of the people and this is best secured by close adherence to law and usage."[18] This letter offers a rare glimpse of Davis's view of the Confederate situation. The underdeveloped South, like the Trans-Mississippi Department, needed to become self-sustaining in manufactures, food production, and other ways, but to bring that about would require "the exercise of extraordinary powers," and Davis saw "the people," whose support was crucial to the war effort, as sticklers for "law and usage." Davis felt confined by popular opinion in the South, as he read it.

But Davis may well have misread popular opinion, for there is evidence of longing for order in the South as well as for liberty, and he had been offered a glimpse of it in the requests for martial law in 1862. In the end, even his misconception proved no barrier to embracing "extraordinary powers" when he felt threatened by organized resistance in the Confederacy. Davis *was* hardening on this subject. In the summer of 1863 he began to use the term *tories* to describe the domestic enemy in East Tennessee, and he felt the need of Judah Benjamin's "summary justice" to deal with them.[19] The adoption of harsh measures came easier and easier to him. As he casually told the Confederate commander at Zollicoffer, Tennessee, the officer, if short on cavalry, should "not hesitate to impress horses especially of tories." Davis did not bother to spell out how military men in the field were to identify tories.[20]

For the most part, Davis put East Tennessee out of his mind, but he could not help worrying about North Carolina.[21] Governor Zebulon Vance seemed disinclined to realize the internal danger in his state and to meet it. As early as 28 July 1863, Davis replied to a warning from Vance about the peace movement led by William Woods Holden, "This is not the first intimation I have received that Holden is engaged in the treasonable purpose of exciting the people of North Carolina to resistance against the Government, and cooperation with the enemy." But Davis was not "aware whether he has gone so far as to render him liable to criminal prosecution."[22]

Davis fretted about Holden, but because of yet another crisis of 1863, the gross inflation of the currency and the inadequacy of taxation, Davis came to develop broadly useful arguments for ignoring limitations of the constitution made wholly impractical by the circumstances of war. By 1863 it appeared as though the Confederate government would be incapable of taxing two-thirds of the wealth of the country because it was held in land and slaves. To tax such property was to lay a direct tax, and according to the constitution, direct taxes had to be proportionate to the population of the states, and the population had to be determined by a census. The Confederacy was in no condition to conduct a census enumeration, yet the burden of financing the war would otherwise fall unfairly on a tiny sector of the economy.

In the president's message to Congress of 7 December 1863, he explained his willingness to sign into law taxation measures that would under peaceful circumstances be unconstitutional. Davis now used language that sounded very like the language of Abraham Lincoln: "What else would this be in effect than to increase the burthen of those who are the heaviest sufferers by the war, and to make our own inability to protect them from invasion, as we are required to do by the Constitution, the ground for adding to their losses by an attempted adherence to the letter, in violation of the spirit of that instrument?" Davis had ridiculed such language two years before when Lincoln used it.[23]

Political circumstances in North Carolina might well move Davis further toward violating the letter to maintain the spirit of the constitution. In a letter to Vance, written 30 December 1863, Davis alluded to President Lincoln as "that despot," but he went on to warn Vance that too much conciliation in North Carolina now would lead the governor "to the use of force to repress treason" later.[24]

North Carolina frightened and preoccupied Davis as East Tennessee never could. One North Carolina case, that of the political prisoner Eli Swanner, reveals the shape of Davis's thinking. Swanner was a forty-three-year-old resident of Beaufort with a wife and six children, apparently an avowed Union man, twice arrested, who readily announced his desire to be sent north. Arrested the second time in 1863, Swanner, after the usual examination by a War Department commissioner, was sent to Richmond and ordered to be confined for the war. Vance demanded a trial for the man in North Carolina, and the state legislature adopted Swanner's cause, passing a resolution demanding his return to the state. The War Department in Richmond had little sympathy for Swanner; even the lenient B. R. Wellford Jr. called him "an avowed Tory" and said that he would cause as much harm as possible if released. Nevertheless, Davis returned the prisoner to North Carolina along with a long letter of explanation to Vance on 22 January 1864.

Swanner, the president pointed out, was "avowedly disloyal" and lived in a part of North Carolina overrun by the enemy. He was just the sort to act as guide and informant to Union forces attacking Confederate pickets or raiding the area for plunder. Davis also pointed out:

> If such persons are to be put upon a footing with the most loyal citizens, and treated with the tenderest regard to the strict law of treason, you see how impossible it will be to procure testimony sufficient for their conviction. Before an overt act is committed they must not be touched out of a nice and scrupulous regard for the right of the citizen. After the commission of the act, they are screened and protected within the enemy's lines. I cannot conceal from Your Excellency my opinion of the inexpediency of permitting such persons to go at large unmolested. Still, in deference to the declared wishes of the General Assembly of North Carolina, and with an earnest desire to promoting harmony and good feeling between the State and Confederate authorities, I accede to your request, and have directed the said Eli Swanner to be returned to North Carolina for examination and trial.[25]

Davis conceded nothing on principle in the Swanner case, and in a way the letter to Vance served as notice that the president's mind was made up. He was apparently willing to let Vance publish the letter in a newspaper.[26] Besides, Davis had a plan to take care of Swanner. If the North Carolina authorities discharged him, the man, under the latest conscription law, could "be enrolled and sent to a company of N.C. serving in Virginia or Tennessee."[27]

Davis's letter to Vance about the Swanner case was roughly the equivalent of Lincoln's letter of June 1863 to Erastus Corning and others about Clement Vallandigham—in which the U.S. president asked whether he would be forced to shoot a simple-minded soldier boy who deserted while not being able to touch the wily agitator who induced the boy to desert.

Mention of the Vallandigham case offers a jarring reminder of how far behind Davis had left the ideology of civil liberty by the summer of 1863. Lincoln banished the troublesome dissenter to the Confederate lines in June 1863, and President Davis had to deal personally with the Vallandigham problem when he came into the Confederacy. Yet Davis never mentioned Clement Vallandigham in a public proclamation, message, speech, or letter during the war. The ultimate Democratic martyr to the Republican despotism in the North went without official comment from Jefferson Davis, an unimaginable omission in 1861 or 1862 when Davis had been attempting to depict the Confederacy as a haven from Yankee despotism.

But in 1863, civil liberties were increasingly in the way of the policies Davis felt necessary to save what was left of the Confederacy. Finally, in February 1864, Davis sent a special message to Congress, formally requesting the end of civil liberties in the Confederacy. Asking to renew his authority to suspend the writ of habeas corpus, Davis offered this blunt explanation: "It has been our cherished hope—and hitherto justified by the generous self-devotion of our citizens—that when the great struggle in which we are engaged was passed we might exhibit to the world the proud spectacle of a people unanimous in the assertion and defense of their rights and achieving their liberty and independence after the bloodiest war of modern times without the necessity of a single sacrifice of civil right to military necessity. But it can no longer be doubted that the zeal with which the people sprang to arms at the beginning of the contest has, in some parts of the Confederacy, been impaired by the long continuance and magnitude of the struggle." Davis went on to say that "discontent, disaffection, and disloyalty" were abroad in the land. Civil rights would have to be sacrificed to military necessity.[28]

Davis even referred to "public meetings . . . in some of which a treasonable design is masked by a pretense of devotion to State sovereignty"—a rare hint that the familiar rhetoric of states' rights was no longer acceptable at face value in the South. Davis explained the need for suspension as "a remedy plainly contemplated by the Constitution." He pointed out that all the powers of the constitution, "extraordinary as well as ordinary," were intended to be used when required. "And," he added, "a suspension of the writ when demanded by the public safety is as much a duty as to levy taxes for the support of the Government."[29]

Davis seemed to be arguing the case for the first time. He did not say that Congress had previously authorized the suspension, presumably settling the questions of constitutionality and propriety under less dramatic circumstances. Davis did not point out that previous suspensions had gone unchallenged by the state supreme courts. It was not the case that suspension was merely "contemplated" in the constitution; as a matter of fact, the writ of habeas corpus *had been* suspended already in the Confederacy's brief constitutional history. Moreover, Davis did not quote the constitution or identify the enabling situation of invasion or rebellion now clearly at hand in the Confederacy. Davis was developing constitutional amnesia, and the disease would get worse over the years.

This message might lead one to believe that civil rights had never been sacrificed to military necessity in the Confederacy before 1864. Yet the president had himself issued a dozen orders sacrificing civil liberty to military necessity in 1862 and early 1863. To Davis those proclamations were defenses against particular invasions or threats from without, or they were concessions to undeveloped conditions on the frontiers of the Confederacy. Only in 1864 did he confess the need for protection from disloyalty within the heart of the Confederacy. In his mind these cases were somehow different and required that he start the argument over again.

The only way to reconcile the anomalies in Davis's position is to see in his mind a distinction between martial law as applied in the various proclamations of 1862 and early 1863 and the suspension of the writ of habeas corpus. The former seemed to him the law used during sieges and contained nothing political about it. The latter was aimed at political opposition to the war effort. It is not a distinction that would be found compelling by civil libertarians, perhaps, and it made no difference at all to the inmates in Castle Thunder and Salisbury. The constitution of the Confederate States of America made no such distinction. But the distinction allowed Davis to continue to see himself as one who maintained constitutional rectitude until conditions became impossible and to cultivate his image as an apostle of constitutional purity for the rest of his long life.

Abraham Lincoln, for his part, never had to change his policy on civil liberties. From the beginning to the end of the Civil War he adhered to the policy that seemed best suited to holding on to what he already had. Even with the border states secured to the Union by late 1862, similar limitations on civil liberties appeared necessary to enforce conscription.

Historians could not help but notice the differences in Confederate and Union ideologies and policies—the Union restricting liberty from the earliest moment to the very end of the war, while the Confederacy made a great point of its maintenance of civilian rights in the midst of war almost to the very end. Dwelling more on what the presidents said than what they did, historians assumed that Confederates valued white civil liberties more than Northerners did and that Confederate leaders had more reverence for the constitution.

Such a conclusion ignores behavior and the realities of power.[30] Actually, Abraham Lincoln and Jefferson Davis acted alike as commanders in chief when it came to the rights of the civilian populace. Both showed little sincere interest in constitutional restrictions on government authority in wartime. Both were obsessed with winning the war. Both ultimately obeyed their great national mandates to hold on to the territory they had.

CONCLUSION

THE PARADOX OF CONFEDERATE HISTORIOGRAPHY

THE WRITTEN CONSTITUTIONAL HISTORIES of the two sides in the American Civil War have from the very start gone in opposite directions. In the case of the North, as a carryover from Republican allegations during the war and immediately after, historians retained for a time a belief in the conspiracy of a vast, disloyal fifth column that was met, in part, by military arrests of civilians and other restrictions of civil liberty. Over the course of the twentieth century, historians have diminished the importance of internal dissent in the North during the war. The major achievement of revisionist historiography in this century has been to rehabilitate the reputation of the Democracy as a loyal opposition and to show that Republican allegations of extensive disloyalty in the North were mistaken or malevolent smears of the Democrats.

That development brought a disjunction in constitutional history, as it was well known that the Lincoln administration had made prisoners of thousands of civilians. As the vision of extensive disloyalty in the North vanished, so too did justification for military arrests of civilians in the North. For a time, Abraham Lincoln's reputation verged dangerously near accusations of dictatorship, but in the end the North's political prisoners proved to have been exaggerated in importance. Many came from occupied territory in the Confederacy, and many more from border states, especially Missouri, where internal civil war raged.

The historiography of the Confederacy went in the opposite direction. The imposition of Lost Cause mythology after the war to resist Reconstruction and racial equality helped create a myth of southern white society unified behind the war effort. The same immediate needs of the Reconstruction period determined that the white South protect itself with constitutional arguments, and a reputation for consistent constitutional rectitude—even during the war for Confederate existence—proved useful. Jefferson Davis's very identity became self-consciously merged with strict constitutional values. And historians subsequently adorned the whole southern people with the mantel of Davis's constitutionalism. The greatest student of Confederate constitutional, judicial, and legal history, William M. Robinson Jr., could as late as 1941 declare that "the Confederate people . . . by nature were lovers of constitutional forms."[1]

But twentieth-century Confederate historiography increasingly took as its task the discovery and description of conflict within Confederate society. Beginning most notably with Frank Owsley in 1925, historians of the Confederacy found numerous challenges to the Lost Cause myth of unity of white society during the war. At first it came as an unpleasant surprise to Southerners. Owsley did not "dwell upon the heroism and unselfishness in the Confederacy which has been the theme of countless volumes," and his book was therefore "misunderstood as being an unfriendly attack."[2] Seventy years later, the delineation of conflict within Confederate society, often depicted along lines of social class, constitutes a major theme of Confederate historical writing.

Constitutional history, however, remained frozen in the assumptions of the Lost Cause past. It failed to develop along with the history of Confederate society, economy, and politics. The result was as anomalous as the result for northern history. In the case of the Confederacy, the reader is presented with the image of a society rent by domestic resistance and dissent, of great violence and pervasiveness in certain regions, but conversely with the image of a government that refused to adjust constitutional forms to meet these stupendous problems. Instead, the Confederate president is usually proclaimed a "constitutionalist."

Confederate constitutional history would surely have caught up with the social, economic, and political history of the Confederacy had there not been a curious problem of evidence. Confederate political prisoners were not conveniently documented in prison lists digested in the *Official Records* in the 1880s from the Confederate archives captured at war's end. They were nowhere to be found, if sought in a logical manner. A handful of documents sat in the National Archives' collections of prison records, but they seemed notable mainly as a contrast to the uncountably vast records for political prisoners in the North. The existence of the habeas corpus commissioners was unknown until World War II, their role remained unclear even afterward, and manuscript records of their day-to-day work went undiscovered.

The documents necessary to uncover the number and identity of the Confederacy's political prisoners lay among the letters written to the Confederate secretaries of war—*as though they were letters merely, filed by the name of the commissioner, and having no readily recognizable indication that they were prison records.* Only when they were read and their contents systematically digested could the real history of the Confederate constitution be revealed at last.

Under the pressures of a war for national existence, the Confederate Constitution proved as "flexible" as the Constitution of the United States, on which it was modeled. And the white people of the South embraced order and sacrificed liberty as readily as Northerners did. Indeed, what the British consul in Washington said of the people under the Lincoln administration could as accurately have been said of the people under the Davis administration: they seemed to favor "placing their own lives and liberties . . . without any reserve, into the hands of the officers of the army." They were "recklessly applauding the suspension, without law, of all their liberties." The government "sends any one it pleases to a Fortress."

The observation, of course, was not strictly true of *either* the North or the South during the war, but it was as true of the one as the other. The exaggerated perception of the foreign observer owed its existence to the sharp contrast he saw between the society at war and the liberties that Americans, in both the North and South, had ordinarily enjoyed in peacetime.

To the current-day observer, the fate of liberty in the Confederacy seems equally anomalous when compared with the shrill professions of devotion to liberty and southern rights prevalent in the political debates on the eve of the war. Those defensive political statements from southern leaders in the 1850s cannot be taken at face value. They obscured much in southern society. They created an image, perhaps, of a society "obsessed with the idea of slavery" and ever fearful in a paranoid way "of an imminent loss of freedom."[3] The angry face and distraught emotions southern politicians showed the North and the world hid the normal face and sensible resolve of the southern white people. When war came, those people made the necessary sacrifices, including many civil liberties.

The supposed contrast between the fate of liberty in the North and South during the Civil War was substantially a construct of southern leaders after the war, as figures once at loggerheads politically—even as odd a couple as Jefferson Davis and Alexander H. Stephens—came to agree on a strategy of contrasting the supposed despotic tendencies of the North with the consistent history of concern for liberty in the South. In the absence of readily available evidence to the contrary from Confederate archives, they managed to fool posterity for a long time.

The South, even the white South, was never a monolith, however, in the period of the Confederacy or at any other time. As Reconstruction drove Davis and Stephens together in constitutional doctrine after the war, Zebulon Vance, for one, had opposite reflections on the history of the Confederacy. In a remarkable oration before a G.A.R. post in Boston in 1886, Vance reflected on reasons for internal discontent in the old Confederacy:

> It had been supposed that the war would be fought through without any disturbances of the ordinary functions of civil government, or any strain upon the muniments of their civil rights. But so soon as the fortunes of the Confederacy began to ebb; so soon as the superior numbers and resources of the North began to be seriously felt, the managers of the South came to feel the necessity of resorting to extraordinary means, and this feeling of serenity was rudely disturbed. Political discontent and distrust began to prevail. Perhaps in this respect we made the initial mistake of the whole secession movement: a mistake, the fatality of which increased day by day to the end. We started out without revolution of any kind, with all the machinery of society, State and Federal, in complete operation. There was simply a transfer of the central authority from the United States to the Confederate States of America. . . . In

thus avoiding the alarms of revolution and giving assurance to the timid of the security of society at the outset, a great point was undoubtedly gained. But this was dearly paid for. These smoothly flowing conditions could not of course be maintained. No consideration was given to the dangers of that coming period when hard necessity should compel the setting aside of civil rights and peaceful forms, and the substitution of the harsh features of revolution—at a moment, too, when the government most needed the warm support of public opinion. Looked at simply with a view to success, in my opinion the seceding States should have faced the most ultra measures of revolution at the very start; they should have formed no National government and should have bound themselves by the shackles of no constitution.[4]

Other circumstances worked to give credibility to the historical image of the Confederacy as a haven of constitutional rectitude. There were numerous institutional and customary differences between the North and South, and most of these, as chance would have it, worked to the South's advantage in this debate. Thus, for example, the North still had on the books the Alien Enemies Act of the Federalist era but could not use it in the Civil War because the North was attempting to prove that its enemies were not aliens. Therefore the military prisons of the North swelled with southern-born citizens and southern residents from occupied areas. For the Confederates, there was no ideological or constitutional problem with defining as enemy aliens people from the North who happened to be in the Confederacy. The Alien Enemies Act of the Confederate States of America of 8 August 1861 served at first to banish from the Confederacy many potential political prisoners of northern birth. Later it made simpler the detention of citizens of northern birth who ran afoul of Confederate internal security measures.

The most important institutional difference was African-American slavery. Slavery effectively put under permanent arrest the people of the South with the most potential for disloyalty. If the Alien Enemies Act made a difference of thousands of political prisoners between North and South, slavery made a difference to be measured in millions. If we take the slave population of the Confederacy as roughly three million, that figure is equal to the entire population of the troublesome states of Maryland, Missouri, and Kentucky. If the Lincoln administration could have kept under similar conditions to slavery all the people of Maryland, Kentucky, and Missouri, it could have substantially eliminated these three states as a breeding ground of political prisoners. That would have eliminated in turn the principal spur to suspension of the writ of habeas corpus—the border state strategy, the majority of trials by military commission, and the largest group of political prisoners outside occupied Confederate territory. It would have radically altered the record of the Lincoln administration on civil liberties, diminishing its political prisoners to scattered cases, most of them stemming from the enforcement of conscription.

In that event there would be no numerical disparity between North and South in terms of political prisoners, just as there was no marked disparity in the spirit of measures taken to deal with dissent and disloyalty. To be sure, most of the 4,108 southern prisoners came from border areas, but then most northern arrests came from border areas and occupied territory. The two societies were more alike than unlike in the way they handled civil liberties. They were far more alike than their subsequent historical reputations would indicate. Lincoln was no "dictator," and Jefferson Davis was no "constitutionalist."

Therefore, the political prisoners on both sides seem much alike. They came mostly from border areas—in the Confederacy, especially Tennessee and Virginia. North Carolina's ocean borders exposed that state to Union invasion, too. Many prisoners came from areas near the military fronts. Conscription has been a serious problem for any American government that used it, and the Confederacy proved no exception. The government arrested citizens as conscripts or deserters or for aiding desertion. The prisoners did not represent an organized fifth column, through many in East Tennessee and in western Virginia proved ready to fight for the other side. Many were arrested as spies by both governments, but few could be proved to be spies. If the Lincoln administration managed to detain Rose O'Neal Greenhow for a time, the Confederate government nabbed agent Timothy Webster and hanged him. But there were not many other success stories in foiling espionage. The Confederacy did not have to contend with blockade runners, as the North did. On the other hand, the lack of a legal tender act caused special problems for the Confederacy. Most surprising of all, the Confederacy at a greater rate than the North arrested persons who held opposition political views at least in part because they held them, despite the Confederacy's vaunted lack of political parties. Such arrests were more common before 1863 while memories of the votes on secession remained fresh.

The final statistics broke down this way. The cause of arrest cannot be determined in 23.9 percent of the cases. What is listed as cause in many other instances is vague indeed: "suspicion," "suspicious character," "disloyalty," and "dangerous character," for example. But even accepting such vague charges, we find that Union men accounted for 11 percent of the prisoners for whom a charge was noted, excluding those who could not possibly have been arrested for their votes in 1860 and 1861, the African-American prisoners. That 11 percent figure includes as well many arrested for northern sympathies expressed in other ways than voting for antisecession political parties. Investigations of the white prisoners proved that at least 10.9 percent proved to be alien enemies. These were often longtime residents of the South or northern civilians who followed the Federal armies too closely—merchants, teamsters, curiosity seekers, and the like. The commonest circumstance of arrest was going to or coming from enemy lines—at least 16.2 percent of the cases of white Confederate citizens for whom a cause of arrest can be ascertained. The true number is much greater because it was common to pick up a person for suspicious movements and then incarcerate the citizen for some more specific charge. Problems of conscription or desertion caused a substantial percentage of the arrests, but no determination is possible because many cases were resolved by sending the prisoner to the conscription officer, and that remains the only notation in the record. There were almost no newspaper reporters or editors among the political prisoners—a circumstance that supports the common assertion that freedom of the press was a reality under Jefferson Davis.

Make no mistake about it: most of the political prisoners discussed in this book were Confederate States prisoners, more than half of them at one time or another inmates at the Eastern District Military Prison in Richmond under the very noses of the administration and Congress. In the early days of martial law in Richmond—before the novelty wore off—their arrests and releases were frequently mentioned in the Richmond newspapers read by the government officials resident in the capital. Thomas C. Hindman may have been beyond Richmond's immediate control, but no Arkansas prisoners form part of the 4,108 on whom this book is based. The prisoners discussed here were for the most part the responsibility of the Davis administration in Richmond.

The vital evidence now reveals what really happened: the Confederate government restricted civil liberties as modern democratic nations did in war. We did not know this until now, partly because the evidence, lying in improbable archives, was easily overlooked. We also did not know because the very creators of the Confederate state later retouched its image, painting over the scenes of arrest and imprisonment to present what seemed to them a prettier picture of a people united in a long history of constitutionalism and uncompromising dedication to southern rights. That image was as false as any forgery and misled later historians, but the true canvas presenting a rougher image is now emerging into view. The next step should be its full integration into an accurate narrative of Confederate history.

NOTES

ABBREVIATIONS

Letters Letters Received by the Confederate Secretary of War, 1861–1865, RG 109, National Archives, microcopy 437, 150 reels

OR *The War of the Rebellion: A Compilation of the Official Records of the Union and Confederate Armies,* 128 vols. (Washington DC: Government Printing Office, 1880–1902)

INTRODUCTION

1. Lawrence H. Mathews to Leroy Pope Walker, 19 April 1861, Letters, no. 379-1861, reel 1. The arrest occurred on the day of the formal surrender ceremony at the fort in 1861. Mathews wrote under the name "Nemo" for the *Pensacola Observer*.

2. B. F. Eppes to James A. Seddon, 17 March 1863, Letters, E(WD)36, reel 90.

3. Kenneth Radley, *Rebel Watchdog: The Confederate States Army Provost Guard* (Baton Rouge: Louisiana State Univ. Press, 1989), pp. 74–101.

4. Richard C. Wade, *Slavery in the Cities: The South, 1820–1860* (New York: Oxford Univ. Press, 1964), p. 107; Kenneth M. Stampp, *The Peculiar Institution: Slavery in the Ante-Bellum South* (New York: Alfred A. Knopf, 1956), p. 149.

5. E. Merton Coulter, *William G. Brownlow: Fighting Parson of the Southern Highlands* (Chapel Hill: Univ. of North Carolina Press, 1937), p. 17.

6. Arthur James Lyon Fremantle, *Three Months in the Southern States: April–June, 1863* (1864; reprint, Lincoln: Univ. of Nebraska Press, 1991), pp. 127, 134–35.

7. Southern Historical Society, *Southern Historical Society Papers,* 52 vols. (Richmond: Virginia Historical Society, 1876–1959), vol. 51 (1958), ed. Frank E. Vandiver, p. 26.

8. Law and Oldham quoted in Thomas B. Alexander and Richard E. Beringer, *The Anatomy of the Confederate Congress: A Study of the Influence of Member Characteristics on Legislative Voting Behavior, 1861–1865* (Nashville: Vanderbilt Univ. Press, 1972), pp. 170–71. See also speech in Congress, 4 Oct. 1862, in Southern Historical Society, *Southern Historical Society Papers,* vol. 47 (1930), p. 46.

9. Ibid., p. 47.

10. *Charleston Courier,* 11 Feb. 1862, 6 March 1862. The Richmond reporter for the *Charleston Mercury,* however, pronounced a verdict against the passport system after a year's trial on 14 Oct. 1862.

11. Speech in Congress, 16 May 1864, in Southern Historical Society, *Southern Historical Society Papers,* 51:81.

12. *OR,* 4:3:280.

13. R. D. Craighead to George W. Randolph, 5 Oct. 1862, Letters, C(WD)1027, reel 40.

14. O. H. Sears to James A. Seddon, 19 Oct. 1864, Letters, S(WD)438, reel 142.

15. J. F. Gibson to C. P. Clayton, ca. June 1862, Letters, G(WD)361, reel 48.

16. L. G. Reid to Leroy Pope Walker, 21 July 1861, Letters, no. 2449-1861, reel 5.

17. M. W. Clusky to James A. Seddon, 15 Nov. 1864, Letters, S(WD)481, reel 142.

18. John B. Jones, *A Rebel War Clerk's Diary at the Confederate States Capital*, 2 vols. (Philadelphia: J. B. Lippincott, 1866), 2:133.

19. *Communication of the Secretary of War . . . Jan. 27, 1864 [relative to the "domestic passport system"]* (Richmond VA, 1864).

20. Kenneth Radley emphasizes the "political repercussions" and criticism aroused by the system, hazarding the opinion that this further "divisive issue" ultimately "harmed the war effort." See *Rebel Watchdog*, pp. 89, 100. Yet the very difficulty Radley had defining the origins and extent of the system was caused by the scarcity of mentions of the system in the documentary record—a sign of relatively few protests.

21. Richard Bensel, "Southern Leviathan: The Development of Central State Authority in the Confederate States of America," in Karen Orren and Stephen Skowronek, eds., *Studies in American Political Development: An Annual*, vol. 2 (New Haven CT: Yale Univ. Press, 1987), p. 135. The congressman, quoted by Bensel, was J. T. Leach, who spoke on 27 Jan. 1865. See Southern Historical Society, *Southern Historical Society Papers*, vol. 52 (1959), ed. Frank E. Vandiver, p. 242.

Part One: Liberty and Order

1. Frank E. Vandiver, *Jefferson Davis and the Confederate State* (Oxford: Clarendon Press, 1964), pp. 21–22.

2. Emory M. Thomas, *The Confederacy as a Revolutionary Experience* (Englewood Cliffs NJ: Prentice Hall, 1971), pp. 58–59.

3. William C. Davis, *Jefferson Davis: The Man and His Hour* (New York: Harper Collins, 1991), p. 704. See also Clement Eaton, *Jefferson Davis* (New York: Free Press, 1977), p. 273.

4. Vandiver, *Jefferson Davis and the Confederate State*, p. 21.

5. Frank E. Vandiver, "The Civil War as an Institutionalizing Force," in Vandiver, Martin Hardwick Hall, and Homer L. Kerr, *Essays on the American Civil War* (Austin: Univ. of Texas Press, 1968), p. 81.

6. Thomas, *Confederacy as a Revolutionary Experience*, pp. 63, 64.

7. Emory M. Thomas, *The Confederate Nation, 1861–1865* (New York: Harper & Row, 1979), pp. 152, 150.

8. Richard Franklin Bensel, *Yankee Leviathan: The Origins of Central State Authority in America, 1859–1877* (Cambridge: Cambridge Univ. Press, 1990), pp. 95, 142, 144. Bensel shows the "modern" affinity for a view of constitutional flexibility in the Confederacy in his reliance on Curtis Arthur Amlund, *Federalism in the Southern Confederacy* (Washington DC: Current Affairs Press, 1966), which argued that there was a substantial abandonment of states' rights doctrines of government as the Confederacy developed.

9. See, for example, Wayne K. Durrill, *War of Another Kind: A Southern Community in the Great Rebellion* (New York: Oxford Univ. Press, 1990).

10. Paul D. Escott, *After Secession: Jefferson Davis and the Failure of Confederate Nationalism* (Baton Rouge: Louisiana State Univ. Press, 1978), pp. 190–91.

11. Escott, *After Secession*, p. 137.

12. Ibid., p. 178.

13. E. M. Thomas, *Confederate Nation*, pp. 150, 264 n; Frank Owsley, *State Rights in the Confederacy* (1925, reprint, Gloucester MA: Peter Smith, 1961), p. 171; for the history of legislation, see John B. Robbins, "The Confederacy and the Writ of Habeas Corpus," *Georgia Historical Quarterly* 55 (1971): 83–101.

Chapter 1: The Rogue Tyrant and the Premodern State

1. In the most recent general history of the Confederacy Arkansas disappears as a subject after the vote for secession. It makes a brief reappearance in the Battle of Pea Ridge, 6 March 1862, but that battle is featured as the event that lost *Missouri*, without mention of its effects on Arkansas. See E. M. Thomas, *Confederate Nation*, pp. 87, 94, 124. Arkansas is mentioned more often in Frank E. Vandiver, *Their Tattered Flags: The Epic of the Confederacy* (New York: Harper's Magazine Press, 1970), but it is characterized as a "remote domain" (p. 96). Thomas does not mention Hindman; Vandiver mentions him only as a "tardy" subordinate at Chickamauga (though he mentions his successor in Arkansas, Theophilus Holmes; pp. 247, 193).

2. No one deals with the 1863 report as a statement of political thought, though all historians writing on Civil War Arkansas use it as a source. Though Hindman's modern biographers defend his policies as a "viable alternative" to the "lackluster state rights approach," they do not call attention to the remarkable qualities of the report. Diane Neal and Thomas W. Kremm, *Lion of the South: General Thomas C. Hindman* (Macon GA: Mercer Univ. Press, 1993), pp. 159–60. William L. Shea uses it also but dismisses Hindman as a fanatic; see Shea, "1862: 'A Continual Thunder,'" in Mark K. Christ, ed., *Rugged and Sublime: The Civil War in Arkansas* (Fayetteville: Univ. of Arkansas Press, 1994), p. 39.

3. Kenneth C. Martis, *The Historical Atlas of the Congresses of the Confederate States of America: 1861–1865* (New York: Simon & Schuster, 1994), p. 40; Carl H. Moneyhon, *The Impact of the Civil War and Reconstruction on Arkansas* (Baton Rouge: Louisiana State Univ. Press, 1994), p. 33; Donald B. Dodd and Wynelle S. Dodd, *Historical Statistics of the South, 1790–1970* (University: Univ. of Alabama Press, 1973). Though containing extensive upland areas, Arkansas has been neglected in the revival of interest in such areas, which has focused on "Appalachia."

4. Moneyhon, *Impact of the Civil War on Arkansas*, p. 13.

5. *OR*, 1:13:23.

6. Richard M. McMurry, *Two Great Rebel Armies: An Essay in Confederate Military History* (Chapel Hill: Univ. of North Carolina Press, 1989), pp. 22–23, 26–28.

7. *OR*, 1:13:29–30.

8. Ibid., p. 31.

9. Ibid.

10. Ibid., p. 32.

11. Ibid.

12. Ibid., p. 33; *OR*, 1:10:2:558–59.

13. *OR*, 1:13:33–34.

14. Ibid., p. 34.

15. Ibid., p. 38.

16. Ibid., p. 39.

17. Ibid.

18. Bobby L. Roberts ignores Hindman's justification by precedent when he states that Hindman's "only excuse for this patently illegal act was that many citizens and state officials favored it and that there had been an abdication of duties by many civil authorities." Roberts, "General T. C. Hindman and the Trans-Mississippi District," *Arkansas Historical Quarterly* 32 (1973): 308.

19. *OR*, 1:13:39–40.

20. *OR*, 1:10:2:298, 373.

21. Neal and Kremm, *Lion of the South*, pp. 94–102.

22. Michael B. Dougan, *Confederate Arkansas: The People and Policies of a Frontier State in Wartime* (University: Univ. of Alabama Press, 1976), p. 85.

23. Neal and Kremm, *Lion of the South*, pp. 1–66.

24. Ezra J. Warner, *Generals in Gray: Lives of the Confederate Commanders* (Baton Rouge: Louisiana State Univ. Press, 1959), pp. 137–38.

25. *OR*, 1:22:1:83.

26. Martis, *Historical Atlas*, p. 22.

27. Not a hint of this side of Beauregard appears in the narrowly military biography written by T. Harry Williams, *P. G. T. Beauregard: Napoleon in Gray* (Baton Rouge: Louisiana State Univ. Press, 1954), but see the following: G. T. Beauregard to W. Warren Johnson, 3 May 1862 (copy of telegram); T. C. Hindman to W. Warren Johnson, 4 May 1862 (copy); Hindman to Johnson, 13 May 1862; Hindman to Johnson, 4 June 1862 (copy). The actual destruction was recorded carefully in lists sent to the quarter master general out of fear that the records might be destroyed in the Union invasion. Johnson sent a record of over seventy pages of reports of cotton destroyed in Arkansas in 1862. Letters, J(WD)III, reel 131. See also *OR*, 1:13:40.

28. Bobby L. Roberts justifies Hindman's recruitment policies and cotton burning as military necessities but insists that he brought about his own undoing by the declaration of martial law. Roberts repeatedly depicts martial law as a "usurpation" (p. 310) and a "patently illegal" (p. 308) act. It was his "greatest excess" (p. 310) and was "totally illegal." Roberts, "General T. C. Hindman." Yet Davis did not directly rescind Hindman's order. Davis, though he wanted Holmes to replace Hindman and to back away from martial law, was willing to acquiesce in imposing martial law if the Arkansas delegation desired it.

29. *OR*, 2:2:1402, 1403, 1404, 1417.

30. Neal and Kremm, *Lion of the South*, p. 115; Warner, *Generals in Gray*, pp. 257–58. Holmes's letter to Davis about Hindman is referred to in Walter Lee Brown, *A Life of Albert Pike* (Fayetteville: Univ. of Arkansas Press, 1997), p. 411.

31. Carl H. Moneyhon emphasizes the weakness of the economy in *The Impact of the Civil War in Arkansas*. The more comprehensive treatment of military and political events comes in Michael B. Dougan, *Confederate Arkansas: The People and Policies of a Frontier State in Wartime* (University: Univ. of Alabama Press, 1976). Both share a "total war" interpretation of Arkansas Civil War history: the state in their view faced total war and was unequal to its demands either economically or because of its individualistic frontier culture and belief in states' rights. In such a scheme of interpretation Hindman becomes something of a hero. Moneyhon: "Hindman was gone, but his policies of total war continued during the remaining years of the war"

(p. 111). Dougan: "Yet the Civil War was so nearly a total war that" states' rights "helped in undoing her valiant sons" (p. vii). The only study closely focused on the question is pro-Hindman and pro–martial law for the circumstances; see Leo E. Huff, "The Martial Law Controversy in Arkansas, 1861–1865: A Case History of Internal Confederate Conflict," *Arkansas Historical Quarterly* 37 (1978): 147–67.

32. For the succession of orders from 10–30 June 1862, see Neal and Kremm, *Lion of the South,* pp. 121, 132; *OR,* 1:13:385, 846.

33. *OR,* 1:22:1:145–46.

34. *OR,* 1:13:874.

35. Ibid.

36. T. Michael Parrish and Robert M. Willingham Jr., *Confederate Imprints: A Bibliography of Southern Publications from Secession to Surrender* (Austin TX: Jenkins, and Katonah NY: Gary A. Foster, n.d.), esp. pp. 451–525; "A Bibliography of Habeas Corpus Pamphlets from the Civil War," *Lincoln Lore* 1793 (July 1988).

37. *OR,* 1:53:822; Davis's rebuke was apparently written by one of his staff following suggestions from the president. See Lynda Lasswell Crist, ed., *The Papers of Jefferson Davis,* 15 vols. (projected) (Baton Rouge: Louisiana State Univ. Press, 1971–), vol. 7, 1861, p. 275.

38. Parrish and Willingham, *Confederate Imprints,* pp. 440, 497.

39. Albert Pike, *Address to the Senators and Representatives of the State of Arkansas in the Congress of the Confederate States* (Shreveport? LA, 1863), pp. 1–2.

40. Ibid., pp. 3–4.

41. Ibid., pp. 13–14, 20.

42. *OR,* 1:15:779–83.

43. *OR,* 1:13:861.

44. Ibid., pp. 934, 936–37.

45. Ibid., p. 941.

46. Ibid., p. 849.

47. Ibid., p. 856.

48. Ibid., p. 855.

49. Ibid., p. 44.

50. Ibid., p. 886.

51. Ibid., p. 915.

52. *OR,* 1:22:2:803; for Hindman's resentment of Randolph, see p. 785, for example.

53. Arkansas delegation endorsing letter from Governor Flanagan to Robert W. Johnson, 21 Jan. 1863, Letters, F(WD)82, reel 91.

54. Arkansas delegation to Jefferson Davis, 17 Feb. 1863, Letters, F(WD)82, reel 91.

55. *OR,* 1:13:900–901.

56. Ibid., p. 901.

57. Robert L. Duncan, *Reluctant General: The Life and Times of Albert Pike* (New York: E. P. Dutton, 1961); Alvin M. Josephy, *The Civil War in the American West* (New York: Alfred A. Knopf, 1991), esp. 360–61; David Y. Thomas, *Arkansas in War and Reconstruction, 1861–1874* (Little Rock: Arkansas Division, United Daughters of the Confederacy, 1926), pp. 184–88, 320. Pike's most recent and most careful biographer depicts the conflict with Hindman as originating in a territorial dispute. See W. L. Brown, *Life of Albert Pike,* pp. 405ff.

58. *OR*, 1:13:936. The Pike letter appears in an appendix of documents that arrived too late for inclusion in their proper order in the *OR*.

59. Ibid., p. 867. W. L. Brown, *Life of Albert Pike*, p. 426.

60. *OR*, 1:53:848.

61. Richard B. McCaslin deals with martial law, trials by military commission, and other evidence of desire for order in another remote Confederate state in *Tainted Breeze: The Great Hanging at Gainesville, Texas, 1862* (Baton Rouge: Louisiana State Univ. Press, 1994). He attributes the hangings both to vigilantism and Confederate policy.

62. *OR*, 1:53:846–47.

Chapter 2: Alcohol and Martial Law

1. Phoebe Yates Pember, *A Southern Woman's Story: Life in Confederate Richmond* (1879; reprint, Bell I. Wiley, ed., St. Simons Island GA: Mockingbird Books, 1974), p. 25. Alcohol has been neglected as a factor in Civil War history, both for the North and the South.

2. William M. Robinson Jr., "Prohibition in the Confederacy," *American Historical Review* 37 (October 1931): esp. 50–51.

3. Ian R. Tyrrell, "Drink and Temperance in the Antebellum South: An Overview and Interpretation," *Journal of Southern History* 48 (1982): 497–509 (quotation on p. 509, emphasis added). Tyrrell's notion that temperance was stymied by the numerical weakness of the likely reform class (see p. 501) assumes that temperance was a class movement motivated by desires to discipline the working classes.

4. Besides Tyrrell see Paul E. Johnson, *A Shopkeeper's Millennium: Society and Revivals in Rochester, New York, 1815–1837* (New York: Hill & Wang, 1978), pp. 57, 115, 127, 131–33, and W. J. Rorabaugh, *The Alcoholic Republic: An American Tradition* (New York: Oxford Univ. Press, 1979), pp. 202–5.

5. C. C. Pearson and J. Edwin Hendricks, *Liquor and Anti-Liquor in Virginia, 1619–1919* (Durham NC: Duke Univ. Press, 1967), p. 152. James Benson Sellers said, "The Civil War served both to accelerate and to retard the temperance movement in Alabama." *The Prohibition Movement in Alabama, 1702–1943* (Chapel Hill: Univ. of North Carolina Press, 1943), p. 40.

6. Sellers, *Prohibition Movement in Alabama*, p. 41.

7. A full assessment of the role of alcohol in the Confederacy lies well beyond the scope of this book, which deals with the subject only as it affected questions of civil liberty and order.

8. *Charleston Courier*, 19 Feb. 1862.

9. Ibid., 26 Feb. 1862.

10. V. Sulakowksi to Leroy Pope Walker, 11 Aug. 1861, Letters, no. 3249-1861, reel 7.

11. Samuel McCorkle et al., petition, ca. 19 March 1862, Letters, M(WD)201, reel 59, and B(WD)564, reel 83.

12. William Wright, John McRae, and John Strange to Jefferson Davis, 28 March 1862, Jefferson Davis Papers, Special Collections, Perkins Library, Duke University; Crist, ed., *Papers of Jefferson Davis*, 7:120.

13. John Taylor to Albert T. Bledsoe, 4, 5, 6 March 1862; Charlottesville citizens' petition, n.d., all in Letters, T(WD)44, reel 74; William B. Mallory to George W. Randolph, 24 July 1862, Letters, M(WD)999, reel 61.

14. G. W. Lee to George W. Randolph, 18 Oct. 1862, Letters, L(WD)651, reel 58.

15. J. Sullivan to George W. Randolph, 20 Sept. 1862, Letters, S(WD)930, reel 72.

16. J. Harford to Jefferson Davis, 4 Oct. 1862, Letters, H(WD)1155, reel 53; G. W. Lee to George W. Randolph, 9 Aug. 1862, Letters, L(WD)496, reel 58, and 11 Nov. 1862, L(WD)1862, reel 58.

17. J. R. John to Thomas Hill Watts, 1 Oct. 1862, with Randolph and Davis endorsements, Letters, J(WD)434, reel 55.

18. James M. Calhoun to George W. Randolph, 3 Oct. 1862, Letters, C(WD)1038, reel 40.

19. See in the *Richmond Dispatch,* for example, "Rowdyism in Richmond," 5 Feb. 1862, "Consumption of Corn—The Whiskey Distillers," 9 Feb. 1862, "Groggeries," 13 Feb. 1862, and "Serious Events—A Remedy Necessary," calling for martial law to take care of drunken soldiers and officers, passports, and spies, 28 Feb. 1862. For the *Richmond Enquirer,* see "Drunk and Disorderly," 7 Feb. 1862. For the *Richmond Examiner,* see "Vice in Richmond," 25 Jan. 1862, and "Whiskey," 27 Jan. 1862.

20. *Richmond Enquirer,* 7 March 1862; James G. Scott and Edward A. Wyatt IV, *Petersburg's Story: A History* (Petersburg VA, 1960), p. 104.

21. James D. Richardson, ed., *The Messages and Papers of Jefferson Davis and the Confederacy Including Diplomatic Correspondence, 1861–1862,* 2 vols. (rev. ed., Allan Nevins, ed., New York: Chelsea House–Robert Hector, 1966), 1:222.

22. R. B. Lawrence to Jefferson Davis, 15 April 1862, Letters, L(WD)164, reel 57; Eli Phlegan et al. to secretary of war, ca. 13 Feb. 1862, no. 11119-1862, reel 27.

23. *Charleston Courier,* 19 Feb. 1862.

24. Thomas E. King to Jefferson Davis, 14 Feb. 1862, Letters, no. 1212-1862, reel 56.

25. Rufus W. Folger to Jefferson Davis, 18 Feb. 1862, Letters, F(WD)27, reel 46; Crist, ed., *Papers of Jefferson Davis,* vol. 8, *1862,* p. 73.

26. Joseph Taylor to Jefferson Davis, 15 June 1864, Letters, T(WD)140, reel 143.

27. A. G. Graham to Jefferson Davis, 3 April 1862, Letters, G(WD)186; Graham to George W. Randolph, 10 April 1862, Letters, G(WD)192; Thomas Hill Watts to George W. Randolph, 19 April 1862, Letters, G(WD),192, reel 47; John S. Rowland to George W. Randolph, 20 Oct. 1862, Letters, R(WD)661, reel 69. Rowland was superintendent of the Western and Atlantic Railroad in Atlanta.

28. W. H. Christian to Jefferson Davis, 2 Oct. 1862, Letters, C(WD)1029, reel 40; Henry M. Bowyer, petition to secretary of war, 10 Feb. 1862, B(WD)24, reel 31. Other requests for the extension of martial law to combat alcohol came from citizens of Madison County, Virginia, and the city council of Augusta, Georgia. T. H. Humphries et al. to Jefferson Davis, ca. 10 April 1862, Letters, H(WD)231, reel 50; Crist, ed., *Papers of Jefferson Davis,* 8:146; and *OR,* 1:14:478–79, 497.

29. B. M. Ednery to George W. Randolph, 15 Nov. 1862, Letters, E(WD)212, reel 45.

30. *OR,* 1:51:2:482.

31. Ibid.

32. *Charleston Courier,* 19 Feb. 1862.

33. Ibid., 3 April 1862.

34. *Richmond Dispatch,* 12 March 1862.

35. *Richmond Enquirer,* 8 July 1863.

36. Crist, ed., *Papers of Jefferson Davis,* 8:146; and *OR,* 1:14:478–79, 497.

37. Collier's ideas are examined in chapter 3.

38. See S. S. Satchwell to George W. Randolph, 25 Sept. 1862, Letters, S(WD)1106, reel 73. Surgeon Satchwell could act because General Theophilus Holmes had imposed martial law in Wilson, North Carolina, where the hospital was located.

39. *OR*, 1:14:489.

40. Northrup endorsement on J. C. Commack to commanding general, 11 Nov. 1862, Letters, C(WD)1237, reel 41; Northrup endorsement on Alexander H. H. Stuart to George W. Randolph, 5 Aug. 1862, Letters, S(WD)762, reel 72.

41. E. Griswold to George W. Randolph, 15 Oct. 1862, Letters, G(WD)717, reel 49.

42. Crist, ed., *Papers of Jefferson Davis*, 8:447.

43. *Acts of the General Assembly of the State of Virginia, 1861–2* (Richmond VA: William F. Ritchie, 1862), pp. 101–2.

44. Major B. P. Noland endorsement on J. P. Barksdale to secretary of war[?], 1 Feb. 1865, Letters, B(WD)69, reel 146.

45. See, for example, List of medicines required at the Medical Purveyors Department, C. S. Navy, Letters, M(WD)852, reel 105.

46. James Thomas Flexner, *George Washington in the American Revolution (1775–1783)* (Boston: Little, Brown, 1967), p. 220 n.

47. James Lyons to George W. Randolph, 17 June 1862, Letters, M(WD)756, reel 61.

48. *Richmond Dispatch*, 14 June 1862.

49. Randolph endorsement on Alexander H. H. Stuart to George W. Randolph, 5 Aug. 1862, Letters, S(WD)762, reel 72.

50. C. Vann Woodward, ed., *Mary Chesnut's Civil War* (New Haven CT: Yale Univ. Press, 1981), pp. 551, 550.

51. Alexander H. H. Stuart to George W. Randolph, 5 Aug. 1862, Letters, S(WD)762, reel 72.

52. Lewis G. Harvie to James A. Seddon, 5 Jan. 1863 [misdated 1862], Letters, H(WD)23, reel 94.

53. Alexander H. Stephens, *A Constitutional View of the War between the States*, 2 vols. (Philadelphia: National Register, 1868–70), 2:786–88. This is the letter referred to by Albert Pike in the previous chapter.

54. N. G. Swan to ———, 20 Aug. 1863, Letters, S(WD)537, reel 112.

55. Benjamin B. Nash to Charles Fowler with endorsement by John H. Winder, 31 March 1863, N(WD)52, Letters, reel 105.

56. [Virginia] *Acts, 1861–2*, pp. 101–2; [supplemental bill supplying date of first act] *Acts of the General Assembly of . . . Georgia, . . . November and December, 1863 . . . also, Extra Session of 1864* (Milledgeville: Boughton, Nisbet & Barns, 1864), p. 21; *Acts of . . . the General Assembly of Alabama . . . October and . . . November, 1862* (Montgomery: Montgomery Advertiser Book & Job Office, 1862), p. 43; *Acts and Resolutions Adopted by the General Assembly of Florida, . . . 1862* (Tallahassee: Dyke & Carlisle, 1862), p. 58; *Public Laws of the State of North Carolina, Passed . . . 1861– . . . 65* (Raleigh: William E. Pell, 1866), pp. 20–21; *Laws of Mississippi* (n.p., n.d.), p. 63; *Acts Passed by the Twenty-seventh Legislature of . . . Louisiana . . . December, 1862 and January, 1863* (Natchitoches: Times Office, 1864), p. 29; H. P. N. Gammel, ed., *The Laws of Texas, 1822–1897* 10 vols. (Austin: Gammel Books, 1898), 5:702.

57. S. S. Barber to John C. Breckinridge, 27 March 1865, Letters, B(WD)125, reel 146.

58. May Spencer Ringold, *The Role of the State Legislatures in the Confederacy* (Athens: Univ. of Georgia Press, 1966), p. 43.

59. But see, for example, Michael P. Johnson, *Toward a Patriarchal Republic: The Secession of Georgia* (Baton Rouge: Louisiana State Univ. Press, 1977), and William W. Freehling, *The Road to Disunion: Secessionists at Bay, 1776–1854* (New York: Oxford Univ. Press, 1990).

Part Two: The Confederate Bench and Bar

1. Eugene D. Genovese, *Roll, Jordan, Roll: The World the Slaves Made* (New York: Vintage, 1976), p. 26.

2. Vernon Burton, "Society," in Richard N. Current, ed., *Encyclopedia of the Confederacy,* 4 vols. (New York: Simon & Schuster, 1993), 4:1489.

3. Even legal historian Lawrence M. Friedman is somewhat bewitched by the image of the "lawyer-statesman"; see Friedman, *A History of American Law* (New York: Simon & Schuster, 1973), p. 271.

4. Charles S. Sydnor, "The Southerner and the Laws," *Journal of Southern History* 6 (Feb. 1940): 7.

5. The nature of the frontier bar—freewheeling or clinging to outdated forms—is itself a matter of debate. See Lawrence M. Friedman, *A History of American Law* (New York: Simon & Schuster, 1973), esp. pp. 138–47; Elizabeth G. Brown, "The Bar on a Frontier: Wayne County [Michigan], 1796–1836," *American Journal of Legal History* 14 (1970): 154–55; William W. Blume, "Civil Procedure on the American Frontier," *Michigan Law Review* 161 (1957): 209; and Raymond T. Zillmer, "The Lawyer on the Frontier," *American Law Review* 27 (1916): 30–41.

6. See Maxwell Bloomfield, *American Lawyers in a Changing Society, 1776–1876* (Cambridge: Harvard Univ. Press, 1976), pp. 271–301; Kermit Hall, "West H. Humphreys and the Crisis of the Union," *Tennessee Historical Quarterly* 34 (1975): 48–69; B. Patricia Dyson, "Contract Stability in Wartime: The Example of the Confederacy," *American Journal of Legal History* 19 (1975): 216–31.

7. Edward A. Pollard, *Life of Jefferson Davis, with a Secret History of the Southern Confederacy* . . . (Philadelphia: National Publishing, 1869; reprint, New York: Books for Libraries Press, 1969), pp. 310, 327.

8. Bloomfield, *American Lawyers in a Changing Society,* pp. 271–301.

9. William M. Robinson Jr., *Justice in Grey: A History of the Judicial System of the Confederate States* (Cambridge: Harvard Univ. Press, 1941), p. 625.

10. Hall, "West H. Humphreys," p. 69.

11. Dyson, "Contract Stability in Wartime," p. 231.

12. Jennifer Van Zant, "Confederate Conscription and the North Carolina Supreme Court," *North Carolina Historical Review* 72 (1995): 75. This article provides the only lucid explication of the North Carolina cases and is essential to understanding civil liberty in the Confederacy.

13. Pollard likely exaggerated Marshall's income from habeas corpus work as well as the number of such cases tried by the Confederate States district attorney. The records of the

Confederate district court were burned, but there are numerous references in the press. See *Richmond Enquirer,* 27 Sept. 1864, 18 Oct. 1864, 25 Oct. 1864, 3 Nov. 1864, and 20 Jan. 1865.

14. The *American Journal of Legal History* did not publish a single article on the Confederacy from 1987 through 1995, and only two articles on Confederate legal history have appeared in the thirty-nine-year career of that journal.

Chapter 3: Liberty and the Bar of the Confederacy

1. See Matthew S. Warshauer, "In the Beginning Was New Orleans: Andrew Jackson and the Politics of Martial Law," (Ph.D. diss., American Studies, Saint Louis University, 1997).

2. See Carl B. Swisher, *The Oliver Wendell Holmes Devise: History of the Supreme Court of the United States,* vol. 5, *The Taney Period, 1836–64* (New York: Macmillan, 1974), p. 845. See also William M. Wiecek, "The Great Writ and Reconstruction: The Habeas Corpus Act of 1867," *Journal of Southern History* 36 (1970): 533. Thanks to Professor Barry Cushman of the University of Virginia Law School for help with this question.

3. William Griffee Brown, *History of Nicholas County West Virginia* (Richmond VA: Dietz Press, 1954), p. 119.

4. Max R. Williams and J. G. de Roulhac Hamilton, eds., *The Papers of William Alexander Graham,* 8 vols. (Raleigh: North Carolina Office of Archives and History, 1957–92), vol. 5, *1857–1863* (1973), pp. 403–4.

5. Robinson, *Justice in Grey,* pp. 91–107, 279–288.

6. Kenneth C. Martis, *The Historical Atlas of the Congresses of the Confederate States of America: 1861–1865* (New York: Simon & Schuster, 1994), visually exaggerates Union occupation by including states like Kentucky and Missouri, which were claimed but never actually controlled by the Confederacy.

7. Bloomfield, *American Lawyers in a Changing Society,* pp. 291–92. See also Robinson, *Justice in Grey,* p. 283.

8. Bloomfield, *American Lawyers in a Changing Society,* p. 291.

9. Dunbar Rowland, ed., *Jefferson Davis, Constitutionalist: His Letters, Papers and Speeches,* 10 vols. (Jackson: Mississippi Department of Archives and History, 1923), 6:166; *Richmond Enquirer,* 3 Nov. 1864 and 20 Jan. 1865; *Black's Law Dictionary* (St. Paul MN: West, 1968), p. 876.

10. R. R. Collier to George W. Randolph, 27 Oct. 1862, Letters, C(WD)1142, reel 40.

11. R. R. Collier to George W. Randolph, 3 Nov. 1862, Letters, C(WD)1160, reel 41.

12. Crist, ed., *Papers of Jefferson Davis,* 8:479–80; see also *OR,* 2:4:591.

13. R. R. Collier to James A. Seddon, 24 Nov. 1862, with enclosed clipping, Letters, C(WD)1230, reel 41.

14. R. R. Collier to Jefferson Davis, 23 Dec. 1862, Letters, C(WD)7, reel 84. Collier showed the Cooper letter about Moore and Handly to another liquor seller tried by court-martial, one Jacob T. Crowder, who thought he should be released on account of it. See Crowder to Seddon, 1 Dec. 1862, Letters, C(WD)1266, reel 41.

15. R. R. Collier to Jefferson Davis, 23 Dec. 1862, with endorsement of 30 Dec. Letters, C(WD)7; Collier to James A. Seddon, 5 Jan. 1863, Letters, C(WD)18, reel 84; Bloomfield, *American Lawyers in a Changing Society,* p. 343; and G. S. Boritt, "Was Lincoln a Vulnerable Candidate

in 1860?" *Civil War History* 27 (1981), 43 n. My thanks to Frank J. Williams for help on this point.

16. See D. C. Glenn to R. R. Rhodes, 12 Nov. 1862, Letters, G(WD)838, reel 49 (advice); Crist, ed., *Papers of Jefferson Davis*, 7:144 (recommendation), 8:350 (request for appointment). For a biographical sketch of Glenn, see ibid., 2:301.

17. D. C. Glenn to Jefferson Davis, 1 Sept. 1863, Letters, G(WD)365, reel 93.

18. John B. Robbins, "The Confederacy and the Writ of Habeas Corpus," *Georgia Historical Quarterly* 55 (1971): 90.

19. Johnston recognized the need for a large army to save Vicksburg before he knew General Pemberton was besieged there. See Johnston to Pemberton, *OR*, 1:24:3:888. Pemberton knew also; see Pemberton to Johnston, 19 May 1863, p. 892.

20. M. R. Clark to George W. Randolph, 21 Oct. 1862, Letters, C(WD)1150, reel 40.

21. D. C. Glenn to James A. Seddon, 17 June 1863, Letters, G(WD)275, reel 93.

22. D. C. Glenn to Thomas Hill Watts, 17 June 1863, Letters, G(WD)275, reel 93.

23. Thomas Hill Watts to James A. Seddon, 22 June 1863, Letters, G(WD)275, reel 93.

24. *OR*, 1:24:3:785; Stephen A. Forbes, "Grierson's Cavalry Raid," in *Transactions of the Illinois State Historical Society for the Year 1907* (Springfield: Illinois State Historical Library, 1908), p. 111.

25. Rowland, ed., *Jefferson Davis, Constitutionalist*, 5:491 n.

26. Jefferson Davis to Joseph E. Johnston, 18 May 1863, in Rowland, ed., *Jefferson Davis, Constitutionalist*, 5:489.

27. Ibid., 5:491.

28. Ibid., 6:3.

29. William H. Hancock to Ethelbert Barksdale, 15 June 1863, Letters, G(WD)275, reel 93.

30. Ethelbert Barksdale to Jefferson Davis, 27 June 1863, Letters, G(WD)275, reel 93.

31. D. C. Glenn to R. R. Rhodes, 10 Aug. 1863 with endorsements by Davis and Seddon, Letters, G(WD)365, reel 93; Glenn to James A. Seddon, 20 July 1864, Letters, G(WD)175, reel 128.

32. F. Garvin Davenport, ed., "Judge Sharkey Papers," *Mississippi Valley Historical Review* 20 (1933): esp. 83–87; and Davenport, ed., "The Essay on *Habeas Corpus* in the Judge Sharkey Papers," *Mississippi Valley Historical Review* 22 (1936): esp. 243–45. Glenn, incidentally, regarded Sharkey as a traitor in 1863.

33. On this role of lawyers, see Mark E. Steiner, "The Lawyer as Peacemaker: Law and Community in Abraham Lincoln's Slander Cases," *Journal of the Abraham Lincoln Association* 16 (1995): esp. 1–3.

34. John Gill Shorter to James A. Seddon, 19 Oct. 1863, Letters, G(WD)400, reel 93; and Benjamin Gardner to Shorter, 11 Oct. 1863, Letters, G(WD)400, reel 93.

35. *Black's Law Dictionary*, p. 161.

36. Robert M. Barton to James A. Seddon, 4 May 1863, Letters, J(WD)157, reel 98.

37. John A. Gilmer to Zebulon Vance, 15 Dec. 1863, and Hugh A. Cole to John A. Gilmer, 15 Nov. 1863, Letters, W(WD)60, reel 144.

38. 60 *North Carolina*, 78 (1863).

39. 60 *North Carolina*, 80 (1863).

40. 60 *North Carolina*, 180 (1863).

41. 60 *North Carolina*, 194 (1863); Williams and Hamilton, eds., *Papers of William Alexander Graham*, 5:433–34, 435–36, 439, 445–46, 453, 473, 483–84, 493–94, 527; Case of R. J. Graves, Letters, W(WD)40, reel 115, and Graves to James A. Seddon, 15 Dec. 1862, S(WD)209, reel 110; *OR*, 2:5:794–800.

42. J. B. Jones, *A Rebel War Clerk's Diary at the Confederate States Capital*, 2 vols. (Philadelphia: J. B. Lippincott, 1866), 2:117–18.

43. Kenneth Radley, "Military Justice," in Current, ed., *Encyclopedia of the Confederacy*, 3:1039. Judge advocates served in military courts with the armies to enforce the articles of war.

44. D. B. Harris to Lucius B. Northrup, 20 June 1863, with numerous endorsements, Letters, H(WD)441, reel 96.

45. *OR*, 4:2:967.

46. They apparently did so in North Carolina in 1863, where Thomas Bragg was hired. See Thomas Bragg to James A. Seddon, 25 June 1863, Letters, reel 82.

47. 60 *North Carolina*, 181 (1863).

48. 60 *North Carolina*, 517 (1864).

49. E. W. Upshaw to ?, 20 April 1864, Letters, A(WD)20, reel 146 (copy).

50. Joel M. Acker to A. R. Lawton, 18 Oct. 1864, Letters, A(WD)20, reel 146.

51. T. S. Haymond to Jefferson Davis, 14 Feb. 1865, with endorsement by J. A. Campbell, Letters, N(WD)18, reel 150.

52. Economic historians largely ignore the legal problems and chastise the Confederate government instead for failing to take the economic measures necessary for the currency's ready acceptance. See, for example, Douglas B. Ball, *Financial Failure and Confederate Defeat* (Urbana: Univ. of Illinois Press, 1991), esp. p. 176.

53. *OR*, 1:15:772.

54. R. H. Forrester to J. B. Villepigue, 3 July 1862, Letters, H(WD)70, reel 52. Hawkins attributed his problem to Van Dorn's orders but appears to have been arraigned before their official publication.

55. Case of S. M. Hawkins, J. B. Villepigue to George W. Randolph, 31 Aug. 1862, Letters, H(WD)70, reel 52. Anti-Semitism was common among Civil War generals.

56. Samuel M. Hawkins to George W. Randolph, 15 July 1862, Letters, H(WD)70, reel 52.

57. E. S. Fisher, draft opinion, 15 July 1862, Letters, H(WD)70, reel 52.

58. Endorsement by R. G. H. Kean, 28 Aug. 1862, Letters, H(WD)70, reel 52.

59. Samuel M. Hawkins to George W. Randolph, 4 Aug. 1862, Letters, H(WD)70, reel 52.

60. Samuel M. Hawkins to George W. Randolph, 9 Aug. 1862, Letters, H(WD)70, reel 52.

61. Robert H. Forrester to George W. Randolph, 14 Aug. 1862, Letters, H(WD)70, reel 52.

62. For problems in everyday transactions, see case of Mark Vall, M. J. Saffold report of 1 Oct. 1863, Letters, S(WD)605, reel 112; case of George W. Adams, report of S. S. Baxter, 25 July 1862, Letters, B(WD)811, reel 34; and case of Robert Garrett, arrested 6 March 1863, Letters, P(WD)161, reel 106.

63. Case of George W. Adams, report of S. S. Baxter, 25 July 1862, Letters, B(WD)811, reel 34.

64. For the importance of ending substitution and drafting principals, see William Blair, *Virginia's Private War: Feeding Body and Soul in the Confederacy* (New York: Oxford Univ. Press, 1998), esp. p. 103.

Chapter 4: "Unaffected by . . . the Condition of Our Country"

1. J. G. de Roulhac Hamilton, "The State Courts and the Confederate Constitution," *Journal of Southern History* 4 (1938): 425–48; Memory F. Mitchell, *Legal Aspects of Conscription and Exemption in North Carolina, 1861–1865* (Chapel Hill: Univ. of North Carolina Press, 1965); Van Zant, "Confederate Conscription," pp. 54–75. Van Zant's lucid article made this chapter possible by opening the meaning of Pearson's decisions for any historical practitioner.

2. Van Zant, "Confederate Conscription," p. 75.

3. Ibid., p. 62.

4. In North Carolina the issue was complicated by the question of whether justices had the power only in vacation or whether the court itself had the power during regular term. See *In the matter of Bryan, 60 North Carolina,* 49 (1863).

5. J. Mills Thornton III, "Fiscal Policy and the Failure of Radical Reconstruction in the Lower South," in J. Morgan Kousser and James M. McPherson, eds., *Region, Race, and Reconstruction: Essays in Honor of C. Vann Woodward* (New York: Oxford Univ. Press, 1982), pp. 352–53.

6. *In the matter of Austin, 60 North Carolina,* 186 (1863). On stingy taxpayers, see John J. Duff, *A. Lincoln, Prairie Lawyer* (New York: Rinehart, 1960), p. 174.

7. Vernon Burton emphasized the connection between legal and political careers in "Society," in Current, ed., *Encyclopedia of the Confederacy,* 4:1489.

8. One-volume histories mentioning Pearson include Clement Eaton, *A History of the Southern Confederacy* (1954; reprint, New York: Free Press, 1965), pp. 256, 267; Charles P. Roland, *The Confederacy* (Chicago: Univ. of Chicago Press, 1960), p. 129 (Judge James D. Halyburton is also mentioned); and E. Merton Coulter, *The Confederate States of America, 1861–1865* (Baton Rouge: Louisiana State Univ. Press, 1950), pp. 123, 392 (Halyburton also mentioned). Pearson was not mentioned in the book that first called attention to internal dissent as a cause of Confederate defeat, Frank L. Owsley's *State Rights in the Confederacy.* William M. Robinson Jr. gives him only one sentence in *Justice in Grey,* p. 616.

9. J. G. de Roulhac Hamilton, "Pearson, Richmond Mumford," in *Dictionary of American Biography,* 20 vols. (New York: Charles Scribner's Sons, 1934), 14:360–61. In Reconstruction he became a Republican and less stalwart in his defense of habeas corpus privilege than he had been during the war. See especially Hamilton, *Reconstruction in North Carolina,* Studies in History, Economics and Public Law Edited by the Faculty of Political Science of Columbia University, vol. 58 (New York: Columbia University, 1914), esp. p. 511.

10. The political interpretation was Hamilton's in "The State Courts and the Confederate Constitution," pp. 431, 434–35, 438.

11. An alternative explanation, offered by Van Zant, is the proximity of Richmond Hill to the Confederate military prison in Salisbury. But arrested conscripts were often held in camps of instruction or the guard house; they were not actually imprisoned. Petitioners sought Pearson's court from many miles away. Van Zant, "Confederate Conscription," p. 58 n.

12. Rowland, ed., *Jefferson Davis, Constitutionalist,* 6:167.

13. Hamilton, "Pearson," in *Dictionary of American Biography,* 14:360–61.

14. Robinson, *Justice in Grey,* pp. 73, 74, 72, 92; *60 North Carolina,* 13 n (1863).

15. *60 North Carolina,* 182 (1863); *In the matter of Curtis, 60 North Carolina,* 194 (1863); *60 North Carolina,* 31, 40 (1863).

16. *In the matter of J. C. Bryan, 60 North Carolina, 60 (1863).*

17. Richard Bardolph said that "Pearson seemed to deny the constitutionality of the conscription laws themselves as well as the means used to enforce them." Bardolph, "Inconstant Rebels: Desertion of North Carolina Troops in the Civil War," *North Carolina Historical Review* 41 (1964): 185. John G. Barrett said that Pearson thought conscription unconstitutional and felt it was no crime to desert. Barrett, *The Civil War in North Carolina* (Chapel Hill: Univ. of North Carolina Press, 1963), p. 242. See also Roland, *The Confederacy*, p. 129.

18. *In the matter of Irvin, 60 North Carolina, 72 n (1863).* See W. Buck Yearns and John G. Barrett, eds., *North Carolina Civil War Documentary* (Chapel Hill: Univ. of North Carolina Press, 1980), pp. 150–53.

19. Thomas Bragg to James A. Seddon, 28 June 1863, Letters, B(WD)486, reel 82. On the issue of jurisdiction for a state court in conscription matters, see Van Zant, "Confederate Conscription," pp. 58, 60, 63 n; *In the matter of Bryan, 60 North Carolina, 17 (1863).*

20. See Mitchell, *Legal Aspects of Conscription*, p. 46; *OR*, 1:18:887; 1:25:2:747–49; 1:51:2:709, 711–12, 717; M. M. Manly to James A. Seddon, 7 April 1863, Letters, M(WD)673, reel 104.

21. *Public Laws of the State of North Carolina, Passed . . . 1863* (Raleigh: W. W. Holden, 1863), pp. 11–12. See also *Public Laws of the State of North Carolina, Passed . . . 1864–'65* (Raleigh: Carmon & Holden, 1865).

22. *In the matter of D. L. Russell, 60 North Carolina, 391 (1864).* Hamilton in his able sketch of Pearson properly emphasizes the judge's lack of interest in precedent and his emphasis on logic and deduction. Hamilton, "Pearson," in *Dictionary of American Biography*, 14:360–61.

23. 60 *North Carolina*, 370, 372–73 (1864); Van Zant, "Confederate Conscription and the North Carolina Supreme Court," pp. 69–70. Van Zant's reading of this and subsequent cases is unequaled in clarity, and I rely on it entirely. See also her surefooted and clearheaded analysis of the case titled *In the matter of Spivey*, where Pearson let a conscript officer continue to hold the petitioner because the officer, probably by chance, gave the proper response to the writ and called Spivey a "prisoner" held in an "attempt to avoid service" and not a "conscript."

24. *In the matter of Bryan, 60 North Carolina, 57 (1863).*

25. *In the matter of Cain, 60 North Carolina, 517–19 (1864).* Pearson argued that a contrary position would make "the President . . . a *dictator.*"

26. *Walton v Gatlin, 60 North Carolina, 317 (1864);* and *Walton v Gatlin, 60 North Carolina, 331 (1864)* (Pearson quotation at pp. 353–54).

27. *William D. Johnson v Peter Mallett, 60 North Carolina, 413 (1864).*

28. *Seth Bridgman v Peter Mallett, 60 North Carolina, 493–96 (1864).*

29. Ibid., pp. 496–97.

30. Ibid., pp. 497–502.

31. *Matthew Johnson v Peter Mallett, 60 North Carolina, 502–5 (1864).* Battle's reasoning here was different. He found a conflict of judicial authority as the Confederate judge Halyburton thought such exemption all right, but a Petersburg circuit court judge named Joynes did not. He felt empowered to "adopt the strong convictions" of his "own mind" in such a case.

32. Van Zant, "Confederate Conscription," p. 75.

33. Vandiver, *Their Tattered Flags*, p. 266; Mitchell, *Legal Aspects of Conscription*, p. 84.

34. *In the matter of Huie, 60 North Carolina, 165 (1863).*

35. Works of the populist school of Confederate history rarely consider the other side of

conscription, the way in which the government gradually made it less and less favorable to the upper classes.

36. Van Zant, "Confederate Conscription," p. 67; *Ex parte Walton*, 60 *North Carolina*, 367–68 (1864).

37. Van Zant, "Confederate Conscription," p. 68; *Gatlin v Walton*, 60 *North Carolina*, 354 (1864).

38. Edward Younger, ed., *Inside the Confederate Government: The Diary of Robert Garlick Hill Kean* (1957; reprint, Baton Rouge: Louisiana State Univ. Press, 1993), p. 138.

39. James A. Seddon to Zebulon B. Vance, 5 March 1864, *OR*, 4:3:197–98.

40. Jefferson Davis to Thomas Bragg, 7 March 1864, *OR*, 4:3:200–201.

41. Mark E. Neely Jr., "Justice Embattled: The Lincoln Administration and the Constitutional Controversy over Conscription in 1863," in Jennifer M. Lowe, ed., *The Supreme Court and the Civil War*, special issue of *Journal of Supreme Court History* (Washington DC: Supreme Court Historical Society, 1996), pp. 47–61.

42. Van Zant, "Confederate Conscription," p. 75.

43. Yearns and Barrett, *North Carolina Civil War Documentary*, p. 152.

44. Robert R. Heath to James A. Seddon, 2 March 1864, Letters, H(WD)166, reel 129.

45. See Braswell D. Deen Jr. and William Scott Henwood, *Georgia's Appellate Judiciary: Profiles and History* (Norcross GA: Harrison, 1987), p. 3; Dunbar Rowland, *Courts, Judges, and Lawyers of Mississippi, 1798–1935* (Jackson: Mississippi Department of Archives and History and Mississippi Historical Society, 1935), p. 78; John B. Galbraith, *Reports of Cases . . . in the Supreme Courts of Florida, at Terms Held in 1862–'3–'4*, vol. 10 (Tallahassee: Dyke & Sparhawk, 1864); J. S. G. Richardson, *Reports of Cases . . . in the Court of Appeals and Court of Errors of South Carolina*, vol. 13 (Charleston: E. J. Dawson, 1866); Thomas H. Coldwell, *Report of Cases . . . in the Supreme Court of Tennessee during the Years 1860–61*, vol. 26 (1867; reprint, St. Louis: Gilbert Books, 1881); John W. Shepherd, *Report of Cases . . . in the Supreme Court of Alabama, . . . 1861 . . . [to] 1863*, vol. 38 (Montgomery AL: Barret & Brown's Book and Job Office, 1867); L. E. Barber, *Reports of Cases . . . in the Supreme Court of Arkansas, . . . 1862 [to] . . . 1867*, vol. 24 (Little Rock: Woodruff Printing, 1889).

46. See *Reports of Cases . . . in the Supreme Court of Louisiana*, vol. 16 (1861–62) (New Orleans: Bloomfield & Steel, 1866); Peachy R. Grattan, *Reports of Cases Decided in the Supreme Court of Appeals of Virginia*, 1 July 1861 to 1 April 1865 (Richmond: J. W. Randolph & English, 1867).

47. A majority of Confederate states chose their justices by popular election.

48. Rowland, *Courts, Judges, and Lawyers*, p. 79. J. G. de Roulhac Hamilton used the scarcity of constitutional cases in Confederate state courts as proof that liberty was rarely threatened. He realized, however, that the North Carolina Supreme Court posed a problem for such an interpretation. He attempted to explain away the contrary evidence by pointing to the state's "highly individualistic population, containing a considerable element which had been lukewarm towards the Confederacy from the beginning." But other states lukewarm on secession caused no similar problems. Hamilton, "The State Courts and the Confederate Constitution," *Journal of Southern History* 4 (Nov. 1938), 431, 434–35, 438. For humor see Van Zant, "Confederate Conscription," p. 71.

49. J. Mills Thornton III, *Politics and Power in a Slave Society: Alabama, 1800–1860* (Baton Rouge: Louisiana State Univ. Press, 1978), p. xviii.

Chapter 5: Ghosts of the Dead Habeas Corpus

1. See Alwyn Barr, ed., "Records of the Confederate Military Commission in San Antonio, July 2–October 10, 1862," *Southwestern Historical Quarterly* 70 (1966–67): 93–109, 289–313, 623–44, and 71 (1967): 247–77. Newspapers noted the early courts-martial in Richmond without adverse comment. See, for example, *Richmond Enquirer,* 7 Oct. 1861, 12 Nov. 1861, 19 Nov. 1861, and 6 Dec. 1861.

2. *OR,* 2:2:1373. See Robinson, *Justice in Grey,* pp. 387–89.

3. James Lyons to L. P. Walker, 2 Sept. 1861 and 6 Sept. 1861, Letters, no. 3918-1861, no. 4012-1861, reel 8. Tucker appears never to have served.

4. *OR,* 4:3:204. Military officials made various appointments of persons to review civilian cases, though it is not possible to ascertain whether any appointments came as a result of section 2 of the Habeas Corpus Act of 13 October 1862. Thus Charles A. Stringfellow, the assistant adjutant general in Knoxville, appointed L. P. Mynatt to "inquire into the charges against all civilians charged in violations of the laws of the Confederate States" and to "report in writing your opinion as a lawyer who should be released on account of the vagueness or frivolousness of the accusations or the want of evidence . . . and who should be confined for trial." *OR,* 2:4:920. An appointment made before the October act called for a military commission to examine charges against political prisoners in Columbia [Mississippi?]. See George William Brent to D. W. Adams, 18 June 1862, *OR,* 2:3:892.

5. James Lyons report, 12 Dec. 1861, Letters, no. 8371-1861, reel 18.

6. Letters, reel 23.

7. Sydney S. Baxter to George W. Randolph, 24 July 1862, Letters, B(WD)806, reel 34.

8. Bill of S. S. Baxter, 24 July 1862, B(WD)806, reel 34.

9. S. S. Baxter, Suggestions on martial law, 29 April 1862, Letters, B(WD)488, reel 33.

10. Case of Daniel F. Dulaney, Letters, C(WD)1001, reel 88.

11. Report of S. S. Baxter, 5 Jan. 1861, B(WD)9, reel 81; *OR,* 2:5:804.

12. Robert O. Dixon to Jefferson Davis, 3 Sept. 1862, with endorsement by Randolph, Letters, L(WD)519, reel 58.

13. J. B. Baldwin to James A. Seddon, 2 March 1863, B(WD)9, reel 81.

14. S. S. Baxter to John B. Baldwin, March 1863, Letters, B(WD)267, reel 82.

15. James A. Seddon to Zebulon Vance, 27 Dec. 1862, *OR,* 2:5:798.

16. *OR,* 2:5:837, 852.

17. Henry Foote to John H. Winder, 21 Dec. 1863, with endorsement by James A. Seddon, Letters, F(WD)30, reel 126.

18. Henry Foote to James A. Seddon, 15 Jan. 1864, Letters, F(WD)30, reel 126.

19. B. R. Wellford Jr., to Sydney S. Baxter, 20 Jan. 1864, Letters, C(WD)154, reel 123.

20. Southern Historical Society, *Southern Historical Society Papers,* 51:116, 155, 199–200.

21. Robinson, *Justice in Grey,* pp. 386–87.

22. Ibid., p. 383.

23. Ibid., pp. 410–11.

24. What Robinson cited as evidence for the continuation as "special" commissioners proved nothing of the kind. Campbell's letter appointing Peter Hamilton on 30 July 1864, for example, mentioned nothing about concluding cases. See *OR,* 2:7:515–16, 4:3:225, 4:3:210. See Robinson, *Justice in Grey,* 411 n.

25. See Noel Fisher, "'The Leniency Shown Them Has Been Unavailing': The Confederate Occupation of East Tennessee," *Civil War History* 40 (1994): 290; Robinson, *Justice in Grey*, p. 385.

26. Letters, no. 8371-1861, reel 18.

27. Letters, no. 8382-1861, reel 18.

28. Case of M. Chapman, Letters, C(WD)605, reel 112.

29. Case of Henry H. Cowdry, Letters, C(WD)605, reel 112, reel 123; RG 109, chap. 9, vol. 100, National Archives; OR, 2:6:917; H. H. Cowdry to Isaac H. Carrington, n.d., Dept. of Henrico Papers, 1861–1864, Virginia Historical Society, Richmond. Cowdry moved to Alabama, left when the war began, but returned to retrieve his family in 1863, when he was arrested.

30. Case of John C. Gilliland, Letters, B(WD)163, reel 31.

31. Ibid.

32. Affidavit of Rebecca J. Burr and P. M. Gabbent, Letters, B(WD)163, reel 31.

33. Case of Joel Mayhue, Letters, C(WD)617, reel 86.

34. Case of Robert Tyson, Letters, reel 143; Prisoners Brought Before Vowles and Sands, 1864, RG 109, chap. 9, vol. 229, National Archives.

35. Case of Charles A. Thatcher, Letters, F(WD)133, reel 46, W(WD)126, reel 115.

36. Case of John Miller, Letters, B(WD)509, reel 121.

37. The widely cited article is Robert Neil Mathis, "Freedom of the Press in the Confederacy: A Reality," *Historian* 37 (1975): 633–48.

38. Clement Eaton, *The Freedom-of-Thought Struggle in the Old South*, rev. ed. (New York: Harper & Row, 1964). Study of the Confederate press has not closely examined the continuity of antebellum self-restraint during the war, but see J. Cutler Andrews, *The South Reports the War* (Princeton NJ: Princeton Univ. Press, 1970), pp. 540–41.

39. Case of Frank Smyth, Letters, no. 3423-1861, reel 8; *OR*, 2:2:1382.

40. Case of Gabriel Cueto, Letters, B(WD)1424, reel 36, C(WD)1223, reel 41, B(WD)14, reel 81; *OR*, 2:5:775.

41. Williams and Hamilton, eds., *Papers of William Alexander Graham*, vol. 6, *1864–1865* (Raleigh: North Carolina Department of Cultural Resources, Division of Archives and History, 1976), p. 97.

42. Case of T. S. Whitaker, Letters, W(WD)410, reel 145.

43. This is the usual excuse for excess; see Fisher, "'Leniency Shown Them Has Been Unavailing,'" p. 291.

44. Case of Daniel F. Dulaney, Letters, C(WD)1001, reel 88, D(WD)65, reel 125. Other arrests for sedition include John C. Smyth, Letters, C(WD)984, reel 88; Fielding Boggs, Letters, B(WD)163, reel 31; Joseph A. Alderson Jr., Letters, B(WD)1527, reel 37; Duggan, *OR*, 2:1:834; John Frost, Letters, B(WD)27, reel 81; Dr. John A. Hannah, *OR*, 2:6:18, and Letters, H(WD)404, reel 95; James Johnson, Affidavit of Thomas Oldham, Aug. 1863, Dept. of Henrico Papers. See also John Goddard, Letters, V(WD)37, reel 143; B. S. Herndon to Isaac H. Carrington, 20 Feb. 1864, Dept. of Henrico Papers, and RG 109, chap. 9, vol. 229, National Archives; Jefferson T. Main, Letters, B(WD)163, reel 31; Charles Williams, *OR*, 2:4:861; and William J. Walker, Letters, no. 9291, reel 21.

45. William D. Hennen to John A. Campbell, 6 July 1863, Letters, H(WD)549, reel 96.

46. Ibid.; case of Jesse Rogers, Letters, H(WD)529, reel 130.

47. *OR*, 2:6:30.

48. Case of William Gallycan, Letters, H(WD)197, reel 129.

49. William D. Hennen to J. A. Campbell, 22 Sept. 1863, Letters, H(WD)622, reel 129; report of 2 March 1864, Letters, H(WD)373, reel 129.

50. Case of Robert Ramsey, Letters, H(WD)194, reel 129.

51. Case of Andrew Gray, Letters, H(WD)402, reel 130.

52. Robinson, *Justice in Grey,* p. 411 n.

53. Case of J. P. Lawrence (also John Weaver and Joseph Pharis), Letters, L(WD)69, reel 133, and L(WD)72, reel 149. These prisoners had counsel. Leovy offered mercy in the cases of Joshua Bishop, Letters, L(WD)71, reel 149, and David Hall and Andrew Iddings, Letters, L(WD)75 and 74-½, reel 149.

54. Henry J. Leovy to James A. Seddon, 4 Nov. 1864, *OR,* 4:3:815.

55. *OR,* 4:3:815.

56. *OR,* 4:3:819–20.

57. Percy Walker to James A. Seddon, 21 Jan. 1863, Letters, frame 301, reel 115.

58. Case of James B. Miller, and Peter Hamilton to James A. Seddon and to J. A. Campbell, 5 April 1864, Letters, H(WD)225, H(WD)230, and H(WD)261, reel 129.

59. Peter Hamilton to James A. Seddon, 23 April 1864, with Seddon endorsement, H(WD)280, reel 129.

60. J. B. Magruder memo, Letters, no. 3371-1861, reel 7.

61. See, for example, John P. Frank, *Lincoln as a Lawyer* (Urbana: Univ. of Illinois Press, 1961), p. 24; Duff, *A. Lincoln, Prairie Lawyer,* p. 168; Bloomfield, *American Lawyers in a Changing Society,* p. 242.

62. *OR* , 1:52:2:648. Jessie Pearl Rice, *J. L. M. Curry: Southerner, Statesman and Educator* (New York: King's Crown Press, 1949), p. 44.

63. Jabez L. M. Curry to James A. Seddon, 15 June 1864, Letters, C(WD)405, reel 124.

64. J. L. M. Curry, *Civil History of the Government of the Confederate States with Some Personal Reminiscences* (Richmond VA: B. F. Johnson, 1901), p. 31.

65. Ibid., p. 32.

Part Three: Dissent

1. Jefferson Davis, *The Rise and Fall of the Confederate Government,* 2 vols. (New York: D. Appleton, 1881), 2:304, 306.

2. Charles P. Roland, *The Confederacy* (Chicago: Univ. of Chicago Press, 1960).

3. Vandiver, *Their Tattered Flags.*

4. Thomas, *Confederate Nation,* p. 125; Thomas does not deal with East Tennessee after mentioning the section's opposition to secession of the state.

5. Clement Eaton, *A History of the Southern Confederacy,* (1954; reprint, New York: Free Press, 1965), pp. 40–42, 163. See also Coulter, *Confederate States of America,* pp. 84–86.

6. Thornton, *Politics and Power in a Slave Society,* p. 437. Emphasis on economic hardships late in the war has a similar effect.

7. Eric Foner, *Reconstruction: America's Unfinished Revolution, 1863–1877* (New York: Harper & Row, 1988), pp. 13, 14, 15.

8. Escott, *After Secession,* p. 137.

9. Foner, *Reconstruction,* p. 18.

10. See Gary W. Gallagher, *The Confederate War: How Popular Will, Nationalism, and Strategy Could Not Stave Off Defeat* (Cambridge: Harvard Univ. Press, 1997), esp. p. 3.

Chapter 6: The Politics of Pastoralism in East Tennessee

1. See W. Todd Groce, "The Social Origins of East Tennessee's Confederate Leadership," in Kenneth W. Noe and Shannon H. Wilson, eds., *The Civil War in Appalachia: Collected Essays* (Knoxville: Univ. of Tennessee Press, 1997). The restoration of East Tennessee to Confederate history is in progress on several fronts. See Noel Fisher's book-length treatment, *War at Every Door: Partisan Politics and Guerrilla Violence in East Tennessee, 1860–1869* (Chapel Hill: Univ. of North Carolina Press, 1997), and two other articles in Noe and Wilson, eds., *Civil War in Appalachia*: Peter Wallenstein, "Helping to Save the Union: The Social Origins, Wartime Experiences, and Military Impact of White Union Troops from East Tennessee," and Robert Tracy McKenzie, "'Oh Ours Is a Deplorable Condition': The Economic Impact of the Civil War in Upper East Tennessee." These works appeared while this book was being revised for publication. Previously, interest was high from the 1930s to the 1950s. See Coulter, *William G. Brownlow;* Thomas Alexander, *Thomas A. R. Nelson of East Tennessee* (Nashville: Tennessee Historical Commission, 1956); Verton M. Queener, "Origin of the Republican Party in East Tennessee to 1867," *East Tennessee Historical Society Publications* 13 (1941): 66–90, and "East Tennessee Sentiment and the Secession Movement, November 1860–June 1861," 20 (1948): 59–83. Quiet decades followed with the rise in reputation of Jefferson Davis and modernization theories.

2. East Tennessee was a departmental designation of the Confederate government. The *OR* uses the term extensively. Some older histories retain index entries for "East Tennessee" as though it had attained, like West Virginia, a separate political identity. See, for example, Coulter, *Confederate States of America*. A revival of interest in the subject began with Charles Faulkner Bryan Jr., "The Civil War in East Tennessee: A Social, Political, and Economic Study" (Ph.D. diss., University of Tennessee, Knoxville, 1978); and Daniel Crofts, *Reluctant Confederates: Upper South Unionists in the Secession Crisis* (Chapel Hill: Univ. of North Carolina Press, 1989).

3. Fisher, "'Leniency Shown Them Has Been Unavailing,'" pp. 280, 290. The logical comparison is with Missouri, where northern forces occupied their own state, and not with Federal policies in East Tennessee.

4. Charles F. Bryan Jr., "'Tories' amidst Rebels: Confederate Occupation of East Tennessee, 1861–1863," *East Tennessee Historical Society Publications* 60 (1988): 4.

5. "It was not Yankee manifestos, but hunger and hardship, that first tested the commitment of the plain folk to the old order in the occupied South," argues Stephen V. Ash in *When the Yankees Came: Conflict and Chaos in the Occupied South, 1861–1865* (Chapel Hill: Univ. of North Carolina Press, 1995), p. 177.

6. See maps and charts in Stephen V. Ash, *Middle Tennessee Society Transformed, 1860–1870* (Baton Rouge: Louisiana State Univ. Press, 1988); and John Cimprich, *Slavery's End in Tennessee, 1861–1865* (University: Univ. of Alabama Press, 1985). Bryan includes Fentress County in East Tennessee in "The Civil War in East Tennessee." See also Fisher, *War at Every Door,* pp. 8, 200 n (for mention of Fentress and White Counties). The region was antisecessionist, but

six of the counties were secessionist. For statistics on wealth and slaveholding, see Ash, *Middle Tennessee Society Transformed*, pp. 10–11. Though Ash uses East Tennessee only for comparison, his book is valuable.

7. William G. Brownlow, *Sketches of the Rise, Progress, and Decline of Secession: With a Narrative of Personal Adventures among the Rebels* (Philadelphia: George W. Childs, 1862), p. 210 (emphasis added).

8. Mary Emily Robertson Campbell, *The Attitude of Tennesseans toward the Union, 1847–1861* (New York: Vantage, 1961), p. 175. Bryan also makes the point that the majority of East Tennesseans lived in a valley in landscapes not unlike those in Middle Tennessee. Bryan, "Civil War in East Tennessee," p. 8.

9. Richard McCormick, *The Second American Party System: Party Formation in the Jacksonian Era* (Chapel Hill: Univ. of North Carolina Press, 1966), p. 235.

10. Oliver Temple called attention to the "noteworthy" quality of the political leadership and listed many others who enjoyed distinguished political careers. Temple, *East Tennessee and the Civil War*, p. 361.

11. Crofts, *Reluctant Confederates*, p. 149.

12. Campbell gave the Sevier vote as 1,243 to 69; the more lopsided figure was Temple's. The total vote exceeded the total vote in the presidential election the previous November; according to the *Tribune Almanac*, 1,230 voters turned out in Sevier in November 1860.

13. Vote totals are based on figures compiled from Temple, *East Tennessee in the Civil War*, and Campbell, *Attitude of Tennesseans toward the Union*, as well as the *Tribune Almanac*. Figures for some counties vary a little from source to source.

14. Bryan maintains that early policy was set by Tennessee governor Isham Harris, who gave up on conciliation when the August 1861 election results showed little drift toward supporting secessionist leaders in the region. Bryan points to some arrests of civilians that preceded the bridge-burning revolt of November. Bryan, "Civil War in East Tennessee," pp. 71, 80.

15. *OR*, 2:1:840–41.

16. *OR*, 2:1:842. The quotation provided the title of Noel C. Fisher's article on East Tennessee, "'The Leniency Shown Them Has Been Unavailing.'"

17. *OR*, 2:1:858.

18. See *OR*, 2:1:844–45.

19. *OR*, 2:1:848.

20. Brownlow, *Rise, Progress, and Decline of Secession*, facing p. 301.

21. *OR*, 2:2:1392. Benjamin's hanging-by-the-bridge order was quoted in later war propaganda—for example, see Edward Everett, *Account of the Fund for the Relief of East Tennessee; with a Complete List of the Contributors* (Boston: Little, Brown, 1864), pp. 14–15—but faded quickly from memory.

22. Rowland, ed., *Jefferson Davis, Constitutionalist*, 5:40.

23. Crist, ed., *Papers of Jefferson Davis*, 7:437.

24. Wallenstein, "'Helping to Save the Union,'" p. 13.

25. *OR*, 2:1:858.

26. *OR*, 2:1:852.

27. Nathaniel G. Taylor, a Carter County politician and refugee who agitated for East Ten-

nessee relief in the North during the war, estimated that Confederate authorities had made prisoners of some 5,000 East Tennesseans—an impossibly high figure. See Everett, *Relief of East Tennessee,* p. 15. The 660 names I have found in surviving records, on the other hand, are too few in number. The records surveyed include National Archives, RG 109, chap. 9, 219-½, manuscript, "Record of Political Prisoners, Department of East Tennessee, 1862"; the Letters Received by the Confederate Secretary of War, 1861–1865; the *Official Records*; standard published works on East Tennessee; and *Message of the President . . . Feb. 11, 1863 . . . Listing Civilians in Custody in Richmond* (Richmond VA, 1863) and . . . *Feb. 27, 1863 . . . List of Civilian Prisoners at Salisbury* (Richmond VA, 1863), hereafter cited as *Message.*

28. Of the 660, place of arrest was determined for 436. The Green County area accounted for 42.7 percent with its 186 prisoners. Knox and Sevier accounted for another 52 prisoners. Together these two areas accounted for over half, 54 percent, of the prisoners for whom place of arrest is known.

29. East Tennessee arrest records come mainly from three groups: first, those among the 303 in the report to Congress; second, a well-described group of 58 from records made by habeas corpus commissioner William D. Hennen from August 1863 to April 1864, and third, others compiled from the remaining Letters Received by the Confederate Secretary of War. The National Archives record of East Tennessee prisoners contains little information beyond their names.

30. Case of George M. Billingsley, Letters, W(WD)126, pt. 2, reel 115.

31. The point about poverty is made in Bryan, "Civil War in East Tennessee," pp. 132–35.

32. Brownlow, *Rise, Progress, and Decline of Secession,* pp. 212–13.

33. Bryan, "Civil War in East Tennessee," pp. 13–16. The Switzerland analogy captured the imagination of northern sympathizers. See Everett, *Relief of East Tennessee,* p. 11; Fisher, *War at Every Door,* pp. 18–21.

34. Of 73 prisoners, 24 were family men, and 41 records had no information.

35. Theodore F. Lang, *Loyal West Virginia from 1861 to 1865* (Baltimore: Deutsch, 1895), p. 8.

36. Oliver P. Temple, *Notable Men of Tennessee from 1833 to 1875: Their Times and Their Contemporaries* (New York: Cosmopolitan Press, 1912), pp. 192–93; Temple, *East Tennessee in the Civil War,* pp. 66–78.

37. James M. Sharp to Confederate commander at Dandridge, 16 Feb. 1864, Letters, H(WD)196, reel 129.

38. Brownlow, *Rise, Progress, and Decline of Secession,* p. 129.

39. Ibid., pp. 49–50.

40. Temple, *East Tennessee and the Civil War,* p. 558.

41. Brownlow, *Rise, Progress, and Decline of Secession,* p. 321.

42. Robert Bonner reminded me of the unattractive features of the army alternative.

43. Cases of Payne, Letters, C(WD)484, reel 86, and W(WD)126, second report, reel 115; Stockbridge, Letters, B(WD)139, reel 81; Beard, Letters, W(WD)126, pt. 2, reel 115; Brown, Letters, W(WD)126, pt. 2, reel 115; Caton, Letters, W(WD)126, pt. 2, reel 115; E. Fortner, Letters, C(WD)611, reel 86; Johnson, Letters, W(WD)126, pt. 2, reel 115; Kelly, Letters, W(WD)126, pt. 2, reel 115; Ledger, Letters, W(WD)126, pt. 2, reel 115; Miller, Letters, W(WD)126, pt. 2, reel 115; Thornhill, Letters, W(WD)126, pt. 2, reel 115; Tucker, *OR,* 2:4:950, and Letters, B1417–1862, reel 36; Shanks, *OR,* 2:4:950, and Letters, B1417–1862, reel 36; E. Walker, Letters, B(WD)533, reel 83,

and W(WD)126, pt. 2, reel 115; H. Walker, Letters, B(WD)533, reel 83, and Letters, W(WD)126, pt. 2, reel 115; S. Fortner, Letters, W(WD)126, pt. 2, reel 115.

44. Cases of Mercer, Letters, B(WD)138, reel 81; McGuire, Letters, B(WD)139, reel 81; Williams, Letters, B(WD)139, reel 81; Kenny, Letters, B(WD)138, reel 81 and OR, 2:4:890, 950.

45. Brownlow, *Rise, Progress, and Decline of Secession,* pp. 319, 324.

46. Daniel Ellis, *Thrilling Adventures of . . . , the Great Union Guide of East Tennessee . . . Written by Himself* (New York: Harper & Brothers, 1867), p. 189. See also Alexander, *Thomas A. R. Nelson of East Tennessee,* pp. 104–5.

47. Queener emphasized isolation and ignorance. Foner tends to depict the southern uplanders as precapitalist subsistence farmers with communitarian motives.

48. Ellis, *Thrilling Adventures,* pp. 13–14.

49. Fisher, "'Leniency Shown Them Has Been Unavailing,'" p. 289.

50. Ellis, *Thrilling Adventures,* p. 85. For another Brownlow statement, see Crofts, *Reluctant Confederates,* p. 159. In Washington County, North Carolina, a Unionist in the summer of 1861, well before the imposition of conscription, warned that when war came, "the rich people were going to make the poor people do all the fighting." Durrill, *War of Another Kind,* pp. 40–41.

51. Ellis, *Thrilling Adventures,* pp. 121, 176.

52. Richard N. Current, *Lincoln's Loyalists: Union Soldiers from the Confederacy* (Boston: Northeastern Univ. Press, 1992), p. 215.

53. "More than anything else, . . . it was the North's growing radicalism that alienated many Unionists. . . . For many . . . Unionists, emancipation was the final straw." Ash, *When the Yankees Came,* p. 120.

54. Alexander, *Thomas A. R. Nelson of East Tennessee,* p. 97. For examples of antiabolition deserters from the Federal army, see cases of James B. Crey, John Master, and Moses Vanway, Letters, C(WD)482, reel 86; Harry Jones, Bennett Williams, Richard Johnson, Charles Earhart, Letters, B(WD)626, reel 83.

55. Letters, W(WD)126, supplemental report, 23 Feb. 1863, reel 115.

56. For Brownlow's early desire to ignore the slaves and get on with conquering "their white masters," see *New York Tribune,* 9 Sept. 1862.

57. *New York Tribune,* 6 Oct. 1862.

58. Roy P. Basler, ed., *The Collected Works of Abraham Lincoln,* 9 vols. (New Brunswick NJ: Rutgers Univ. Press, 1953–55), 5:319 n. Another upper South spokesman for Unionist emancipation was J. William Demby of Arkansas, who said, "We go . . . for depriving the rebel master of his slave, and every other species of property, as one of the measures of punishment for his treason. We heartily approve of . . . the President of the United States, in all measures deemed needful for the suppression of the rebellion." See Demby, *Mysteries and Miseries of Arkansas; or, A Defence of the Loyalty of the State* (St. Louis, 1863), p. 71. For an account that properly reminds us of the importance of Lincoln's exemption of Tennessee from the Emancipation Proclamation but overemphasizes the animosity of East Tennessee political leaders to emancipation, see William C. Harris, *With Charity for All: Lincoln and the Restoration of the Union* (Lexington: Univ. Press of Kentucky, 1997), pp. 54–57.

59. See W. Todd Groce, "The Social Origins of East Tennessee's Leadership," in Noe and Wilson, eds., *Civil War in Appalachia,* esp. p. 48.

Chapter 7: Persistent Unionism in Western Virginia and North Carolina

1. *OR*, 2:1:851.

2. I am indebted to Stephen V. Ash, *When the Yankees Came* for a realization of the importance of Unionism. Here I deal with the Unionists before occupation by Federal forces.

3. Boyd B. Stutler, *West Virginia in the Civil War* (Charleston WV: Education Foundation, 1963), esp. p. vii.

4. Charles Henry Ambler, in *A History of West Virginia* (New York: Prentice-Hall, 1933), devotes 38 pages to constitutional and political questions, 6 to military operations, and none to civilian conflicts (pp. 295–311, 335–41). James C. McGregor, *The Disruption of Virginia* (New York: Macmillan, 1922), devotes 12 of 328 pages to "war sentiment" in the area. Richard O. Curry, in *A House Divided: A Study of Statehood Politics and the Copperhead Movement in West Virginia* (Pittsburgh: Univ. of Pittsburgh Press, 1964), has but 4 of 200 pages on guerrilla warfare in western Virginia.

5. James M. McPherson, *Battle Cry of Freedom* (New York: Oxford Univ. Press, 1988), pp. 297–98.

6. Edward Conrad Smith, *The Borderland in the Civil War* (New York: Macmillan, 1927), p. 219, suggests that West Virginia Unionism was important for keeping Maryland in the Union, but the influence must have run the other way.

7. Curry, *House Divided*, p. 53.

8. *OR*, 2:2:1466, 1469.

9. Although Ash uses the term *resistance* frequently, he does not emphasize its opposite, *collaboration*, in *When the Yankees Came*. Kenneth M. Stampp comes close in "The Southern Road to Appomattox," in *The Imperiled Union: Essays on the Background of the Civil War* (New York: Oxford Univ. Press, 1980), pp. 264–65, where he contrasts "the behavior of Confederate civilians" in occupied areas with "the problems that plagued the German Nazis" from "an organized underground that . . . made life precarious for collaborators and German military personnel." I learned about collaboration from Richard Cobb, *French and Germans, Germans and French: A Personal Interpretation of France under Two Occupations, 1914–1918/1940–1944* (Hanover, N.H.: Univ. Press of New England, 1983).

10. Case of J. W. Butler, *Message*, 27 Feb. 1863; *OR*, 2:2:1424; and Letters, reel 115; case of Samuel Gordon, Letters, B(WD)448, reel 33.

11. Letters, no. 9095-1861, reel 20; Curry, *House Divided*, p. 53.

12. Otey Fellows of Fayette County, Letters, B(WD)678, reel 33, and W(WD)126, reel 115; Benjamin Roby Sr., of Hardy County, no. 9170, reel 20; and Samuel Currence of Barbour County, no. 3535, reel 7.

13. S. S. Baxter report of 16 May 1862, Letters, B(WD)756, reel 34.

14. Problematic exceptions include Allan Richmond, only twenty, who was identified as an avowed Union man in 1863 but who was arrested with his brother, whose Unionism may have caused the identification. Their father was a notorious Union man. Letters, C(WD)500, reel 86. Dutchell Gabrill was also identified as a Union man but was only twenty years old (Letters, B(WD)461, reel 82); and James Kincaid was recorded as sixteen years old and a Union man.

15. Cases of Hiram Atkin and Peter Atkin, Letters, B(WD)160, reel 81.

16. James Lyons report, 12 Dec. 1861, Letters, no. 8371-1861, reel 18.

17. L. D. Morrall petition for Currence, 19 Aug. 1861, Letters, no. 3535-1861, reel 7.

18. James Lyons report, 12 Dec. 1861, Letters, no. 8371-1861, reel 18.

19. *OR*, 2:2:1447, 1448.

20. *OR*, 2:2:1478. Stover remained in prison in February 1863.

21. *OR*, 2:2:1448.

22. Report of Isaac H. Carrington, 2 Jan. 1864, Letters, C(WD)1044, reel 88; List of Citizen Prisoners to Be Examined, 5 Jan. 1864, Dept. of Henrico Papers. See also cases of Hiram Atkins, Hiram Bean, Peter Hoofman, S. Martigny, J. B. Nixon, William Rakes, J. S. Wilson, all in Letters, C(WD)1044, reel 88.

23. Warner, *Generals in Gray*, p. 147.

24. *Communication from the Secretary of War . . . February 11, 1864, [transmitting papers relating to the trial and conviction of W. E. Coffman]* (Richmond VA, 1864), pp. 4, 7, 8.

25. Wade Keys to James A. Seddon, 18 Nov. 1863, Letters, K(WD)127, reel 99. The question should have been settled long before. See James E. Ford to Leroy Pope Walker, 2 Aug. 1861, Letters, no. 2783-1861, reel 6. Samuel Cooper believed as late as November 1862 that the fifty-seventh article could subject civilians to military trial. *OR*, 2:4:950–51. Sydney S. Baxter concluded by the spring of 1862 that it could not; see Baxter to George W. Randolph, 29 April 1862, Letters, B(WD)488, reel 33. As late as August 1863, another commissioner, Isaac Carrington, thought it could, but B. R. Wellford Jr. thought not; he reviewed the commissioners' recommendations in most cases and was close to the assistant secretary of war. Case of Abraham Doughty, Letters, C(WD)598, reel 86. With some writers on military law, the application of the fifty-seventh article to civilians is still considered an open question. See Lee S. Tillotson, *The Articles of War, Annotated* (Harrisburg PA: Military Service, 1942), p. 169.

26. Coffman had been charged with being "in regular correspondence with the enemies of the Confederate States . . . Furthermore, that he has been, for a long time, in the habit of lurking in the neighborhood of Confederate States forces, and giving the information and intelligence, gained thereby, to the enemies of the . . . Confederate States." *Communication from the Secretary of War*, p. 3.

27. Keys to Seddon, 18 Nov. 1863, Letters, K(WD)127, reel 99. The Coffman affair, though the subject of a report published by the Congress (and later duly listed in standard bibliographies of Confederate imprints), has not heretofore been examined.

28. Michael Fellman, *Inside War: The Guerrilla Conflict in Missouri during the American Civil War* (New York: Oxford Univ. Press, 1989), pp. 97, 99–100.

29. Case of William Cruickshanks, Baxter report of 23 April 1862, Letters, B(WD)447, reel 33; *OR*, 2:2:1424.

30. Case of Samuel B. Cutlip, *Message; OR*, 2:2:1425; Baxter report of 25 April 1862, Letters, B(WD)448, reel 33. See also Stutler, *West Virginia in the Civil War*, pp. 43, 131–34, 141–46. To see Heth in a different light, read Phillip Shaw Paludan, *Victims: A True Story of the Civil War* (Knoxville: Univ. of Tennessee Press, 1981).

31. *OR*, 1:16:1:1146; see also pt. 2, p. 182.

32. He was explaining the wrongful arrest of Caleb N. Stevenson; *OR*, 2:2:1465.

33. *OR*, 1:10:2:323–24; 1:7:89; 1:16:1:785; 1:25:2:763.

34. *OR*, 1:27:1:290, 702.

35. *OR*, 1:43:2:264.

36. *OR*, 1:43:1:639.

37. *OR*, 1:42:2:885.

38. Letters, B(WD)162, reel 31.

39. Cases of Legrand B. Collier, Letters, C(WD)611, reel 86; Samuel Currence, Letters, no. 3535-1861, reel 7; S. Dickinson, *OR*, 2:5:822; George W. Fox, *OR*, 2:2:1443; Hiram Hale, Letters, B(WD)64, reel 81; William M. C. K. Smith, Letters, no. 9780-1862, reel 22; F. Stover, *OR*, 2:2:1442, and Letters, no. 9171-1861, reel 20; Moses Weddell, Letters, L(WD)264, reel 133; James Jackson, Letters, B(WD)190, reel 81, C(WD)48, reel 122, reel 82, reel 86; Charles Morrison, Letters, B(WD)64, reel 81, and B(WD)481, reel 82.

40. Jack Temple Kirby, *Poquosin: A Study of Rural Landscape and Society* (Chapel Hill: Univ. of North Carolina Press, 1995), pp. xi–xii, 23, 145, 160–61. Kirby does not focus especially on political history and relies on Wayne Durrill's study of neighboring Washington County, North Carolina, for descriptions of "class warfare" in the area. On voting, see Daniel W. Crofts, *Old Southampton: Politics and Society in a Virginia County, 1834–1869* (Charlottesville: Univ. Press of Virginia, 1992), p. 146.

41. John Bankhead Magruder to Samuel Cooper, 23 and 24 Jan. 1862, with endorsement by Governor John Letcher, Letters, nos. 10209, 10211, reel 24. Letcher refused to intervene and thus to protect his citizens, saying that Magruder had to decide whether the people posed a military threat. If they did, Magruder was to arrest them himself.

42. In Nansemond County, the vote was 477 for Bell to 429 for Breckinridge and 1 for Douglas; in Norfolk, 704 for Bell to 447 for Breckinridge and 52 for Douglas; in Princess Anne, 451 for Bell to 379 for Breckinridge and 16 for Douglas. *The Tribune Almanac and Political Register for 1861* (New York, 1861), p. 51.

43. Genovese, *Roll, Jordan, Roll*, p. 43.

44. Eugene Weber, *Peasants into Frenchmen: The Modernization of Rural France, 1870–1914* (Stanford CA: Stanford Univ. Press, 1976).

45. J. M. Morehead to Leroy Pope Walker, 26 Aug. 1861, Letters, no. 4020-1861, reel 8.

46. Case of G. S. Bolton, Letters, B(WD)64, reel 81.

47. Statement of H. B. Short, Letters, B(WD)64, reel 81.

48. *Tribune Almanac*, p. 48.

49. Case of David Stowe, Baxter report of 24 Feb. 1863, Letters, B(WD)173, reel 81. Stowe refused to take the Confederate oath of allegiance.

50. Paul D. Escott mentions "swamps, pocosins, and Carolina bays of the coastal plain" as areas of resistance. See Escott, *Many Excellent People: Power and Privilege in North Carolina, 1850–1900* (Chapel Hill: Univ. of North Carolina Press, 1985), p. 71. See also Durrill, *War of Another Kind*, esp. pp. 7–11.

51. Case of Thomas Kennedy, Letters, W(WD)126, reel 115. Wellford apparently arranged for Kennedy to write to his wife to sell their property and go north.

52. Robin E. Baker, "Class Conflict and Political Upheaval: The Transformation of North Carolina Politics during the Civil War," *North Carolina Historical Review* 69 (1992): 148–78; Escott, *Many Excellent People*, p. 27 ("class tension and conflict . . . became prominent in the 1860s"); Wayne K. Durrill, *War of Another Kind*. For more political interpretive schemes, see Marc W. Kruman, "Dissent in the Confederacy: The North Carolina Experience," *Civil War*

History 27 (1981): 293–313; George C. Rable, *The Confederate Republic: A Revolution against Politics* (Chapel Hill: Univ. of North Carolina Press, 1994).

53. Letters, C(WD)485, reel 86; reel 87; W(WD)126, pt. 2, reel 115.

54. Letters, C(WD)577, reel 86; W(WD)126, pt. 2, reel 115.

55. Davis said he professed Unionism under advice of fellow prisoners and would take the Confederate oath. He was fifty-four. Dept. of Henrico Papers; Letters, B(WD)481, reel 82; C(WD)575, reel 86; W(WD)126, pt. 2, reel 115.

56. Letters, W(WD)126, pt. 2, reel 115; reel 83; reel 86.

57. Letters, C(WD)536, reel 86.

58. Case of George Morley, Dept. of Henrico Papers.

59. Letters, B(WD)232, reel 82.

60. Letters, T(WD)449, reel 75; C(WD)165, reel 85; W(WD)126, reel 115. Other Quakers arrested were E. W. Hassell, a conscript trying to get north to avoid military service, S(WD)484, reel 142; Francis Winslow, B(WD)462, reel 82; and N. T. Perkins, C(WD)165, reel 85.

61. *Message of the President . . . Communication from the Secretary of War Covering a List of the Civilian Prisoners . . . at Salisbury* (Richmond VA, 1863), hereafter cited as *Message;* Case of Isom Wood, Letters, W(WD)126, reel 115. B. R. Wellford Jr. doubted Wood's sanity and arranged his exchange for a northern civilian.

62. Case of James Sinclair, Letters, S(WD)94, reel 140.

63. *Message;* Letters, W(WD)126, reel 115. Loftin was arrested in part because he had influence over poor men in the area.

64. Letters, W(WD)126, reel 115. Harboring deserters was not an indictable offence.

65. Letters, W(WD)126, reel 115.

66. Harold M. Hyman and William E. Wiecek, *Equal Justice under Law: Constitutional Development, 1835–1875* (New York: Harper & Row, 1982), p. 236. This chapter title echoes Thomas B. Alexander, "Persistent Whiggery in the Confederate South, 1860–1877," *Journal of Southern History,* 27 (Aug. 1961): 305–29.

Chapter 8: A Provincial Society at War

1. The title of this chapter and the focus on a divided society owe much to Carl Degler, *The Other South: Southern Dissenters in the Nineteenth Century* (New York: Harper & Row, 1974), though I tend not to identify dissenters as antislavery people as much as Degler does.

2. Thomas, *Confederate Nation,* pp. 188–89.

3. Cases of Edward Bradley Jr., James Bradley, W. Hart, Lambert Sampson, Thomas Sampson, and Lewis Simpson, Report of S. S. Baxter for 4 Sept. 1862, Letters, B(WD)994, reel 34.

4. Clipping from *Houston TriWeekly Telegraph,* enclosed in William Preston Johnston to the secretary of war, 8 Nov. 1862, Letters, J(WD)440, reel 55. But compare the mass hangings and detentions of Sioux Indians in Minnesota in 1862. See Mark E. Neely Jr., *The Last Best Hope of Earth: Abraham Lincoln and the Promise of America* (Cambridge: Harvard Univ. Press, 1993), p. 150.

5. *OR,* 2:6:1053.

6. Edwin Forbes, *Thirty Years After: An Artist's Memoir of the Civil War* (1890; reprint, Baton Rouge: Louisiana State Univ. Press, 1993), p. 233.

7. Ibid., p. 223.

8. D. W. Vowles to John H. Winder, 11 April 1864, Letters, D(WD)57, reel 144.

9. *OR*, 2:6:1053; RG 109, chap. 9, vol. 100, National Archives.

10. Prisoners received at Castle Thunder, 25 Feb. 1863–14 June 1864, RG 109, chap. 9, vol. 100, National Archives.

11. D. G. Cooper to Commander of post, Meridian, 23 Sept. 1863, Letters, C(WD)928, reel 88.

12. This contradicts the findings in Bell I. Wiley, *Southern Negroes, 1861–1865* (New Haven CT: Yale Univ. Press, 1938), pp. 38–43.

13. Stephen Thomas, RG 109, chap. 9, vol. 100, National Archives.

14. Notes by Isaac H. Carrington, Dept. of Henrico Papers.

15. Samuel Jones to Samuel Cooper, 22 April 1862, Letters, J(WD)79, reel 97.

16. Thomas M. Jones to James A. Seddon, 12 April 1862, Letters, J(WD)79, reel 97.

17. Jackson Morton to E. Ferrand, 6 May 1862, Letters, reel 60.

18. Samuel Cooper endorsement on Thomas M. Jones to James A. Seddon, 12 April 1862; unsigned defense of Ebenezer (a slave), Letters, J(WD)79, reel 97.

19. Seddon endorsement on Culpeper County citizens' petition, 22 Aug. 1864, Letters, B(WD)542.

20. Samuel Brooke, a free black man from Orange Court House, Virginia, arrested 5 May 1863. Dept. of Henrico Papers.

21. Douglas Southall Freeman, *R. E. Lee: A Biography*, 4 vols. (1935; reprint, New York: Charles Scribner's Sons, 1963), 3:56–57.

22. Edwin B. Coddington, *The Gettysburg Campaign: A Study in Command* (New York: Charles Scribner's Sons, 1968), pp. 153–54.

23. Case of Amos Barnes, Letters, C(WD)1025, reel 88. Barnes claimed that he had aided Confederates to capture alleged runaways, had been promised release, and was held by mistake with men he had helped the Confederates capture.

24. Kenneth M. Stampp, "Southern Road to Appomattox," pp. 246–69; Charles Grier Sellers Jr., "The Travail of Slavery," in *The Southerner as American* (New York: E. P. Dutton, 1966), pp. 40–71; and Richard E. Beringer et al., *Why the South Lost the Civil War* (Athens: Univ. of Georgia Press, 1986), pp. 336–67.

25. Case of James (or Joseph) Cavanaugh (or Brunagh), Letters, B(WD)758, reel 83, and C(WD)218, reel 123; Notes by Isaac M. Carrington, Dept. of Henrico Papers.

26. Case of Levi Bennett, Letters, C(WD)64, reel 122; Dept. of Henrico Papers. See also case of Edward Hopkins, Letters, C(WD)536, reel 86.

27. Case of L. Fedler, Letters, B(WD)756, reel 34.

28. Case of Allen Leonard, Letters, W(WD)126, reel 115; no. 3672-1861, no. 3862-1861, reel 8.

29. Case of Auguste Sheran, Letters, B(WD)43, reel 81; *OR*, 2:5:816.

30. Case of Edward Barnes, *OR*, 2:2:1468; Letters, C(WD)605, reel 86, and W(WD)126, reel 115; Turner-Baker Case no. 3087.

31. Case of F. Rush, Dept. of Henrico Papers. For other prisoners described as insane, see the cases of George Brannon, RG 109, chap. 9, vol. 219-½, National Archives; James Dutton, Letters, no. 10678-1862, reel 25, and *OR*, 2:2:1483; John Monroe, *OR*, 2:2:1425; Martin Newly, Letters, B(WD)190, reel 81; Anthony Rader, *OR*, 2:2:1432; John Rhett (or Wright), RG 109, chap. 9, vol. 229, National Archives; Daniel Somers, Letters, B(WD)232, reel 82; Asa Craig, Letters,

H(WD)622, reel 96; Lawrence Tibney, Letters, B(WD)190, reel 81; Thomas A. Ramsay, *OR,* 2:2:1432; Joe Brummeau (or Bromaugh), Letters, B(WD)758, reel 83; J. Frerkin, RG 109, chap. 9, vol. 229, National Archives; W. Bridwell, RG 109, chap. 9, vol. 229, National Archives; John DeLancey, Letters, W(WD)126, supp. report, reel 115; J. S. Davis, RG 109, chap. 9, vol. 229, National Archives; J. Dalton, RG 109, chap. 9, vol. 229, National Archives; James Harvey, Letters, H(WD)528, reel 130; George Horne, Letters, H(WD)272, reel 129; William Kirby (or Holt), Letters, H(WD)528, reel 130; A. Bailey, *Message,* 27 Feb. 1863; Thomas C. McDonough, Letters, C(WD)612, reel 86, W(WD)126, reel 115, and *OR,* 2:2:1461; Isom Wood, Letters, W(WD)126, reel 115; John McClelland, Letters, W(WD)126, reel 115.

32. Case of Benjamin Carney, Letters, C(WD)468, reel 86.

33. Case of Robert Morton, *OR,* 2:6:447.

34. Case of Daniel Wolff, Letters, C(WD)42, reel 122, and RG 109, chap. 9, vol. 100, National Archives.

35. Case of Felix Hinkle, Letters, no. 9170-1861, reel 20.

36. Report of S. S. Baxter, 28 March 1862, Letters, B(WD)444, reel 32; *OR,* 2:2:1425.

37. *OR,* 2:3:835.

38. Samuel Horst, *Mennonites in the Confederacy: A Study in Civil War Pacifism* (Scottdale PA: Herald Press, 1967), p. 91. The names come from Horst; there are no arrest records for these figures in the War Department files—further proof that the extent of arrests considerably exceeded the record of 4,108 that could be established for this book. For Quaker troubles with conscription, see John E. Crenshaw to John A. Campbell, 29 Aug. 1863, Letters, C(WD)712, reel 87.

39. Horst, *Mennonites in the Confederacy,* pp. 96–110.

40. Jefferson Davis endorsement on Leroy Pope Walker's "Abstract" of the case of Gaspar Tochman, 2 Aug. 1861, Letters, no. 3746, reel 8.

41. Leroy Pope Walker to Jefferson Davis, 15 Aug. 1861, Letters, no. 3748, reel 8.

42. *OR,* 2:2:1369–70.

43. For insightful analysis of the economic side of alien status—confiscation and sequestration of property—see Bensel, *Yankee Leviathan,* pp. 156–58.

44. Robinson, *Justice in Grey,* p. 385.

45. Ibid., p. 625.

46. *OR,* 2:2:1370.

47. Thus Ella Lonn devotes only one paragraph to the law in *Foreigners in the Confederacy* (Chapel Hill: Univ. of North Carolina Press, 1940), pp. 385–86. She calls it the "act of banishment" but belittles its impact.

48. RG 109, chap. 2, vol. 44, National Archives.

49. Case of Adam Scharrer (Thomas P. Atkinson to John H. Winder, 20 July 1863), Letters, C(WD)497, reel 86.

50. James Magee to George W. Randolph, 10 Sept. 1862, 26 Sept. 1862, 22 Oct. 1862, Letters, M(WD)1444, 1445, reel 63.

51. W. F. Guilbeau, "Note relative à la Situation de Français au Texas," ca. January 1863, Letters, B(WD)37, reel 81.

52. Cridland to George W. Randolph, 24 June 1862, Letters, reel 39, and 2 Oct. 1862, C(WD)1016, reel 40.

53. S. G. French to James A. Seddon, 6 April 1863, with endorsement by Jefferson Davis, F(WD)182, reel 91.

54. Williams and Hamilton, eds., *Papers of William Alexander Graham*, 5:350.

55. *Richmond Dispatch*, 7 March 1862.

56. S. S. Baxter report, 6 Aug. 1864, Letters, B(WD)506, reel 121.

Part Four: Jefferson Davis and History

1. Rowland, ed., *Jefferson Davis, Constitutionalist*, 5:116.

2. Paul D. Escott is at his best in depicting Jefferson Davis in this early period as the architect of an ideology that deemphasized slavery and emphasized constitutional liberty linked to the American past. See Escott, *After Secession*, esp. pp. 34–41.

3. William E. Dodd, *Jefferson Davis* (Philadelphia: George W. Jacobs, 1907), p. 223.

4. Rowland, ed., *Jefferson Davis, Constitutionalist*, 5:122.

5. Ibid., 5:6.

6. Escott, *After Secession*, p. 178; Crist, ed., *Papers of Jefferson Davis*, vol. 9, *January–September 1863*, 44 n. The note includes the fact that Davis suspended the writ of habeas corpus the next day after writing the document for which the note is offered in explanation.

7. Brian Dirck, "Communities of Sentiment: Jefferson Davis's Constitutionalism," *Journal of Mississippi History* 58 (1996): 135–62. The article appeared after the chapter on Davis in this book was written and thus too late for extended comment.

Chapter 9: Jefferson Davis and the Writ of Habeas Corpus

1. James M. McPherson retains a valuable sense of the border state drama in *Battle Cry of Freedom: The Civil War Era* (New York: Oxford Univ. Press, 1988), esp. p. 276. See also Daniel Crofts, *Reluctant Confederates: Upper South Unionists in the Secession Crisis* (Chapel Hill: Univ. of North Carolina Press, 1989).

2. Basler, ed., *Collected Works of Abraham Lincoln*, 4:532.

3. *Official Records of the Union and Confederate Navies in the War of the Rebellion*, 30 vols. (Washington DC: Government Printing Office, 1894–1922), 2:3:293–94.

4. Norman B. Ferris, *Desperate Diplomacy: William H. Seward's Foreign Policy, 1861* (Knoxville: Univ. of Tennessee Press, 1976), p. 117.

5. The article was quoted at length in the *Charleston Courier*, 13 Feb. 1862.

6. J. H. Dillon to S. L. M. Barlow, 27 Sept. 1862, S. L. M. Barlow Papers, Huntington Library, San Marino, California.

7. Rowland, ed., *Jefferson Davis, Constitutionalist*, 5:167, 170.

8. Ibid., 5:40.

9. Ibid., 5:198–99.

10. OR, 1:19:2:601–2. Douglas Southall Freeman provided the reference to Marshall in *R. E. Lee: A Biography*, 4 vols. (New York: Charles Scribner's Sons, 1934), 2:356 n.

11. The important article on the puzzle of the important invasion proclamation is Louis H. Manarin, "A Proclamation: 'To the People of ———,'" *North Carolina Historical Review* 41

(April 1964): 246–51. The new edition of the *Papers of Jefferson Davis* throws no new light on the question.

12. Rowland, ed., *Jefferson Davis, Constitutionalist*, 5:338–39.

13. Freeman, *R. E. Lee*, 2:354; Parrish and Willingham, *Confederate Imprints*, pp. 487, 513; *Charleston Courier*, 3 Jan. 1862, 19 Feb. 1862, 3 Sept. 1862.

14. Davis, *Rise and Fall of the Confederate Government*, 2:333; Rowland, ed., *Jefferson Davis, Constitutionalist*, 5:338.

15. Escott, *After Secession*, p. 175.

16. Rowland, ed., *Jefferson Davis, Constitutionalist*, 5:357.

17. Crist, ed., *Papers of Jefferson Davis*, 8:585; 9:38, 42–43, 44 n, 75, 76 n.

18. Davis to Lee, 28 July 1863, in Rowland, ed., *Jefferson Davis, Constitutionalist*, 5:580.

19. Rowland, ed., *Jefferson Davis, Constitutionalist*, 6:24, 27.

20. Ibid., 6:53.

21. Davis did visit East Tennessee in December 1862, on his way to visit the western army. In brief remarks at the railway station in Knoxville, he said he had "heard it reported that East Tennesseans were disloyal, but he was loth to believe that the land which owned a Jackson, a Coffee and a Carroll, could give birth to men who could prove recreant to their country." *Charleston Courier*, 10 Dec. 1862.

22. Rowland, ed. *Jefferson Davis, Constitutionalist*, 5:577.

23. Ibid., 6:114.

24. Ibid., 6:146.

25. Ibid., 6:159.

26. Ibid., 6:177. Davis would not allow Vance to edit the letter for publication.

27. Case of Eli Swanner, Letters, C(WD)484, reel 86; W(WD)126, pt. 2, reel 115; and S(WD)203, reel 141.

28. Richardson, *Messages and Papers of Jefferson Davis*, 1:360. Despite the forthrightness of Davis's announcement, biographies of Davis and histories of the Confederacy do not always demarcate a clear dividing line on civil liberties at this point. But see Robert McElroy, *Jefferson Davis: The Unreal and the Real*, 2 vols. (New York: Harper & Brothers, 1937), 2:399: "By the beginning of February, 1864, both Davis and Lee appreciated Lincoln's wisdom in early ridding himself of the restrictions imposed by the writ of *habeas corpus*."

29. Rowland, ed., *Jefferson Davis, Constitutionalist*, 6:165, 168.

30. For a compatible analysis, featuring political parties and legislative bodies as well as the rival presidents, see Bensel, *Yankee Leviathan*, pp. 225–33.

Conclusion

1. Robinson Jr., *Justice in Grey*, p. 383.

2. Owsley, *State Rights in the Confederacy*, p. viii.

3. Thornton, *Politics and Power in a Slave Society*, p. xviii.

4. Z. B. Vance, *The Political and Social South during the War: A Lecture Delivered before John A. Andrew Post, No. 15, G.A.R. in Boston, Massachusetts, Dec. 8, 1886* (Washington DC: R. O. Polkinhorn, 1886), p. 14.

INDEX OF POLITICAL PRISONERS

GENERAL INDEX

A Nation Divided: New Studies in Civil War History

Neither Ballots nor Bullets: Women Abolitionists and the Civil War
Wendy Hamand Venet

Black Confederates and Afro-Yankees in Civil War Virginia
Ervin L. Jordan Jr.

Longstreet's Aide: The Civil War Letters of Major Thomas J. Goree
Thomas W. Cutrer

Lee's Young Artillerist: William R. J. Pegram
Peter S. Carmichael

Yankee Correspondence: Civil War Letters between New England Soldiers and the Homefront
Nina Silber and Mary Beth Sievens, editors

Southern Rights: Political Prisoners and the Myth of Confederate Constitutionalism
Mark E. Neely Jr.